McLuhan

Hot & Cool

THE DIAL PRESS, INC. NEW YORK 1967

ACKNOWLEDGMENTS

Acknowledgment is made to the following authors, agents and publishers for permission to reprint material in this book.

"Understanding Marshall McLuhan" by Howard Luck Gossage: reprinted by permission of the author.

"The New Life Out There" by Thomas K. Wolfe, Jr.: reprinted by permission of Thomas K. Wolfe, Jr. c/o Marvin Josephson Associates, Inc. Copyright © 1965 The New York *Herald Tribune*, Inc.

"A Handful of Postulates" by John M. Culkin, S.J.: copyright © 1966 by John Culkin, S.J. Reprinted by permission of the author.

"McLuhan Explains the Media" by Dean Walker: reprinted by permission of the author and *Executive* magazine.

"The Medium and the Message" by Kenneth E. Boulding: reprinted by permission of the author and the *Canadian Journal of Economics and Political Science*.

"Marshall McLuhan: Double Agent" by George P. Elliott: reprinted by permission of the author. Originally published in *The Public Interest*, Summer 1966.

"Notes on the Collective Mind" by Rudolph E. Morris: reprinted by permission of the author and *Renascence*.

"A Modern Sensibility" by Walter Ong, S.J.: reprinted by permission of the author and *Social Order*.

"Explorations" by William Blissett: reprinted by permission of the author. Originally published in *Canadian Forum*, August 1958.

"Joyce, Mallarmé and the Press" by Marshall McLuhan: Copyright 1954 by the University of the South. Originally published in *The Sewanee Review*, Winter 1954.

"McLuhan's Galaxy" by John Freund: reprinted from Journal of Conference on College Composition and Communication, May 1963, by permission of the National Council of Teachers of English.

Untitled review by Patrick D. Hazard: reprinted by permission of the author. Originally published in *Annals*, November 1964.

Untitled review by Dell Hymes: reprinted by permission of the *American Anthropologist*.

"Between Two Galaxies" by Frank Kermode: reprinted by permission of the author. Originally published in *Encounter*, February 1963.

"Evils of Literacy" by A. Alvarez: originally published in the *New States-man*, December 21, 1962. Reprinted by permission.

A review of *The Gutenberg Galaxy* by Dan M. Davin: reprinted by permission from *The Globe and Mail*, Toronto. Reprinted by permission of the author.

"A Structure of Insights" by Raymond Williams: reprinted from *University of Toronto Quarterly*, April 1964, by permission of the University of Toronto Press and the author.

"Philosophy in a Pop Key" by Harold Rosenberg: © 1965 The New Yorker Magazine, Inc. Reprinted by permission of the author and *The New Yorker*.

"Running It Up the Totem Pole" by Dwight Macdonald: reprinted by permission of the author. Originally published in *Book Week*, July 7, 1964.

"Electronic Man" by Christopher Ricks: originally published in the *New Statesman*, December 11, 1964. Reprinted by permission.

"Paradise Regained or McLuhanacy" by Jack Behar and Ben Lieberman: originally published in Teacher's College *Record*, April 1966. Reprinted by permission of *Record* and the authors.

"Architecture for the Electronic Age" by John M. Johansen: reprinted by permission of the author. Originally published in *The American Scholar*.

"The World and Marshall McLuhan" by George Steiner, Jonathan Miller and Andrew Forge: reprinted by permission of the authors and the British Broadcasting Corporation.

"Against McLuhan" by Benjamin DeMott: reprinted by permission of the author and *Esquire* Magazine. © 1966 by Esquire Inc.

"One Culture and the New Sensibility" by Susan Sontag: reprinted from *Against Interpretation* by Susan Sontag by permission of Farrar, Straus & Giroux, Inc. Copyright © 1965 by Susan Sontag. First appeared in *Mademoiselle*. Reprinted by permission of Laurence Pollinger Limited.

Excerpt from "The Use of Poetry and the Use of Criticism" by T. S. Eliot used by permission of Harvard University Press and Faber and Faber Ltd.

Letter from Edmund Carpenter: reprinted by permission of Edmund Carpenter.

Part Six: A Dialogue—Marshall McLuhan and Gerald Emanuel Stearn: originally published in *Encounter* in June 1967.

CONTENTS

PART TWO: THE HONEYMOON OF THE
MECHANICAL BRIDE

suppose crime did pay? is it an accident that the nar-
cissistic heroes like tarzan, superman, cowboys, and
sleuths are weak on social life? is bogart america's
shropshire lad?—mc luhan

PART THREE: EXPLORATIONS IN THE NEW WORLD

why have the effects of media, whether speech, writ-
ing, photography or radio, been overlooked by social
observers through the past 3500 years of the western
world?—mc luhan

PART FOUR: THE GALAXY RECONSIDERED

schizophrenia may be a necessary
consequence of literacy.——mc luhan

PART FIVE: UNDERSTANDING M.

the medium is the message.—mc luhan

PART SIX: A DIALOGUE

*even hercules had to clean the
augean stables but once!—mc luhan*

casting my perils before swains

I am an investigator. I make probes. I have no point of view. I do not stay in one position.

Anybody in our culture is regarded as invited as long as he stays in one fixed position. Once he starts moving around and crossing boundaries, he's delinquent, he's fair game.

The explorer is totally inconsistent. He never knows at what moment he will make some startling discovery. And consistency is a meaningless term to apply to an explorer. If he wanted to be consistent, he would stay home.

Jacques Ellul says that propaganda begins when dialogue ends. I talk back to media and set off on an adventure of exploration.

    I DON'T EXPLAIN—
    I EXPLORE.

    MARSHALL McLUHAN

by space the universe encompasses and swallows me as an atom; by thought i encompass it.

—PASCAL

(Herbert) Marshall McLuhan has started an uncommon international cultural squabble. It may be said that he has more passionate enemies, devoted followers, and enraged critics than almost any other formidable mind of our time. His ideas have provoked such an extraordinary range of critical response that there is emerging a veritable "Grammar of Epithets Directed at McLuhan." Various writers have called him:

> a metaphysical wizard possessed by a spatial
> sense of madness;

> a Canadian Nkrumah who has joined the assault
> on reason;

> a distorter of immature minds and the
> sensibilities of the young;

> the high priest of Popthink who conducts a
> Black Mass (for dilettantes) before the
> altar of historical determinism;

> a writer who has looted all culture, from
> cave paintings to Mad Magazine, for fragments
> to shore up against the ruin of his system;

> a very creative man who hits very large nails
> not quite on the head;

> the most important thinker since Newton, Darwin,
> Freud, Einstein and Pavlov.

By now a kind of McLuhan avant-garde has formed, becoming in the process a self-contained subculture.

McLuhan is a Canadian, a professor of literature, and a convert to Catholicism. Married, the father of six children (four daughters, two sons), he lives in a modest house in a prosaic section of a dull city: Toronto.

Born in 1911 in Edmonton, Alberta, he studied engineering and then literature at the University of Manitoba. His father sold insurance. His mother was an elocutionist of professional standing ("the Ruth Draper of Canada"). According to some accounts, McLuhan read G. K. Chesterton's *What's Wrong with the World* and subsequently embraced Catholicism ("It gives me emotional stability"). His conversion came in the late 1930's while he was studying at Trinity College, Cambridge.

At Cambridge, McLuhan pursued a study of literary influences which were, in time, to shape (perhaps dictate) the synthesis he ultimately achieved. For example, he formed an early and continuing admiration for the techniques and artistic intentions of James Joyce, Erza Pound, and T. S. Eliot. His enthusiasm for Joyce led him back through the genesis of Symbolism to the stylistic parodies of the Elizabethan Thomas Nashe, a writer whom Wyndham Lewis described in *Time and Western Man* as having "a great appetite for words, their punning potentialities" and who also had the ability of "compressing them into pungent arabesques." It was on Nashe that McLuhan wrote his doctoral dissertation, which he presented at Cambridge in 1943.

McLuhan's scholarly pursuit of Joyce's Elizabethan model is revealing. The roles of grammarian and playful lexicographer are essential and convenient vocations for him. His own puns are the result, not of bad taste or lazy verbal construction, but intellectual involvement. To pun is "to consolidate by pounding or ramming down (as earth or rubble, in making a roadway)."

Until recently McLuhan's career appeared to exemplify that of the bright, mobile, ambitious academic. He taught at the University of Wisconsin, St. Louis University, and Assumption College (now Windsor University). Since 1946, he has served as Professor of Literature at the University of Toronto. He has published hundreds of articles in "little" journals and written four books, *The Mechanical Bride : Folklore of Industrial Man* (1951); *The Gutenberg Galaxy : The Making of Typographic Man* (1962); *Understanding*

Media : The Extensions of Man (1964) ; and *The Medium Is the Massage : An Inventory of Effects* (1967).

In fact, it is fashionable to suggest that there are two Marshall McLuhans: one, a rather donnish, slightly eccentric professor, working away in the sheltered, musty precincts of the academy on trivial literary exercises; the other, a wild idiosyncratic Popster who is on to a good thing—media analysis, a subject badly in need of exploration. However persuasive this argument, it breaks down when one examines McLuhan's writings of the past thirty years and sees the consistency of his arguments.

Personal and biographical information about McLuhan is difficult to trace and there is a coy, almost purposeful elusiveness about the man himself. Eric Goldman, conducting a television interview, paused in the midst of a chaotic dialogue and remarked:

Goldman: How is it, Professor McLuhan, that you should
be so concerned with media? Here you are the
son of Baptist parents, convert to Catholicism,
a Canadian student of English literature, formerly
an engineering student and now . . .

McLuhan: Oh, don't bother about that data.

Goldman: Why?

McLuhan: It's all wrong! And, in any case,
quite unnecessary.*

An engaging and comic folklore about McLuhan is emerging, and he has become his own most puzzling metaphor.

There is a perceptible unity of interest and direction in *all* of McLuhan's work before 1962, when *The Gutenberg Galaxy* appeared. A concern with communication of thought, emotion, belief and with the consequences of transmission, man to men, has informed that unity and has forced McLuhan to reflect eventually on every aspect of human existence: sensory, psychic, material.

---

* "The Open Mind," WNBC telecast, May 19, 1966.

Frank Kermode has written that McLuhan's ideas would start a serious debate in a truly literate culture. Many serious and acute commentators believe that McLuhan is posing questions of profound consequence. If he is wrong, it matters. But McLuhan's ideas are not susceptible to the rigid formalism of genteel discussion; the question of right or wrong ("categories, categories") is, in many ways, irrelevant.

This book is not so much a debate as a McLuhan primer—a prologue to argument, a galaxy of opinion. I have drawn together essays and reviews, comments and interviews from a rich (and growing) literature of critical writings (Parts 1, 2, 4, and 5). At the same time, I have chosen to include some essays, a telecast, and a report by McLuhan (Part 3), dating from the years between the publication of *The Mechanical Bride* and *The Gutenberg Galaxy*, to show the early formulation of ideas which were to find full expression in his books. Part 6 is the transcription of a dialogue between McLuhan and myself, in which McLuhan answers some of his critics.

Finally, let me point out that the book has a circulating point of view and need not be read sequentially. The essays included are numbered consecutively, but this does not imply chronological development. This structural peculiarity is not willful, but is entirely, as the reader will see, in keeping with McLuhan's own methods.

GERALD EMANUEL STEARN

McLuhan

Hot & Cool

the NEW WORLD! of

1

marshall mc luhan

as people become more involved they know less and less. —MC LUHAN

T. S. Eliot believed that a poet required not a large but a significant audience. Up until the publication of *Understanding Media*, McLuhan was known in Canada and the United States to a small but learned world as a very imaginative and prolific critic, a teacher of great charm and persuasiveness, and, curiously, a scholar with a playful avocation in the new discipline, "mass communications." "I have been pilfering his ideas for years," Neil Compton wrote in 1965, "and others have been doing it too: It is easy for a practical eye to discern little bits of McLuhan nestling like fossils in the gritty prose of many a literary critic or sociologist."

In Canada, although *The Gutenberg Galaxy* was awarded the Governor General's award—the Canadian equivalent of the Pulitzer Prize—in 1962, McLuhan's reputation was mainly that of a scholarly nuisance and agitated protagonist. But Canadian culture is, at its best, a very fragile thing, shaped by English patronization and American indifference. The strident inferiority complex that informs it was plainly demonstrated when Robert Fulford of the Toronto *Daily Star* wrote, after reading an especially abusive American attack on *Understanding Media*, that these criticisms were all too familiar to Toronto intellectuals who had been saying worse about McLuhan since the 1950's:

> That, of course, is the trouble with U.S.
> intellectuals. Cultural lag: always a
> decade behind the real action.

It was the publication of *Understanding Media* in 1964 that permitted McLuhan a more extensive audience than that of the scholar. A far more accessible, less specialized book than either

1

The Gutenberg Galaxy or *The Mechanical Bride*, it provides an excellent introduction to McLuhan. It has inspired a torrent of criticism. Much of this writing reflects the initial shock of discovery—sometimes almost euphoric, sometimes outraged. The writers of the essays and articles in Part One have used *Understanding Media* as a vantage point from which to discuss McLuhan's ideas in a general way.

Howard Luck Gossage (1), in his essay on "applied McLuhanism," is concerned with the practical, as opposed to the philosophical or cultural aspects of media. His world is one of effects, not motives. Gossage is a San Francisco public relations consultant.

Tom Wolfe (2) is the Court Chronicler of the reign of Modernity. His energies are directed at being "with it"; his affection for the new is competitive. McLuhan, being at once new and, possibly, *great!*, demands wry detachment and cautious enthusiasm ("What if he is right?"). Wolfe's collection of essays, *The Kandy-Colored Tangerine-Flake Streamline Baby*, was published in 1965.

John Culkin, S.J. (3), a committed McLuhanite, is Director of the School of Communications at Fordham University. His essay is concerned with the application of mass media to innovations in education.

Dean Walker (4), a staff writer for the Canadian magazine *Executive*, explores the implications of McLuhan's ideas for business.

Kenneth E. Boulding (5) is a professor of economics at the University of Michigan. His review amusingly reflects the infectiousness of McLuhan's literary and typographical style—even for those somewhat skeptical of his theories.

George P. Elliott (6), a well-known novelist and professor of English at Syracuse University, expresses his hostility and ambivalence, and at the same time shows that he is honestly intrigued by McLuhan.

you can see why the mighty would be curious. —HOWARD LUCK GOSSAGE

1

Marshall McLuhan's *Understanding Media* has possibly the least catchy title for an important book since *Principia Mathematica;* however, it is somewhat easier to read once you have got the hang of it.

The hard part is getting into it. One school of thought says that you should start at page 77, or wherever, and then sit through it again the way you do when you come in on the middle of a movie. Another holds that you should skim through it once, saving your thunderstruck (or indignant) marginal notations for the second time around. The trouble with this is that skimming McLuhan is like trying to fill a tea cup from a firehose; there is likely to be no second time.

It is quite possible, I think, to start cheerfully at the beginning, provided one has some notion going in of what McLuhan is up to. To begin with, what Professor McLuhan means by a "medium" is any extension of man—whether it be a book, an automobile, an electric light bulb, television, or clothes. His theory is that the media a man uses to extend his senses and his faculties will determine what he is, rather than the other way around. To give a simple example: a car is certainly an extension of a man's legs. Moreover, when he drives a car he has in a sense amputated his legs. He is an amputee just as surely as though he had lost his legs first and then looked for a way to get around.

Similarly, by wearing clothes a man eliminates a good many of the functions that his body would have to perform were he naked. Let us consider this proposition in its most extreme form: a native living at the Equator and an Eskimo. The tropical native, because he is naked, has no means of retaining body heat; therefore he must eat constantly or die. He can starve to death in a day or two. The Eskimo, heavily furred, keeps his body heat and can go without food for weeks if necessary. This is not, of course, to suggest

3

that the Indians of the upper Amazon would be better off with long johns and fur coats, or that Eskimos would be better supermarket customers if they ran around in the buff, but that the media a society uses or is forced to use will determine what it is and how it behaves.

Incidentally, we are used to thinking of clothes as something we wear next to our bodies. Objectively, however, clothes are an extension of our skins. For a naked tribesman, the jungle is his clothes. When one of us runs around naked in a heated room, the room itself is clothes, an extension of our skin, a medium. You recall that earlier I said that any medium will tend to amputate the function which it extends? You can test this very easily by walking into a warm house on a cold day. The first thing you do is take off your overcoat.

Now, to carry this one step further, any new medium or extension of man constitutes a new environment which controls what people who live within it do, the way they think, and the way they act. If you wonder why the Russians behave and react differently from us, part of the answer is probably that until quite recently they lived in a pre-literate society, whereas ours has been literate for a very long time. They are historically ear-oriented whereas we are eye-oriented. There is a great difference.

A man who cannot read will pick up all information about what has gone on before and what is happening outside his field of vision by hearing about it. His world will therefore be more diffused and kaleidoscopic than that of the literate, eye-oriented man because the ear cannot be focused and the eye can.

The process of reading—which I suppose we could define as using our eyes to learn about things we cannot see—is dependent on this unique ability of the eye to focus and follow sequentially. Few people have been able to read at any given time during the past few thousand years since writing was invented. It is only recently, since Gutenberg, that literacy has become the general environment for even a small part of the world. Latin America, Eastern and Southern Europe, Asia, and Africa are still either pre-literate or Johnny-come-latelies to reading; their environmental structures are still ear-oriented.

The differences between literate and pre-literate societies are enormous. Not the least of these differences is technological. Mass production did not begin with the industrial revolution, but with the first printed page that Gutenberg pulled off his press. For the first time, items could be mass produced so that one was indistinguishable from another and all of the same value. This was quite a break-through after millennia of making one object at a time and each somehow different from the other.

But more important was the environment imposed by the medium of print itself: one word after the other, one sentence after another, one paragraph after another, one page after another; one thing at a time in a logical, connected line. The effects of this linear thinking are deep and influence every facet of a literate society such as our own.

An ear-oriented society, on the other hand, will neither act nor react in this one-thing-at-a-time fashion, but will tend to receive and express many experiences simultaneously. It is the difference between our baseball, which is surely one thing after another in a logical sequence, and their soccer which is everything happening at once. Perhaps it is why most of the best chess players—and chess is surely everything happening at once, with millions and millions of simultaneous possibilities—come from pre-literate countries. Or why so many atomic physicists are either Hungarians or Americans in their early twenties. Or why teen-agers can listen to the radio full blast, study, and put their hair up in curlers at the same time.

I mention teen-agers because it is becoming abundantly apparent that they are not, as we previously thought, going through a phase. They are a different breed of cat entirely. All sorts of reasons have been given for their emergence as a distinct group, among them prosperity and lack of discipline. And what the hell, I was young once myself. I *was*—but not like that. For one thing I wasn't as smart as that. Also, this teen-age revolution has been going on for quite a few years now and the early crop is getting up in its late twenties. And I wasn't like them when I was twenty-six either.

Well, what has happened? McLuhan's theory is that this is the first generation of the electronic age. He says they are different because the medium that controls their environment is not print— one thing at a time, one thing after another—as it has been for five hundred years. It is television, which is everything happening at once, instantaneously, and enveloping.

A child who gets his environmental training on television—and very few nowadays do not—learns the same way any member of a pre-literate society learns: from the direct experience of his eyes and ears, without Gutenberg for a middle man. Of course they do learn how to read too, but it is a secondary discipline, not primary as it is with their elders. When it comes to shaping sensory perceptions, I'm afraid that Master Gutenberg just isn't in the same class with General Sarnoff or Doctor Stanton.

Despite the uproar over inferior or inept television fare, McLuhan does not think that the program content of television has anything to do with the real changes TV has produced; no more than whether a book is trashy or a classic has anything to do with the process of reading it. The basic message of television is television itself, the process, just as the basic message of a book is print. As McLuhan says, "The medium is the message."

This new view of our environment is much more realistic in the light of what has happened since the advent of McLuhan's "Electric Age." The Gutenberg Age, which preceded it, was one thing after another in orderly sequence from cause to effect. It reached its finest flower with the development of mechanical linkages: A acts on B which acts on C which acts on D on down to the end of the line and the finished product. The whole process was thus fragmented into a series of functions, and for each function there was a specialist. This methodology was not confined to making things; it pervaded our entire economic and social system. It still does, though we are in an age when cause and effect are becoming so nearly simultaneous as to make obsolete all our accustomed notions of chronological sequence and mechanical linkage. With the dawn of the Electric Age, time and speed themselves have become of negligible importance; just flip the switch. Instant speed.

However, our methodology and thought patterns are still, for the most part, based on the old fragmentation and specialism, which may account for some of our society's confusion, or perhaps a great deal of it.

If you are one of those who read McLuhan and find that your independently arrived-at theories not only are confirmed by, but fit neatly into his far broader structure, it is very heady stuff indeed.

It can also be maddening. For right there, in the middle of a paragraph, you are likely to find an apparently extraneous thought of the kind he calls a "probe." The probe is apt to be a flat and final pronouncement about a subject on which the reader just happens to be the World's Greatest Authority. How could McLuhan possibly have known? And as long as he was at it why didn't he amplify it into the five thousand words it deserved?*

McLuhan's defense of his random probes is that if he stopped to develop them he'd never get on with the main body of his work. They occur to him there so he puts them in there. Perhaps he, as an old teacher, also feels the pupils ought to have something to do besides register his conclusions. If so, he is roaringly successful.

He is the only author I know who writes a paragraph that one can read for two hours profitably.

The probe technique does not always work out orally, particularly with small groups. A World's Greatest Expert is liable to grab the probe and run like hell for his own goal leaving the rest of the group—and the ball—up field somewhere. Also, when McLuhan is in exceptionally fine probing fettle, he has probes sticking out of him like a porcupine, which is somewhat baffling to the uninitiated. At such times, a lot of Marshall goes a little way.

Richard Schickel categorized those who balked at McLuhan's

---

* Note on Marshall McLuhan as a conversationalist: when you expound one of your own abstract ideas, he is all rapt attention; it is possible that he also listens. If he wore a hearing aid you would wonder whether he had turned it off. As a non-listener, he is excelled only by Buckminster Fuller, who does wear a hearing aid and does turn it off. Fuller is the champ: One time he interrupted me in the middle of a *question* with, "Do you want an answer or don't you? Very well . . ." He then answered the question; I only wished it had been mine.—H. L. G.

theories in *Harper's* ("Marshall McLuhan, Canada's Intellectual Comet"; November 1965) as the "compulsively literal" and the "compulsively academic." I will grant these, but I would like to add another major grouping which cannot be characterized so invidiously. They are bright and flexible enough, but they long ago made their commitments elsewhere. We might call them the Gutenberg-oriented (McLuhan admits to being one himself by inclination). Their attitude is epitomized by something that Barrows Mussey, an American author living in Germany, wrote me, more as explanation than justification: "The difference between McLuhan and me is that, by temperament—and by experience too—I am the sort who says the Wright brothers will never get it off the ground. He is the one who says that every family in America will have a private plane by 1950."

A major key to McLuhan's prose style and his outlook is to be found in his undoubted stature as a Joyce scholar, which is where he started out while working on his doctorate at Cambridge. He regards *Finnegans Wake* as the most important book of our era and the one that has done the most to chart his own explorations. His immense Joycean joy at snuffling and roiling about in the double-bed of language is evident throughout his work; as is his delight in elaborate puns, some of which are pointed and pregnant (which is to say I get them), while others are so obscurantist as to demand a "Key to McLuhans Wake."

The avalanche of referential material, probes, and indicators within his work is so vast and diverse as to keep his interpreters busy for some time. Since he isn't much given to going back and clarifying, and at any rate isn't terribly good at it, we can also expect a spate of articles with titles like "Understanding Marshall McLuhan," and "Mechanical Brideshead Revisited."

The Mechanical Bride, published in 1951, was his first book on media and his most bizarre. I will not dwell on it more than to say it is a collector's item fetching upward of fifty dollars in mint condition. His second, *The Gutenberg Galaxy*, is what is called an Important Book. It is mosaicked, empyrean, richly larded with magnificent literary substantiations. (McLuhan has total recall of his own and everybody else's material.) While it is not a book I would volunteer to write jacket blurbs for, its basic premise alone is enough to justify it. It is something like Norbert Wiener's *The Human Use of Human Beings*: If you only get the notion of the title you are miles ahead.

I believe McLuhan will endure, for the reason that there is an observable pattern in his work building toward a unified field theory. It is reasonable that he should try, for to account for creation is the proper goal of those who are able to envision it at all; it is the name of the game.

Understanding Media: The Extensions of Man is the first book of what McLuhan intends to be a trilogy. The second will be called *Cliché to Archetype*, and I hope it will be subtitled "The Environment of Man," because that is what it is about. We all know what scorn is reserved for the man who hasn't read the book, only the review, and discusses it anyway? And what really poor form it is for a writer to review a book he hasn't actually read? Here, I am going to excavate a new layer of Hell for myself: I am going to do both to a book which hasn't yet been written. I haven't even seen one page of McLuhan's unfinished manuscript, but he has talked enough about it so that I think I can wing it, chancy though it is:

CLICHÉ TO ARCHETYPE TO CHANCE

Everybody talks about environment but nobody does anything about it. This is because, McLuhan says, "The moment a man recognizes his environment it becomes something else, his 'old environment,' and as such is the content of his new, or true, environment; which, of course, again is unseen."

Has he lost you already? Let's get out the bread crumbs: by "environment," he means that accustomed, unnoticed set of conditions which limits an organism's world at any given moment. In the ordinary course of events, we are not aware of our environment any more than a fish is aware of his. As Father John Culkin of Fordham, a leading McLuhanite, says, "We don't know who it was discovered water, but we're pretty sure it wasn't a fish."

Imagine a series of clear plastic domes, one within another. You can only see them from the outside; from the inside they are invisible. You become aware of an environment—one of these domes that surrounds you—only when you get outside of it. At that point you can see it. But you can't see the one which is *now* above you.

To put it another way, let us suppose that an ant has lived all his young life inside an anthill. He is not really aware that the anthill is his world; it simply *is* his world. So one day they send him off on his first important assignment, to drag back a dead beetle, say. He goes outside the anthill. Two things happen: 1) He sees the anthill for the first time; 2) He becomes aware that the world is a very big place. Does this mean that he is aware of his environment? No, because what he doesn't know is that his anthill is inside a greenhouse. The only way he'll become aware of the greenhouse is if he goes outside it. And even then it won't do him much good, because, you see, the greenhouse is inside the Houston Stadium, and so on. In each instance, you will notice that the old environment becomes content for the newer one, never the other way around. McLuhan, in one of his random conversational probes, notes that this seems to work out even in decor. Victorian furniture fits into a modern room, but a modern piece looks simply awful in a Victorian room.

So, awareness is becoming conscious that there is something higher controlling us than we had thought. The catch is that we can never catch up; we are always one step behind, for everything is contained by something bigger. McLuhan will not, I think, take us on this route, at least not in this book. Perhaps he will in the third leg of his trilogy, but it is hard to say. Although he is a convert to Roman Catholicism he is chary of airing his religious speculations. His concern at this time is not so much with goals as with process.

There are many sorts of environments besides the simple one of physical space which I mentioned: business, political, social, cultural, communications, etc. But for the moment let's just call it all environment. Two things will make us aware of an environment: either it changes or we do. A man who has lost a leg will become aware of steps. A man who has had five martinis may see things he has never seen before. A man who has had ten martinis may see things nobody has seen before.

There is another variety of environmental recognition reserved for those viewing it as outsiders. There are several varieties of what McLuhan calls "anti-environmentals," though I think "extra-environmental" is more descriptive.

An extra-environmental can be a person within a society whose perceptions have not been conditioned to obliviousness of the structure of a given environment. The story of the Emperor's new clothes is a good example. The child, because he was not yet committed to the environmental power set-up, was not committed to see the Emperor's clothes, so he didn't. It was only when the extra-environmental child pointed out that he was naked that the others were able to see it too.

Similarly, a teen-ager with his other-conditioned perceptions will be extra-environmental in our Gutenbergish society.

A second type of extra-environmental is apparently due to an innate deficiency. That is to say that some people are unable to see things in a normal fashion. On the other hand, they will see things that normal people can't. During the Second War, I understand that some aerial observers were recruited because they were colorblind. Their colorblindness made them unable to distinguish things designed for normal eyes, such as camouflage. They'd look down at a quite ordinary stretch of landscape and say, "Hey, there's a gun emplacement!" Because of their disability, their impairment of vision, their eyes were not taken in by the camouflage; all they could see was the thing itself. The extra-environmental thus has a great advantage, assuming he has anything else going for him. His mind isn't cluttered up with a lot of rules, policy, and other environmental impedimenta that often pass for experience. The more experience you have the less able you are to look at a given environment, especially your own, with fresh eyes.

I said earlier that one of the ways that we can become aware of environment is for it to change. However, sometimes an environment can change without our really noticing what has happened.

Part of this is due to a lag in terminology, part to our Mechanical Age commitment to specialists.

Travel, as an example, has changed drastically, and I don't mean that it's just faster. Travel, for the most part, is no longer travel; it is a process which has a beginning and an end but virtually no middle. Travel is not an experience so much as a suspension of experience. Flying in a plane from San Francisco to New York is nothing more nor less than a horizontal elevator ride. One imagines that if we had buildings 3000 miles high, there would be a young woman on the elevators offering us coffee, tea, or milk.

Is terminology all that important? Yes, because to name things is to recognize them; it is the way we learn about our environment. Which brings us to specialism. The specialist is by nature environmental. He is committed to what McLuhan calls a fragmented function within a given process linkage. If his environment changes he will not necessarily become extra-environmental. It is more likely that he will carry his tendency to specialism with him the way a snail does his shell. A born specialist will tend to interpret all experience in the light of his own expertise. *Illustrative story:* One time a cloak and suit manufacturer went to Rome and while he was there managed to get an audience with His Holiness. Upon his return a friend asked him, "What did the Pope look like?" The tailor answered, "A 41 Regular."

If specialism epitomizes the environmental stance, then "generalism" probably covers the extra-environmental. A generalist starts from the outside of a given environment; a specialist works on the inside. McLuhan has a special aversion to specialism; a sign in his office proclaims, "No specialist need apply." This does not mean that he is against professional expertise in the solution of problems, only against its built-in blinkers.

Once you take a problem to a specialist you are wired in to a specialist's solution. However well executed it is, the odds are against its being a real answer. Let us say that your company is having growing pains, and is uncomfortable in its present quarters. So you go to an architect. Let us also suppose that he is a very good architect, broad-thinking, one dedicated solidly to the proposition that form follows function. So he inquires after your needs, your ambitions, your hopes, your fears, what manner of people you are, etc. Do you know what you are going to end up with? A building. Now, a building, however nice, may not be the answer to your problem at all. Perhaps the real answer is to stop expanding, or fire the traffic manager, or everyone stay home and do cottage work connected by closed-circuit TV. But these are generalist solutions, not the sort of thing you expect an architect to come up with. If he did, you'd probably think he was a busybody.

Those who find McLuhan most compatible are those who have already figured out a structure and wonder where it fits in the larger scheme of things. The generalist area looks like this, a circle:

The dot in the middle is you. The area within the circle is your field of specialization; therefore any problem solution (save one by a greater specialist) which fits inside will be unacceptable because you already know all about it, and have probably tried it, and it doesn't work. On the other hand, anything outside the circle is incomprehensible; any solution placed there will simply be inapplicable. The generalist problem-solving area has got to be right on the circumference itself: close enough in so that you get it, far enough out so that you can't pick it to pieces.

McLuhan's terminology accommodates this concept and improves it by expanding it into a process. He would call the inside of the circle "environment," and the outside "anti-environment." You can't really recognize things inside your environment, and you can't really see things outside it; so there we are sitting on the circumference again. The thing that is added by this change in terms is this: you solve problems by expanding the environmental area, by moving the circumference out.

"Cliché to Archetype," McLuhan's main title, deserves an explanation here too. "Cliché" means any environmental element, omnipresent, unnoticed. It becomes noticed when the environment changes. At this point, as it becomes "content" of the new environment, it also becomes an art form. If you live in a room that has cabbage rose patterned wallpaper, you will notice it at first but after awhile, it will become just wallpaper. What was once fresh and new turns into a cliché and assumes its role as part of the environment. Now let us suppose that when you repaper the room, you decide to save a square of the old stuff and have it framed. As a picture it is no longer wallpaper, but content for the new environment.

Something else has happened too: it has become an art form. If it is successful as an art form and is admired and copied—or at any rate persists so that eventually it becomes the one and only from which all others emanate—it constitutes an archetype. Today's archetype was yesterday's art form, day before yesterday's cliché, and the day before that it was the last word.

It is hard to tell how much of the above will turn out to be McLuhan and how much McGuesswork when the book finally comes out. One thing is sure; it covers only a tiny bit of the material therein. . . .

McLuhan's most powerful appeal, in the end, is to those who have thought themselves into a sort of intellectual isolation, who lie awake and groan, "Doesn't anyone else think in the same patterns I do?" For some of these McLuhan does.

suppose he is what he sounds like, the most important thinker since newton, darwin, freud, einstein, and pavlov—what if he is right?

—TOM WOLFE

What if he's right   What ... if ... he ... is ... right   W-h-a-t
i-f h-e i-s r-i-g-h-t

W	IF	R	
H	HE	I	
A	IS	G	?
T		H	
		T	

There are currently hundreds of studs of the business world, breakfast food package designers, television network creative department vice-presidents, advertising "media reps," lighting fixture fortune heirs, smiley patent lawyers, industrial spies, we-need-vision board chairmen, all sorts of business studs who are all wondering if this man, Marshall McLuhan ... is right. ... He sits in a little office off on the edge of the University of Toronto that looks like the receiving bin of a second-hand book store, grading papers, *grading papers*, for days on end, wearing—well, he doesn't seem to care what he wears. If he feels like it, he just puts on the old striped tie with the plastic neck band. You just snap the plastic band around your neck and there the tie is, hanging down and ready to go, Pree-Tide.

But what if—all sorts of huge world-mover & shaker corporations are trying to put McLuhan in a box or something. Valuable! Ours! Suppose he *is* what he sounds like, the most important thinker since Newton, Darwin, Freud, Einstein, and Pavlov, studs of the intelligentsia game—suppose he *is* the oracle of the modern times —*what if he is right*? he'll be in there. It almost seems that way. An "undisclosed corporation" has put a huge "undisclosed sum"

15

into McLuhan's Centre for Culture and Technology at the University of Toronto. One of *the* big American corporations has offered him $5000 to present a closed-circuit—ours!—television lecture on—oracle!—the ways the products in its industry will be used in the future. Even before all this, IBM, General Electric, Bell Telephone were flying McLuhan in from Toronto to New York, Pittsburgh, God knows where else, to talk to their hierarchs about . . . well, about whatever this unseen world of electronic environments that *only he sees fully* is all about.

They all sit in these conference rooms, under fluorescent lights, with the right air-conditioned air streaming out from behind the management-style draperies. Upward-busting hierarch executives, the real studs, the kind who have already changed over from lie-down crewcuts to brushback Eric Johnston-style Big Boy haircuts and from Oxford button-downs to Tripler broadcloth straight points and have hung it all on the line, an $80,000 mortgage in New Canaan and a couple of kids at Deerfield and Hotchkiss—hung it all on the line on knowing exactly what this corporation is all about —they sit there with the day's first bloody mary squirting through their capillaries—and this man with part of a plastic neckband showing at the edge of the collar, who just got through *grading papers,* for godsake, tells them in an *of-course* voice and with *I'm-being-patient* eyes, that, in effect, politely, they all know just about exactly . . . nothing . . . about the real business they're in—

> —Gentlemen, the General Electric Company makes a considerable portion of its profits from electric light bulbs, but it has not yet discovered that it is not in the light bulb business but in the business of moving information. Quite as much as A. T. & T. Yes. Of-course-I-am-willing-to-be-patient. He pulls his chin down into his neck and looks up out of his long Scotch-lairdly face. Yes. The electric light is pure information. It is a medium without a message, as it were. Yes. Light is a self-contained communications system in which the medium is the message. Just think that over for a moment—I-am-willing-to-be—When IBM discovered that it was not in the

business of making office equipment or business machines—
————but that it was in the business
of processing
information,
then it began
to navigate
with
clear
vision.
Yes.

Swell! But where did *this* guy come from? What is this—these cryptic, Delphian sayings: *The electric light is pure information.* Delphian! *The medium is the message. We are moving out of the age of the visual into the age of the aural and tactile . . .*

Oracle!—McLuhan sits in the conference room on the upper deck of an incredible ferry boat that Walter Landor, one of the country's top package designers, has redone at a cost of about $400,000 as an office and design center. This great package design flagship nestles there in the water at Pier 5 in San Francisco. The sun floods in from the bay onto the basket-woven wall-to-wall and shines off the dials of Landor's motion picture projection console. Down below on the main deck is a whole simulated supermarket for bringing people in and testing package impact and all sorts of optometric wonder wards for testing visual reception of metri-bergiarglebargle—and McLuhan says, almost by the way:

"Of course, packages will be obsolete in a few years. People will want tactile experiences, they'll want to feel the product they're getting—"

But!—

McLuhan's chin goes down, his mouth turns down, his eyes roll up in his *of-course* expression: "Goods will be sold in *bins.* People will go right to bins and pick things up and *feel* them rather than just accepting a package."

Landor, the package designer, doesn't lose his cool; he just looks —*what if he is right?*

". . . The human family now exists under conditions of a global village. We live in a single constricted space resonant with tribal drums . . ." That even, even, even voice goes on—

—McLuhan is sitting in the Lombardy Restaurant in New York with Gibson McCabe, president of *Newsweek,* and several other high-ranking communications people, and McCabe tells of the millions *Newsweek* has put into reader surveys, market research, advertising, the editorial staff, everything, and how it paid off with a huge rise in circulation over the past five years. McLuhan listens, then down comes the chin: "Well . . . of course, your circulation would have risen about the same anyway, the new sensory balance of the people being what it is . . ."

Print gave tribal man an eye for an ear.

McLuhan is at the conference table in the upper room of Howard Gossage's advertising firm in San Francisco, up in what used to be a firehouse—they're pretty great converters in San Francisco— and a couple of newspaper people are up there talking about how they are sure their readers want this and that to read—McLuhan pulls his chin down into his neck: "Well . . . of course, people don't actually *read* newspapers. They get into them every morning like a hot bath."

Perfect! Delphic! Cryptic! Metaphorical! Epigrammatic! With this even, even, even voice, this utter scholarly aplomb—with these pronouncements—"Art is always one technology behind. The content of the art of any age is the technology of the previous age"— with all this Nietzschean certitude—McLuhan has become an intellectual star of the West. He is a word-of-mouth celebrity.

Corporation executives are only the beginning of the roster of people in America who stand to be shaken up—*what if he is right?* The university establishments, the literati—McLuhan has already earned the hostile envy of the New York literary establishment— the artists—they like him—scores of little groups of McLuhan cultists—thousands of intellectuals are now studying McLuhan. The paperback edition of his book *Understanding Media* has been an "underground best seller"—that is, a best seller without benefit of publicity—for six months. City planners—

City planners are wondering *what if he*—McLuhan is the prophet of the New Life Out There, the suburbs, housing developments, astrodomes, domed-over shopping centers, freeways, TV families, the whole world of the new technologies that stretches out to the West beyond the old cities of the East. To McLuhan, New York is already obsolete, on its way to becoming not much more than a Disneyland discothèque for the enjoyment—not the big business or the gawking wonder, but the playing around—of the millions out there. They are already living the new life, while New York sits here choking to death in its *old fashion.*

McLuhan has developed a theory that goes like this: The new technologies of the electronic age, notably television, radio, the telephone, and computers, make up a new environment. A new environment; they are not merely *added* to some basic human environment. The idea that these things, TV and the rest, are just tools that men can use for better or worse depending on their talents and moral strength—that idea is idiotic to McLuhan. The new technologies, such as television, have become a new environment. They radically alter the entire way people use their five senses, the way they react to things, and therefore, their entire lives and the entire society. It doesn't matter what the content of a medium like TV is. It doesn't matter if the networks show twenty hours a day of sadistic cowboys caving in people's teeth or twenty hours of Pablo Casals droning away on his cello in a pure-culture white Spanish drawing room. It doesn't matter about the content. The most profound effect of television—its real "message," in McLuhan's terms —is the way it alters men's sensory patterns. *The medium is the message*—that is the best-known McLuhanism. Television steps up the auditory sense and the sense of touch and depresses the visual sense. That seems like a paradox, but McLuhan is full of paradoxes. A whole generation in America has grown up in the TV environment, and already these millions of people, twenty-five and under, have the same kind of sensory reactions as African tribesmen. The same thing is happening all over the world. The world is growing into a huge tribe, a . . . *global village,* in a *seamless web* of electronics.

These are McLuhan metaphors. He started out as an English literature scholar. He graduated from the University of Manitoba in Canada and then got a doctorate in English at Cambridge in England. He wrote his dissertation on the rhetoric of Thomas Nashe, a sixteenth-century English playwright and essayist. In it he led up to Nashe with a massive study of rhetoric from the Greeks on up. He got interested in the way different kinds of speech, written and oral, affected the history of different civilizations. Gradually his field expanded from literature to the influence of communication, all kinds, all the media, on society. He started doing research in psychology, even physiology, sociology, history, economics—everything seemed to come into it. McLuhan was sort of like John Huizinga this way. Huizinga is a historian, Medieval history, chiefly, who discovered "the play element" in history. He ended up with a rather sophisticated sociological theory, in the book *Homo Ludens,* that in many ways is a precursor of the mathematical "game theory" that so fascinates Pentagon war strategists today. McLuhan worked on his communications theory. For about thirty years he was pretty much in obscurity in places like the University of Wisconsin, the University of St. Louis, and the University of Toronto. He published *The Mechanical Bride* in 1951, then *The Gutenberg Galaxy* in 1962; and with that one the McLuhan Cult really started, and *what if he*—?

As McLuhan sees it—in the simplest terms, here is his theory step by step: People adapt to their environment, whatever it is, with a certain balance of the five senses: sight, hearing, touch, smell, and taste. If something steps up the intensity of one sense, hearing for example, the other senses will change intensity too, to try to regain a balance. A dentist, for example, can practically shut off pain—sense of touch—by putting earphones on a patient and pouring intense noise into his ear—sense of hearing.

Every major technology changes the balance of the senses. One of the most explosive of these technologies was the development of the printing press in the fifteenth century. Before that, people's senses still had pretty much the old tribal balance. That is to say, the sense of hearing was dominant. People got their information mainly by hearing it from other people. People who get their information that way are necessarily drawn closer together, in the tribal way. They have to be close to each other in order to get information. And they have to believe what people tell them, by and large, because that is the only kind of information they can get. They are interdependent.

They are also more emotional. The spoken word is more emotional than the written word. It carries emotion as well as meaning. The intonation can convey anger, sorrow, approval, panic, joy, sarcasm, and so forth. This *aural* man, the tribal man, reacts more emotionally to information. He is more easily upset by rumors. His and everybody else's emotions—a collective unconscious—lie very near the surface.

The printing press brought about a radical change. People began getting their information primarily by seeing it—the printed word. The visual sense became dominant. Print translates one sense—hearing, the spoken word—into another sense—sight, the printed word. Print also converts sounds into abstract symbols, the letters. Print is orderly progression of abstract, visual symbols. Print led to the habit of categorizing—putting everything in order, into categories, "jobs," "prices," "departments," "bureaus," "specialties." Print led, ultimately, to the creation of the modern economy, to bureaucracy, to the modern army, to nationalism itself.

People today think of print as if it were a technology that has been around forever. Actually, the widespread use of print is only about two hundred years old. Today new technologies—television, radio, the telephone, the computer—are causing another revolution. Print caused an "explosion"—breaking society up into categories. The electronic media, on the other hand, are causing an "implosion," forcing people back together in a tribal unity.

The aural sense is becoming dominant again. People are getting their information primarily by hearing it. They are literate, but their primary source is the radio, the telephone, the TV set. The radio and the telephone are obviously aural media, but so is television, in McLuhan's theory. The American TV picture has very low definition. It is not three-dimensional, like a movie or a photograph, but two-dimensional, like a Japanese print or a cartoon.

The viewer fills in the spaces and the contours with his mind, as he does with a cartoon. Therefore, the TV viewer is more *involved* in the TV image than in the movie image, he is so busy running over the image with his eye, filling in this and that. He practically reaches out and *touches* it. He *participates;* and he likes that.

Studies of TV children—children of all social classes who are used to getting their information primarily by television—studies of this new generation show that they do not focus on the whole picture, the way literate adults do when they watch a movie. They scan the screen for details; their eyes run all over the screen, focusing on holsters, horses' heads, hats, all sorts of little things, even in the fiercest gun battles. They watch a TV show the way a non-literate African tribesman watches a movie—

But exactly! The TV children, a whole generation of Americans, the oldest ones are now twenty-five years old—they are the new tribesmen. They have tribal sensory balances. They have the tribal habit of responding emotionally to the spoken word, they are "hot," they want to participate, to *touch,* to be involved. On the one hand, they can be more easily swayed by things like demagoguery. The *visual* or *print* man is an individualist; he is "cooler," with built-in safeguards. He always has the feeling that no matter what anybody says, he can go check it out. The necessary information is filed away somewhere, categorized. He can *look* it up. Even if it is something he can't *look* up and check out—for example, some rumor like "the Chinese are going to bomb us tomorrow"—his habit of mind is established. He has the feeling: All this can be investigated—*looked* into. The aural man is not so much of an individualist; he is more a part of the collective consciousness; he *believes.*

To the literate, visual, *print* man, that seems like a negative quality, but to the aural, tribal man, it seems natural and good. McLuhan is not interested in values, but if anything, he gives the worst of it to the literate man who is smug in the belief that his sensibility is the only proper one. The tribal man—the new TV generation—is far more apt at *pattern recognition*, which is the basis of computers. The child will learn a foreign language faster than a literate adult because he absorbs the whole pattern of the language, the intonations and the rhythms, as well as the meaning. The literate man is slowed down by the way he tries to convert the sounds to print in his mind and takes the words one by one, categorizing them and translating them in a plodding sequence.

In formal learning, in schools, that is, the new TV-tribal man is at a great disadvantage, however, given the current teaching methods. As McLuhan sees it—if people think there is a bad drop-out problem in American schools today, it is nothing compared to what it is going to be like in another ten or fifteen years. There will be a whole nation of young psychic drop-outs—*out of it*—from the wealthy suburbs no less than the city slums. The thing is, all these TV-tribal children are *aural* people, *tactile* people, they're used to learning by pattern recognition. They go into classrooms, and there up in front of them are *visual, literate, print*-minded teachers. They are up there teaching classes by subjects, that is, categories; they've broken learning down into compartments—mathematics, history, geography, Latin, biology—it doesn't make *sense* to the tribal kids, it's like trying to study a flood by counting the trees going by; it's *unnatural*.

It's the same way with these *cities* the *print*-minded rulers keep on piling up around them, *more* skyscrapers, *more* freeways pouring into them, *more* people piling into them. Cities are still based on the old idea of using space efficiently, of putting as many activities into a single swath of ground as possible to make it easier for people to move around and do business with each other. To the new drop-out generation and the drop-out generations to come, this idea of lateral space and of moving people around in it doesn't seem very important. Even *visual* people have begun to lose a little of the old idea of space because of the airplane. When somebody gets on a jet in New York and flies to San Francisco in four hours, the time is so short, the idea of the space, the three thousand miles, loses its meaning. It is just like taking a "horizontal elevator," McLuhan says. In Los Angeles, with everybody traveling by car on freeways, nobody talks about "miles" anymore, they just say "that's four minutes from here," "that's twenty minutes from here," and so on. The actual straight-line distance doesn't matter. It may be faster to go by a curved route. All anybody cares about is the time.

For that matter—the drop-out generations will even get rid of the cars, says McLuhan. The car is still largely tied to the idea of space, but the TV-tribal kids aren't. It even shows up in their dances. The new American dances, the twist, the frug, and all that, ignore the geography of the dance floor. The dancers stay in one place and create their own space. They jerk, spasm, hump, and bob around in one place with the sound turned up—aural! tribal!—up into the hot-jolly hyperaesthetic decibles. Eventually, says McLuhan, they will use the same sort of pattern in the way they work. They will work at home, connected to the corporation, the boss, not by roads or railroads, but by television. They will relay information by closed-circuit two-way TV and by computer systems. The great massive American rush-hour flow over all that asphalt surface, going to and from work every day, will be over. The hell with all that driving. Even shopping will be done via TV. All those grinding work-a-daddy cars will disappear. The only cars left will be playthings, sports cars. They'll be just like *horses* are today, a *sport.* Somebody over at General Motors is saying—*What if he is right?*

Whole cities, and especially New York, will end too just like cars, no longer vital to the nation but . . . just playthings. People will come to New York solely to amuse themselves, *do* things, not marvel at the magnitude of the city or its riches, but just eat in the restaurants, go to the discothèques, browse through the galleries—
—McLuhan is having lunch at Lutèce, a French restaurant at 249 East 50th Street, with four of his admirers, three journalists and a movie star. Lutèce is one of the real high-powered, gleaming-toothed places in New York where the culturati, the fashionati, literati, and illuminati of all sorts have lunch. The Big Boys go there. It has real wine stewards. It is so expensive, only the man who has to pay is shown the prices. Everybody else at the table gets a menu with just the dishes listed. Eat 'em up, gleaming teeth. So these people with gleaming teeth, glissando voices, lozenge-shape cuff links, peacock-colored Pucci-print dresses signed "Emilio"

turn the gleams on each other and sit in there and laugh, cozzen, whisper, bat the eyes, look knowingly, slosh their jowls around at each other in the old fight to make it or make it bigger in the biggest city in the world—and McLuhan just sits out in the garden at Lutèce smiling slightly, oblivious to the roiling, wearing a seersucker jacket and the plastic neckband tie, looking ahead as if . . . he were looking through walls.

Well, of course he is! The city—

"Well, of course, a city like New York is obsolete," he says. And all the gleaming teeth and glissando voices are still going *grack grack grack* in the same old way all around, all trying to get to the top of the city that will disappear.

McLuhan was in New York that time because two rather extraordinary men from San Francisco, Howard Gossage and Gerry Feigen, had just begun their ongoing "McLuhan Festival." The original McLuhan Festival was a kind of "happening" or "environment" in an armory at the University of British Columbia, put on by some teachers there. They were part of what is sometimes called "The McLuhan Cult"—esoteric groups of intellectuals who have . . . *discovered* McLuhan, in Canada and in the United States, most of them over the past three years, since *The Gutenberg Galaxy* came out. In the armory they suspended sheets of plastic from the ceiling, forming a maze. Operators aimed light projections at the plastic sheets and at the people walking through them, a movie projector showed a long, meaningless movie of the interior of the empty armory, goofy noises poured out of the loudspeakers, bells rang, somebody banged blocks of wood together up on a podium, somebody else spewed perfume around, dancers flipped around through the crowds, and behind a stretch fabric wall—a frame with a stretch fabric across it—there was a girl, pressed against the stretch fabric wall, like a whole wall made of stretch pants, and *undulating* and humping around back there. Everybody was supposed to come up and *feel it*—the girl up against the stretch fabric —to understand this "tactile communication" McLuhan talks about.

McLuhan Temple! McLuhan in church—the Rev. William Glenesk

brings McLuhan into the pulpit of his church, Spencer Memorial, on Remsen Street in Brooklyn Heights, one week night in a kind of . . . apotheosis of McLuhan cultism. Glenesk is the "hip" Presbyterian minister who has had jazz combos, dancers, sculpture—graven images!—in church. He brought McLuhan in one night and put him in the pulpit and it became . . . cult! like a meeting of all the solitary souls, from the cubicles of the NYU Bronx campus to the lofts of East 10th Street, who had discovered McLuhan on their own. All these artists came in there in the great carved oak insides of the church and sat in the pews, Stanley Vander Beeck the "underground" movie-maker in an orange shirt and red polka dot tie—

"It is a hot night," says McLuhan, speaking from the pulpit. "Therefore, I invite you to move forward. Heat obliterates the distance between the speaker and the audience . . ."

But of course! The heat steps up the tactile sense, diminishes the visual; the audience is no longer at ease sitting back and watching the speaker as though he is separated from them like the usual . . . *visual spectacle*. The artists, Vander Beeck, Larry Rivers the painter, John Cage the composer—they are all *for* McLuhan, even though McLuhan has a paradoxical attitude toward the "modern" arts. On the one hand, he says artists are geniuses who serve as "early warning systems" for changes in society's sensory balance. But at the same time, he says so-called "modern" art is always one technology behind. In the early nineteenth century the Industrial Revolution came in—the MACHINE age. The artist didn't realize that this was a new age, but they *sensed* that some kind of change was taking place, and they resented it—damned machine-cog life —so they reacted by coming up with the modern art of the early nineteenth century: NATURE, all those landscapes, grazing sheep —the content of the previous technology, namely, agriculture. Modern! All these modern artists, Constable and Turner, couldn't understand why nobody had even painted these great spewy albumen cloud banks and shaggy green horizons before. In the early twentieth century the ELECTRONIC age began, and the artists, only fifty or seventy-five years behind, as usual, suddenly discovered cubism and other abstract forms, breaking up objects into planes, spheres, component parts—the content of the MACHINE age, the industrial technology of the nineteenth century. But in any case, the artist's immediately obsolete "modernism" is a sign that *something* is changing in society's sensory balance. The artists seem to like this idea that they are the "early warning," the avant-garde, even if they are moving forward backwards.

They also like his general "culture" orientation. McLuhan started out as an English scholar, after all, and still laces his work with references to Marlowe, Rabelais, Whitman, Cervantes, Francis Bacon, Shakespeare, Joyce. McLuhan's work is really squarely in the area of biology and sociology now, but artists can take to him—he talks their language. It was the same with Freud. Pavlov never caught on with the culturati—all those damned endless clinical descriptions of dog brains. But Freud was "cultural," a lot of great business from Sophocles, Aeschylus, da Vinci, King Oedipus running around, bare-breasted Electra, all those classical lovelies. Freud wrote like an art dealer prospecting in the forbidden lands of brain physiology.

McLuhan talks the same language, and people are willing to undertake massive artistic expressions of his new science of the senses. In the Royal Ontario Museum in Toronto, a McLuhanite named Harley Parker is designing a "pure McLuhan" gallery for displaying invertebrate paleontology, fishes and things, "a gallery of total sensory involvement," Harley Parker says, with the smell of the sea piped in, the tape-recorded sound of waves, colored lights simulating the furzy-plankton undersea green, "not just a gallery of data, but a total experience." In New York, Father John Culkin of Fordham University is considering sort of the same thing, a McLuhan architectural *environment*, only on a much larger scale, a whole communications center at Lincoln Center, the big culture temple.

But with the standard old-line romantic-reactionary literati of New York—that is another story. Old doggies like Dwight Macdonald *recoil* from McLuhan. This man, this pop Guru McLuhan, asserts the supremacy of technology, the environment, over the romantic ego. McLuhan says man succumbs to the new technologies, the new sensory balance the technologies impose, no matter how hard he fights it, even if he doesn't watch the idiot box—*and I don't pay attention to ads*—no matter what. The old doggies put their faces up in the air, with their eyeballs rolled back, looking for God, and moan a few howls there inside their parlor-floor brownstones at this big red fire siren going by, Marshall McLuhan.

Get this man. But if they want to get at McLuhan, they ought to forget the sanctity of the romantic ego, the last gobhead of the literati, and go after him where he is actually vulnerable; one place is his idea of the sensory balance of man and the dominance of one sense over another and so forth. McLuhan is talking straight physiology here, science—and he has not proved that the five senses are actually set up that way. Maybe it can't be proved. As yet, there is no apparatus for measuring just how intensely the human mind is attuned to this or that sense. Knowledge about three of the senses, smell, taste, and touch, is still absolutely primitive. The sense of smell, for example, cannot be measured at all, currently. Perfume makers have to use people they call "noses" to get the right combination for different scents. They put a white smock on THE NOSE and squirt one test batch of hair spray in a tin closet and THE NOSE jumps in there, and then he jumps out of there, and they squirt another batch in the next closet, and THE NOSE jumps in there, and so on and on, with this NOSE in a white smock leaping and diving in tin cubicles—this is sensory *measurement* in the modern age.

The other place they might get McLuhan is in his crazy daredevil weakness for making analogies. He loves the things. He soars around making analogies. The Russians still have a basically aural, tribal sensory balance, and they like to do their spying by ear, hiding microphones in wooden American eagle seals in the American Embassy and so forth. That seems perfectly all right to them, that's natural, but they are scandalized by something like the American U-2 flights—that is *visual* spying, spying by eye. Americans, on the other hand, are basically a visual people; the U-2

flights seem like the natural way to spy, but a mike in the eagle—
that's a scandal to the visual Americans. Beautiful McLuhan rubric
—but . . .

But, all right, he may have missed the mark on this or that, but
McLuhan will remain a major figure in the social sciences if for no
other reason than that he has opened up the whole subject of the
way the new technologies are changing people's thinking, reactions,
life styles, everything. One means, well, one is in a supermarket
and here comes some Adam's-apply carbuncled kid with bad hair
pushing a rolling hamper full of All Detergent Man Mountain
Giant Bonus boxes, and he is not looking where he is going; he is
not *looking* at anything; his eyes are turned off and screened over,
and there is a plug in his skull leading to the transistor radio in the
breast pocket of his shirt, and he is blamming his free hand on the
Giant All boxes, *blam blam ble-blam blam,* keeping time to the
Rolling Stones, *Hey You Get Offa My Cloud;* somewhere inside of
his skull, *blam blam,* plugged into some kind of electronic circuit
out there, another world—and one knows, instinctively, that all this,
is changing people in some kind of way. Sociologists and physiol-
ogists have done practically nothing on the subject. They have done
practically nothing on the way the automobile has changed Americans, as long as cars have been around. Every time sociologists
have a meeting, somebody gets up and says, why doesn't somebody
make a real study of the American automobile? Not just the stuff
about how they're choking our cities or how they made the big
housing developments possible, but how they . . . well, change
people.

Not even with cars! Much less with television, radio, computers
—McLuhan comes on like the only man to reach a huge, hitherto-
unknown planet or something, and there is so much ground to
cover and so little time, all this unknown ground, mothering earth-
quake, swallowing everybody up and they don't even know it. That
is the way McLuhan thinks of it, and he exasperates—

A television executive is up in Howard Gossage's office in the
firehouse in San Francisco, talking to McLuhan and saying how a

couple of things he said don't fit together, they don't hold up; maybe it is the part about the Russian hidden microphones or something. McLuhan pulls his chin down into his neck and opens his right hand like a century plant—

"I'm not offering this as a self-contained theory; I'm making probes. Probes. There is so much here that hasn't even been gone into, I have no interest in debating it point by point along the way. There is so much that hasn't even been *explored*."

Rather grand manner. He won't argue, he just keeps *probing*, he spins off theories and leaves them there for somebody else to debate, moving on all the time on his single track . . . but, of course. The prophet.

A lot of McLuhanites have started speaking of him as a prophet. It is only partly his visions of the future. It is more his extraordinary attitude, his demeanor, his qualities of monomania, of mission—He *doesn't* debate other scholars, much less TV executives. He is not competing for status; he is . . . alone on a vast unseen terrain, the walker through walls, the X-ray eye . . . TV executives. McLuhan even characterizes General Sarnoff, Generalissimo of RCA and NBC, the most powerful man in American communications, a *god* in the TV world, and the eyes of the government, too, for that matter—McLuhan characterizes the good General as one of the "technological idiots." Sarnoff is one of those people who thinks that television is merely a wonderful tool whose impact is merely what a man chooses to do with it.

McLuhan flies all over Canada and the United States to talk to groups of five, six, twelve, well, not twelve, fourteen . . . disciples. Numbers mean nothing to him. If a thousand people suddenly turned up, it might be a bad sign—McLuhan sits in the upper room at the firehouse at a round table with six or eight people, Gossage, Feigen, Mike Robbins of Young & Rubicam, the advertising agency, Herbert Gold, the novelist, Edward Keating, editor of *Ramparts* magazine, not disciples—But what if he is right—and somebody asks McLuhan what he thinks of the *big* communications conference going on in San Francisco at that very moment, at the Hilton Hotel, a thousand people, headed by the great semanticist, S. I. Hayakawa.

"Well . . . they're all working from very obsolete premises, of course. Almost by definition."

By definition?

"Certainly. By the time you can get a thousand people to agree on enough principles to hold such a meeting, conditions will already have changed, the principles will be useless."

McLuhan pulls his chin down into his neck. The Hayakawa conference . . . disappears.

McLuhan may get some of the normal chuckly human satisfaction out of putting down the General Sarnoffs and the Hayakawas of this world and bringing to package design moguls the news that packages have had it and so forth—it is hard to say. More likely, though, he is simply oblivious to the stake other people have in the things he is talking about. He seems oblivous to all the more obvious signs of status where he himself is involved. He just snaps on that Pree-Tide plastic neckband necktie in the morning and resumes his position, at the monomaniacal center of the unseen world . . .

Unseen scholars. McLuhan comes out of a world that few people know about, the world of the liberal arts scholars, the graduate schools, the *carrels*. It is a far more detached and isolated life than any garret life of the artists. Garret life? Artists today spend all their time calling up Bloomingdale's to see if the yellow velvet Milo Laducci chairs they ordered are in yet. Liberal arts scholars, especially in McLuhan's field, English literature, start out in graduate school in little cubicles, known as carrels, in the stacks of the university libraries with nothing but a couple of metal Klampiton shelves of books to sustain them, sitting there making scholarly analogies—detecting signs of Rabelais in Sterne, signs of Byron— would you believe it? in Thoreau, signs of Ovid in Pound, signs of —analogies—hunched over in silence with only the far-off sound of Maggie, a Girl of the Stacks, a townie who puts books back on the shelves—now she is all right, a little lower-class-puffy in the nose, but—only the sound of her to inject some stray, *sport* thoughts into this intensely isolated regimen. In effect, the graduate school scholar settles down to a life of little cubicles, little journals, little money, little chance of notice by the outside world—unless his intense exercises in analogies, mental combinations, bust out with something so . . . electrifying as Marshall McLuhan's.

Even then there is no one in the . . . outside world able to scout scholarly stars, it is all so esoteric. But McLuhan has had Gossage and Feigen, two of the most imaginative characters in San Francisco. Gossage is a tall, pale advertising man with one of the great heads of gray hair in the USA, flowing back like John Barrymore's. Feigen is a psychiatrist who became a surgeon; he is dark and has these big eyes and a gong-kicker mustache like Jerry Colonna, the comedian. He is also a ventriloquist and carries around a morbid-looking dummy named Becky and is able to get into great psychological duels with strangers, speaking through the dummy. Gossage and Feigen started a firm called Generalists, Inc., acting as consultants to people who can't get what they need from specialists because what they need is the big picture. One thing that drew them to McLuhan was his belief in "generalism"—pattern recognition. McLuhan, for example, dismisses the idea of university "departments," history, political science, sociology, and so forth; he considers all that obsolete and works in four or five of the old "fields" at once. It is all one field to him. So Gossage and Feigen invested about $6000 into just taking McLuhan around to talk to people, Big Boys, all sorts, outside the academic world, on both coasts. Gossage says they had nothing particular in mind, no special goal, they just wanted to play it "fat, dumb and happy" and see what would happen.

It all turned out kind of like the way the architect in Evelyn Waugh's *Decline and Fall* describes life as being like one of those whirling discs at the old amusement parks. You get on the disc and it starts spinning and the faster it goes, the more centrifugal force builds up to throw you off it. The speed on the outer edge of the disc is so fast, you have to hold on for dear life just to stay on but you get a hell of a ride. The closer you can get to the center of the disc, the slower the speed is and the easier it is to stand up. In fact, theoretically, at the very center there is a point that is completely motionless. In life, some people won't get on the disc at all.

They just sit in the stands and watch. Some people like to get on the outer edge and hang on and ride like hell—that would be Gossage and Feigen. Others are standing up and falling down, staggering, lurching toward the center. And a few, a very few, reach the middle, that perfect motionless point, and stand up in the dead center of the roaring whirligig as if nothing could be clearer and less confused—That would be McLuhan.

Gossage and Feigen were bringing McLuhan to New York last May, and McLuhan was two days late getting there. He was in Toronto grading papers for two days.

"Grading papers?" says Gossage. Gossage can see the New York panoply of lunches at the Lombardy, lunches at Lutèce, men like Gibson McCabe, and God knows who all else high in the world of communications waiting for McLuhan—and McLuhan holed up imperturbably grading papers. "Listen," says Gossage. "There are so many people willing to invest money in your work now, you'll never have to grade papers again."

"You mean it's going to be fun from now on?" says McLuhan.

"Everything's coming up roses," says Gossage.

In San Francisco, Gossage and Feigen take McLuhan to a "topless waitress" restaurant, the Off Broadway, at the request of some writer from New York in a loud checked suit. Herb Caen, the columnist, is also along. Everybody is a little taken aback. There they all are in the black-light gloom of the Off Broadway with waitresses walking around wearing nothing but high-heel shoes and bikini underpants, and nobody knows quite how to react, what to say, except for McLuhan. Finally, Caen says that this girl over here is good looking—

"Do you know what you said?" says McLuhan, "Good *looking*. That's a visual orientation. You're separating yourself from the girls. You are sitting back and *looking*. Actually, the lights are dim in here, this is meant as a *tactile* experience, but visual man doesn't react that way."

And everyone looks to McLuhan to see if he is joking, but it is impossible to tell there in the gloom. All that is clear is that . . . yes,

McLuhan has already absorbed the whole roaring whirligig into his motionless center. And later in the day, Gossage presents the *pièce de résistance* of the McLuhan Festival, a party in the firehouse. The first floor of the firehouse, now the lobby, is filled, and yet in there Gossage has put a twelve-piece mariachi band, with trumpets . . . *En la Bodega* and the mariachi players stand on the tile in their piped powder blue suits blasting away on the trumpets and *Tout San Francisco* is filing into the firehouse into the face of the—what the hell is Gossage up to now, *Santa Barranza*, mariachi trumpets, the trumpet announcement of the new Darwin-Freud-Einstein, *Grack*, *En la Bodega*. Then McLuhan himself arrives, filing into the firehouse, and there before him is a field of powder blue and . . . yaaaaaaaaaaaaagggghhhhhhh trumpets—and Gossage sits on the stairway with his head thrown back, laughing over the spectacle, but McLuhan—well, let one see here, or, actually, *not* see, the auditory sense is sharply stepped up, the visual fades, just the slightest haze of powder blue—of course! one need only stop struggling with one's eyes, roil, roil, well, of course, it is clear and . . . why not? serene, the new world.

each culture develops its own sense-ratio to meet the demands of its environment.

—JOHN CULKIN, S.J.

3

A HANDFUL OF POSTULATES

Five statements will serve as the fingers that were used in this endeavor to grasp all of reality in a few pages.

1. 1966 B.C.—All the Senses Get Into the Act
2. Art Imitates Life
3. Life Imitates Art
4. We Shaped the Alphabet and It Shaped Us
5. 1966 A.D.—All the Senses Want to Get Into the Act

That Is Really Enough for Any Single Page to Carry

1. 1966 B.C.—All the Senses Get Into the Act

1966 B.C. wasn't a year of any singular importance for our history books, although it was unquestionably a very important year for the moderns of that brave new world. It happens to be a conveniently symmetrical number for a thesis which is partially cyclic.

It gets us back to man before the Phoenician alphabet. We know from our contemporary ancestors in the jungles of New Guinea and the wastes of the Arctic that pre-literate man lives in an all-at-once sense world. The reality which bombards man from all directions was picked up with the omnidirectional antennae of sight, hearing, touch, smell, and taste. The hunters in Robert Gardiner's film tracked the giraffe with across-the-board sensitivity which mystifies Western, literate man. We mystify him too. And it is this cross-mystification which makes intercultural abrasions so worthwhile.

No sense operates in isolation. Vision is partly structured by ocular and bodily movement; hearing by visual and kinesthetic experience. The full sensorium seeks fulfillment in almost every sense experience. All the senses want to get into the act. There is no such thing as a natural sense-ratio among the senses, since the individual is always embedded in a culture and a language which will have preferred sense-ratios. Absolute ratios are impossible to come by, because the observer of any culture is himself imbedded in a culture and a language. Each culture conceals a unique metaphysics; each codifies reality differently. Linguists tell us it's possible to say anything in any language if you use enough words or images, but there's rarely time. The natural course is for a culture to exploit its own biases.

The culture biases of pre-literate man are aural and tactile. This fact is partly a Western outsider's prejudiced view and partly the influence of environment. Under postulate 4, pre-literate man gets a chance to look over the fence to see what our environment has done to us. A brief glance inside an igloo can now tell us something about ourselves. Eskimos see pictures equally well from all angles. They can draw equally well on top of a table or underneath a table. They can draw an accurate map of a coastline after one trip. They have forty or fifty words for the reality we call "snow." They live in a world of acoustic space. They are Eskimos. These individual differences in perception also have their social implications, but these must be left for another day.

Each culture develops its own sense-ratio to meet the demands of its environment. The balance between the senses and, therefore, the perceptual grid of the individual, will always be culture-bound. Each culture experiences reality in a unique manner. It is a question of degree. Some cultures are close enough to each other in perceptual patterns so that the differences pass unnoticed. It is at the poles (literally and figuratively) that the violent contrasts illuminate our own unarticulated perceptual prejudices.

One further observation on our sense experiences. It is almost platitudinous to state that sensation is defined as the resultant experience of the sentient being and not as the input of the stimulus. The sensory *impression* proffered is not the sensory *effect* obtained. Since there is a quantum of sensory energy for any sensory experience, the sense-ratio will differ for different media. Both radio and telephone are auditory media, but they produce different sensory effects. Radio's well-defined sound satisfies the ear and frees the visual energies for intense visual effects. The telephone's poor sound forces a concentration of sensory energy on the act of hearing and has little visual effect. TV and movies are both watched, but with different effects. Since the whole sensorium seeks participation in all sense activity, the senses directly affected by high definition stimuli will tend to become passive, and the senses not stimulated or stimulated by a low definition stimulus will tend to become active. The *effect* is the thing that counts, not the sensuous facts. Content becomes irrelevant in this kind of sensory analysis.

2. Art Imitates Life

Art and technology are extensions of man. Today man has developed extensions for practically everything he used to do with his body. Stone ax for hand. Wheel for foot. Glasses for eyes. Radio for voice and ears. Money is a way of storing energy. All man-made material things can be treated as extensions of what man once did with his body or with some specialized part of his body.

This outering of individual bodily functions is, by definition, since we are at the most developed technological state, now at its most complete stage. Through the electronic media of telegraph, telephone, radio, and television, man has now equipped his world with a nervous system similar to the one within his own body. President Kennedy is shot and the world instantaneously reels from the impact of the bullets. Current concern with the United Nations, the Common Market, ecumenism reflect this organic feel for the new human unity achieved through modern communications media. Current concern with consciousness-expanding drugs perhaps reflects the next frontier for man's outering drives.

Each new invention, by extending one of the human sense organs, necessarily upsets previously achieved sense balances. Until our century these new technologies were closed systems, each operating in isolation from each other. Now in the electric age, the very instantaneous nature of co-existence among our technological instruments has created a crisis quite new in human history. Our extended faculties and senses now constitute a single field of experience which demands that they become collectively conscious. Just as individual consciousness harmonizes a man's sense of life, so now a social or collective awareness of media effects is required for global rationality. Isolationism is dead personally, politically, and socially. Print detribalized man. *The new media retribalize him . . . but now on a global scale.*

3. Life Imitates Art

We shape our tools and thereafter they shape us. Since our tools are extension of our senses, they shape the way we experience reality. William Blake said it: "They became what they beheld." It is because new extensions of man are so upsetting to accepted ways of perceiving reality that the inventors, like the artist, have traditionally been the outsiders. Similarly, the implications of the most revolutionary inventions are seldom immediately perceived because of the human tendency to feel that the future will be a larger or greatly improved version of the immediate past. Man reassures himself that this is so in phrases like "horseless carriage" and "wireless." No more extreme instance of this delusion could be mentioned than our present image of TV as some sort of home movie. A few decades hence it will be easy to describe the revolution in human perception and motivation that resulted from beholding the new mosaic mesh of the TV image.

The formula for hypnosis is "one sense at a time." Each new technology slips by the barrier of consciousness and possesses the power to hypnotize because it isolates the senses. Our excursion into the mesmerizing power of print in our own culture may give us a measure of understanding and sympathy for other entranced people. Hypnosis fills the field of attention by one sense only: Since the theory of a limited quantum of sensory energy holds, all the sense energy rushes to this one sense and thereby dulls the others. Dentists can fill the ear with sound and fill the tooth painlessly. Monkeys can concentrate on food in traps and end up in zoos. Any kind of concentration sets up a new ratio among the senses. The concentration can be derived from an individual, a language, a medium, or a culture. These forms impress themselves on us without benefit of awareness or conscious attention. Their effect on us is quite independent of any theory we may have about them.

It is this ability of media, languages, and cultures to silently impose their presuppositions on their users which makes it so difficult to chart the media grammars. There is no neutral ground, free of biases, where one may insert the fulcrum. The techniques of physics serve well. The nuclei of known atoms are used to bombard the nuclei of unknown substances to reveal their structures. Our age is at last able to do this. The linguists are doing it for languages. The anthropologists are doing it for culture. McLuhan is doing it for the media. All men tend to believe that their way of experiencing reality is the natural way. There was no antidote for this type of provincialism when most men lived out their lives in one culture, using one language, and perhaps two media—speech and writing. Our present abundance has made us aware of our present poverty. We have discovered that we are all culturally deprived because the biases of our culture, language, and media were fixing our senses on limited aspects of a many-splendored reality. Awareness of past prejudice can be a shattering experience, but awareness is the only thread that will lead back to reality.

All perception is selective. We are all experts at discerning other people's patterns of selectivity. Our own are mercilessly hidden from us. Our own personal experience sets up one grid between us and reality. Our culture adds one. Our language and our media system tighten the mesh. No one man, no one culture has a privileged key to reality. This is merely descriptive, not good or bad, just *there*. Like Socratic challenging of assumptions, it can have a disturbing effect on the victims; it can appear to be leading to epistemological scepticism or relativism. As a fact, it can induce a healthy reaction capable to making ugly Americans beautiful; the elite culture humble; the Eskimos respectable; and all of us fully human.

The structural linguists and the cultural anthropologists have sensitized us to the structures and assumptions of language and culture. The idea of the media themselves as prejudged channels of communication is something almost unexamined in our content-oriented habit of analysis. The absence of understanding about the modes of perception imposed by the media is eloquent testimony of their power to hypnotize. The following examples will be somewhat random attempts to break the trance.

Face-to-face speech is the only medium which engages all the senses simultaneously. The Phoenician alphabet (as opposed to the various hieroglyphic, pictographic, and ideographic scripts) busted this nuclear, omnidirectional world of sound into the linear, one-at-a-time patterns of the page. More of this later. Gutenberg invented movable type. His contemporaries viewed this merely as instant and multiple manuscripts. (In the same way, the first Fords had a socket for buggy-whips.) Postulate 4 explores what he really did. The single point of view encouraged by print dissolved under the impact of telegraphy which busted the linearity of print into the mosaic of the front page of the newspaper, information from all directions again. Print makes the eye supreme. Telephone and radio bring the ear back into the game. Radio becomes the nation-

builder because it communicates the fact of national unity instantaneously. Verbally identical messages delivered in print and on
the radio have drastically different effects. The medium is the message. The Kennedy-Nixon TV debates had little to do with content.
A style of life, an image, was up for sale. English is a mass medium. All languages are mass media. All mass media are languages.

Current biblical research is basically a rediscovery of the oral
traditions upon which the Bible is founded. Shocking discovery
—"The Book" is not a book. The oral tradition with its differences from a written tradition provides one of the most fruitful
avenues of literary research. We have just learned again how to
learn foreign languages—by tongue and ear. A famous novel, *The
Caine Mutiny*, appears in four media (book, play, movie, TV).
Each has a different hero: Willi Keith, the lawyer Greenwald, the
United States Navy, and Captain Queeg respectively. Media and
audience biases forced the changes. Children in the first three
grades read (according to a recent test in Toronto) at an average
distance of $6\frac{1}{2}$ inches from the page—significantly closer than
those in the upper grades. Reason: TV. Nothing like the parental
"I told you TV ruins their eyes." This has nothing to do with it. TV
is a low definition medium (poor picture and poor sound); it therefore invites and gets a high degree of psychological involvement.
These kids are trying to get similarly involved with the printed
page. Eerie!

The artists are pretty reliable guides through the media. James
Joyce heralded the end of our ABCED-mindedness with the early
wonders of *Ulysses* and *Finnegans Wake*. Seurat, with his poin-
tillist paintings and Rouault with his stained-glass and light-
through effects prefigured the TV image which is composed of light
through dots. Dickens provided D. W. Griffith with all the techniques of film editing. The way-out artists are giving us reality as
seen from airplanes, from speeding cars, through lenses. Fellini
breaks up chronological time and the barriers between reality and
dream in *8½*. Joyce and Virginia Woolf had already done it in
print. Picasso's playful chickens have the omnidirectional look
about them. Jazz walks all around a few familiar notes and keeps

seeing new things. Pop art alarms the elite by pretending that a Coke and a hamburger have the same canvas rights as a wine bottle and a dead duck.

Walls are being crumbled, not by the messages but by the media: the walls between age groups—all have access to the same vicarious experiences; between nations—the image is international; between in-school and out-of-school—kids learn much more out of school; between subjects in the curriculum—trespassing is the only avenue to meaning. Take any two objects with a betweenness factor and you will find that the barriers were never less relevant. The push is toward a convergent unity. Teilhard de Chardin called it Point Omega.

4. We Shaped the Alphabet and It Shaped Us

Postulate 4. The genies we let out of bottles return to haunt us. As we enter the era of post-literacy, it becomes possible to disengage ourselves for a relatively objective look at the effects of literacy upon us. Cross-media and cross-cultural contrasts also help. The effects are bound to be either meaningless or disturbing since a print-oriented man is using print to communicate to print-oriented men. Operation bootstrap.

Pre-literate man lives in an all-at-once kind of world. It is the world of the ear. Reality comes in from all directions. Time and space are conceived of acoustically. Sung poetry is the great civilizer; oral tradition, the link with the past. Multilevel meanings are the order of the day—there is little literalness (*no lettera*). Words don't refer to things; they are things. Myth explains the many strata of reality. A man's word is binding. A man's memory is phenomenal (by modern standards). The images accompanying his thoughts are auditory. He uses all his senses but within the nuclear and omnidirectional parameters of sound.

The alphabet is a funnel. All sense data must henceforth be squeezed into and through the narrow passage of print. The audible, the pictorial, the tactile, the olfactory—all get translated into the visual and the abstract. The little black marks of the Phoenician alphabet had no semantic meaning beyond their neutral sound.

Reality is squeezed through the funnel of the alphabet. Reality comes out one drop at a time; it is segmented; sequential; it is fragmented along a straight line; it is analytic; it is abridged; it is reduced to one sense; it becomes susceptible to perspective and point of view; it becomes uniform and repeatable. A simple five-second human reaction to a sunset has to be strung out in words for sentence after sentence before one human can tell another what it meant to him. Time and space are busted up into little bits. Zeno comes along with a system that tries to impose the same fragmented grid on the continuum of reality. It sounds logical, but arrows never reach walls because they can never pass through all of Zeno's halfway points. Not much of a theory if one is facing a firing squad.

Gutenberg completed the alphabet revolution. Books speeded up the decoding process we call reading and also made written documents socially available in uniform and multiple copies. Punctuation and pagination came into being. Teachers panic because they can't dictate books which the students already have. Private interpretation becomes theologically possible because for the first time there is something to interpret privately. Print fostered individualism because, as a private teaching machine, it encourages initiative and self-reliance. It created the ideals of inner self-definition and inner goals. It isolated men. They studied alone. They wrote alone and adopted a personal point of view to express themselves to a new audience created by print. Uniform education became possible. All the social habits of uniformity, specialization, and fragmentation were encouraged by the uniform, repeatable, and specialized medium of print.

Sound and sight, speech and print, eye and ear have nothing in common. The human brain has done nothing that compares in complexity with this fusion of ideas involved in linking up the two forms of language. But the result of this fusion is that, once it is achieved in our early years, we are forever after unable to think clearly, independently, and surely about any one aspect of the matter. We cannot think of sounds without thinking of letters; we believe letters have sounds. Verbal images accompany our thought. Gutenberg gave the printed language an authority it has never lost.

Verbal agreements, so meaningful to pre-literate man, must be sealed in writing. Print man plays it by eye. Seeing is believing.

Puns (fun for the ear) become the lowest form of humor. Linear placement in a sentence replaces inflection as a cue to meaning. Good-bye Latin. Dictionaries and standard usage arrive. Wide reading becomes possible. Memorization becomes less necessary.

When slaves turn on their masters, there is a bitterness and lack of logic in their attack which they inevitably regret once they have achieved their freedom. Our civilization is just starting to free itself from the tyranny of print. Print is not a bad thing in itself, but it doesn't merit the continuous monopoly which it has had in the past. Print, like any other finite being, should be asked to do only those things which it can best do.

5. 1966 A.D.—All the Senses Want to Get Into the Act

The new media have busted the linear monopoly of print. Like most revolutions, this one was not led by the establishment. The elite culture, especially the schools, are the vested interest here. Western education is built around the book. Much of our research is patterned on the fragmenting habits of print. Even Freud is culture-bound. Even our movies and TV have not broken the spell of print-oriented man, because they are made by such men. The monopoly of print is over. It's only now a question of ratifying the fact and adapting ourselves and our institutions to the fact. It will not be easy.

Is it worth doing? Is anything else worth doing? Our habits and modes of perception pervade everything we do as men: our inter-personal relationships, our habits of inquiry, our psychological makeup, our work. It's that basic. Our current frantic and almost neurotic concern about literacy is but one example. An *all media literacy* should command the same sense of urgency and commitment. It will if it is understood. Understanding takes time.

What agencies of society should lead the way?

Those two giants who don't speak to each other—the school and the mass media.

Anyone for dialogue?

executives who want this man's insights will get them only on his own terms.

—DEAN WALKER

Marshall McLuhan, professor, has been worrying a lot of people for a long time. He particularly worries executives who are fitfully aware that he is intriguing on subjects they feel should concern them.

They find it hard to evaluate him or come to grips with what he says; many find it still harder to understand why he bothers to say it.

The root of their problem is this: Executives must be primarily and convincingly pragmatic; but McLuhan is a mid-century combination of poet, philosopher, social scientist, scholar, and wit. He is the sort of person they might normally ignore but they are not sure they can because he talks about media, communications, advertising, and social patterns.

Executives are bothered because when they invite the professor to seminars he does not suggest how they might use his insights. In expecting him to, however, they look on him as a manufacturer of products, whereas he really mines raw materials. He loads his boxcars for market from an ore body of perceptions and challenges.

Marshall McLuhan believes he understands the causes of change in society. He continually improves his theory of the roots of past changes and the sources of present ferment. With more time, more work, and more scope for research, he may one day predict future effects from today's hidden causes.

Marx saw economics as society's mainspring. Freud figured sex went a long way. McLuhan sees the key in communications; he can interpret a huge range of historical, cultural, and contemporary phenomena in terms of technological communications advances.

He delivers his interpretations with a mosaic approach that annoys and confuses most readers who are used to arguments being

45

developed "lineally," with effects following cause to seemingly "logical" conclusions. Such lineal preferences, McLuhan believes, are inherited from our previously print-dominated society. In a world of Einsteinian understandings, total-TV, and Picasso, these prejudices roadblock communications and are helplessly "out of phase."

Executives, then, who want this man's insights will get them only on his own terms. To do so takes effort, but if his ideas stand up, pragmatic advantages can follow.

McLuhan is rarely pinned down on anything, which again exasperates harried or hurried executives. He rarely answers questions directly, but uses them as take-off points for a change of direction. As one of his disciples said: "To Marshall, a question is only a ball to be tossed in the air."

An *Executive* panel on one recent evening tried its hand at questioning the professor and kept a note of the balls that he tossed in the air.

They found it exhilarating. They heard plenty of typically extravagant McLuhanisms—"Money is metaphor"; "The medium is the message"; "As people become more involved they know less and less"; "A culture is an order of sensory preferences." These are the sort of unqualified remarks that have delighted headline writers and his critics for years and confused many listeners. But in the mosaic approach each remark must be considered in relationship to whatever else has been said or is yet to be said and, in these terms, each McLuhanism becomes meaningful and valid with study.

The tremendous speed-up in the rate of change in our society, he remarked, gives man his first-ever chance to control his own destiny. Now he can see the patterns of change as they occur and, to an extent, can control or reject them.

The most significant change since man learned to communicate was from "oral" to "lineal" conditioning and then back again. But where it took centuries to change from oral to lineal, the swing back has occurred in a lifetime.

The phonetic alphabet started the swing to the lineal and later the invention of the printing press confirmed it. In the following four hundred years, man's insistence on visual communication—"seeing is believing"—wrenched his other four senses out of alignment. His extreme visual bias affected his logic, his arts, his sciences, and his social patterns, and McLuhan carefully catalogues all this in *The Gutenberg Galaxy*.

And now the pendulum swings the other way and it moves fast enough for McLuhan at least to be aware of it. It is the speed of the change that allows this. "In the next forty years," he predicted, "we will build as much as we have done in the past four thousand. If we go much faster, no building will ever be completed before a part of it is already being pulled down."

There are reasons to welcome the speed-up. The faster you go, the more freedom you can achieve (and when change itself is the only constant, you can also achieve a kind of gyroscopic stability). The new freedom comes through clearer recognition, greater understanding, and a chance for control. In the past, civilizations went down when a new technology arrived. They never knew what hit them because it hit them too slowly, too softly, too imperceptibly. Now changes come fast and hard and, if we care to look, we can see them. This gives us at last some defense, and technology need no longer be a fate.

But to recognize the real changes, as opposed to the effects of change, we have to throw off many accepted ways of thinking and examining situations. Quoting Peter Drucker, McLuhan said: "In any situation, 90 per cent of the events are caused by 10 per cent.

"Now you just can't know that at slow speeds," he explained. "Things have to be moving fast before you can know that only 10 per cent of events cause anything.

"All human beings have a built-in mechanism that stops them looking into that 10 per cent area. In all ages of mankind, they have always turned away from the causative area to the 'problem area' where things are supposed to be 'really happening' for practical guys to attend to. It is in this area where things only seem to be 'happening' that the executive who is above all 'the practical guy' spends his time. It is only here that he feels he is using knowledge pragmatically, that he will have something to show for his efforts. But he is merely solving problems, not eliminating or anticipating them.

"The 90 per cent area is the completely dead area where nothing is causing and everything is caused by. It is the area of all committees and most management. It is the area of things that have to be solved day by day 'to keep the old wheels turning.' This area siphons off most of the talents, most of the brains, and most of the ability.

"To recognize this would have been impossible in business structures fifty years ago. Events moved so slowly that it was like looking at the individual still pictures that comprise a movie. You could never see a pattern of movement if you looked at the stills one at a time; but run them through a projector at speed and any idiot can see it."

McLuhan, of course, is a pattern seeker. He scans superficially an incredibly broad field. *The Gutenberg Galaxy* refers to a libraryful of material and in it all he can plot a pattern of the causes of change in society and even psychologically in man himself. "I think we live in the first age," he told the *Executive* panel, "when change occurs quickly enough to make pattern-recognition possible. For the first time, not just in business history but in human history, we can begin to know something about economic causes and effects because things happen fast."

But the causes, as opposed to the effects, are mostly in that 10 per cent area. "This is the area of the irritating and vulnerable and unpleasant factors in any human situation. This is psychically the area you refuse to look at because it's inconvenient and unpleasant. Take the railways, for example; the irritating and vulnerable part of their activity was trucking. The one area of opportunity in their lives under changing technology was the area of irritation and vulnerability, the truck."

Western man's emphasis on the visual, especially after the invention of printing, changed him completely, the professor is sure. Before print, communicating involved him in living relationships with other people. Even in manuscript culture, writings were normally read slowly and laboriously aloud. But the invention of the printed, reproducible book let man into a new private world. Quietly and alone he could absorb the book's contents. His earlier communal consciousness and participation was replaced by a feeling of privacy, withdrawal, self-containment. Concepts such as freedom began to build. He put his faith into detached analytical knowledge. The neat logic and lineality of letter-after-letter, word-after-word, line-after-line, multiplied indefinitely by mass reproduction in books, led to his concept of unit-after-unit mass production; the physical sameness of each copy of a book led to the concept of market and prices. And the emphasis on the visual altered the previous balance between the senses and altered man's relationships with his surroundings and his fellows.

The end of this print-dominated age was heralded by invention of the telegraph and formally confirmed by the recognition of "curved space" and the new physics in the early twentieth century. Now this new electric age is rearranging men's sense ratios and the world is changing as a result. Yet even a century after the telegraph arrived, the only ones among us who appear to recognize the cause and extent of the change are Marshall McLuhan and some of the better poets and painters. Most of us still cannot see the vital 10 per cent for the insignificant 90 per cent in our way. It is the form of the new media that is important: The contents are irrelevant. . . .

"Involvement" is a key word in the new electrical age. Involvement makes the printed newspaper an "oral" rather than a lineal medium. The newspaper front page exposes you simultaneously to news on all subjects from all over the world. The stories are set in print, but the format is electric and the news has been collected by telegraph.

"You may know very little about the newspaper you read this morning," he said, "but you read it in order to plunge, to involve yourself, in the communal bathtub. Nobody reads a newspaper intelligently or critically. That's not what it is for. It's there for a communal sense of sharing something, for splashing around in. 'C'mon in, the water's fine,' or 'This morning it's not so good.' This is participation, involvement."

McLuhan says that, as you get more involved in something, you understand it less, but he means "understand" in the old lineal sense of having a detached or "logical" point of view, an "explanation," a coherent summary.

"Since TV, Quebec has changed its own image, has a totally new image of itself. One that's much more tightly organized, very much more complex, and deeper than the previous image it had." He applies this thinking to corporate image as readily as to political image. As it becomes thicker and deeper it becomes less intelligible to those involved. That is, they don't have such a detached, analytical, from-the-outside knowledge. They don't have a perspective, a fixed point of view.

"This is true too of goal-seeking and goal-making. As people become more deeply involved in a situation, they see that they have no goals at all. And so, in this electric age which involves us so deeply in every aspect of ourselves and simultaneously in all aspects of other people, we know less and less about what we want to do.

"The world we lived in prior to the electric age was very abstract, very specialized, very fragmented," he said. Even the idea of "a job" results from print technology and biases. "Jobs are one of the most extreme forms of specialism and fragmentation in human history. There were no 'jobs' in the Middle Ages. There were no 'jobs' in the ancient world. There were only roles. Jobs came in with printing and highly specialized human organization."

The executive in the post-literate world, just as in that pre-literate world, has a role rather than a job. He never really stops work, nor by old-line definitions does he ever exactly start. That's why executive remuneration is such a problem. How do you pay a man for filling a role, for being completely involved?

And all situations completely involve all other situations. This is the new lesson from the physicists who talk about "electrical field," where everything reacts simultaneously on everything else. This is the new essence of existence, the new bias that replaces the lineal bias. You cannot realistically say one thing "causes" another in an electrical field: Everything happens simultaneously.

"Any electrician will tell you that there is no electricity in a wire. Electricity isn't contained in anything; it is merely a changing relationship among objects, including the molecular parts of the wire. No electricity flows through a wire. But we can't grasp this. In our visually oriented world, we cannot envisage electricity at all, nor the effects of electricity. The reason that nearly everybody in the world, except a few artists, is hopelessly out of phase is that he tries to organize his life visually whereas the whole electric age is a nonvisual phenomenon.

"We try to visualize all the time because it is the only training we've had. Naturally we try to use the part we're competent in because we're totally illiterate in the other areas. And this visualization teaches us to make connections between things. We think that everything should be in its proper place and in proper relationship to other things."

All this, of course, is very abstract and why should the executive or anyone else care? Because, says McLuhan, it helps you control. These abstracts are about the 10 per cent area which causes things to happen in the 90 per cent area, with which, in the past, you have been almost entirely concerned.

"Nobody, except perhaps an atomic physicist or two, ever planned changes. Everyone else says: 'Let's just try it and wait and see what happens.' That's the old visual technology. When something works, advertisers ask themselves: 'What did we do that time?' They still don't know anything about advertising because they don't know anything about media. When they step up the intensity of some medium and get some crazy kickback, they don't know what happened.

"And in fact, of course, they get the really big effects from suddenly dropping the intensity of a medium, because then they get involvement. It's like listening on the telephone—you have to give it all your attention."

Just as fragmentation, division of labor, mechanical mass production all followed from print, so do automation and radical changes in marketing and consumption patterns follow from electronics in our new post-literate age.

"Post-literacy is not the same as pre-literacy. On the other hand, we do coexist with many parts of the world today, like India and China, that are pre-literate.

"For the sake of getting industrialized, China is making a bid at getting literate. Russia pushed further along into literacy than she had been. It is this stepping up of the visual component in Russian life that follows literacy that makes Russians interested in markets, consumer goods, organization. You can't even have markets on a pre-literate level. The entire concept of a uniform price comes from print. In the post-literate world we have finished with that concept too. People are terrified of automation because they can see no liaison between work and remuneration and markets. And there isn't any. They'll have totally new markets. Currency was merely a technology to relate fragmented uniform goods to fragmented uniform jobs. What happens to currency in the post-literate age? You get the credit card."

McLuhan bothers executives because they cannot define him, and he has a comment on that problem too. "One of the failings of a visually oriented world is the need to classify. I consider my role is to hit upon as many relative things as I can with my perceptions in any field at all. I just try to chart, grope, plot, find; and not to actually translate that sort of perception, that sort of finding, into a material that is immediately acceptable to a specialized audience of some sort." It is the failure to accept McLuhan on these terms that has caused so much resentment. "I don't think it is conceivable," he added, "that one could find out anything that could not somehow be used."

McLuhan uses the word "myth" extensively to refer to the shorthand, almost symbolic "package understandings" we are continually developing in these days of complex field situations. And of course he himself, probably deliberately, speaks and writes mythically. His shorthand can only become clear as you get familiar with his whole background of writings and study.

"There's a huge gap. People live mythically but they still don't think mythically. They go on thinking fragmentarily and analytically. Our businesses are still conducted on principles that are far removed from their actual needs. That's why the psychiatrist's couch is so filled with clients. There is this huge gap between the way people live and the way they think, between the image they

have of their living and the actual form of their lives and relationships to other people. Because electricity offers a sort of extension
of our entire nervous system, we are deeply involved with other
people but we still have a built-in pattern of private noninvolvement. Jt's a legacy of literacy and we get filled up with guilt feelings: 'I'm not living right'; 'I'm not giving'; 'I'm not loving
enough.'

"The theater of the absurd is a dramatization of this situation.
People come on stage and do things and say things and nobody
listens and nobody pays any attention to what they are doing. And
we all live like that from day to day, whereas in actual fact the
situation requires another form of behavior in which we respond
readily and freely to other people and other needs. We're not conditioned that way yet; we're conditioned to staying apart: to stay
out and stand off. It fills the John Birchers with horror to discover
they live in a world in which they have to be involved with other
people."

A famous McLuhanism is: "The medium is the message." Television, for example, affects you far more by what it is than by
what it offers. Yet what it is remains the 10 per cent overlooked
area to most people: What it says is the 90 per cent that most people are concerned about. "You could say that in any situation the
area of innovation, of novelty, of new impact is always small. But
everything affects everything else simultaneously. It's like having
a bouquet in the room—it affects every part of the room—the rugs,
the air, everything.

"The thing that does change the world, that shifts people's perceptions around and really makes them look and feel differently,
is the 10 per cent area in any situation. In media, that is the form
and not the content, and no one pays any attention to it at all."

The McLuhan mythic statements (he told *Executive*, for example: "We're moving out of a world of visual classification of knowledge and the education of individuals into a world of singing
commercials and traveling encyclopedias") are all examples of
compression of language; and compressed language is always
poetic. The professor is quite happy to be called a poet. "If you are

given the problem of compressing a whole news story into a six or eight word headline, you are almost forced to write poetically. The content of speech is not speech but a whole ballet of mental faculties. When you utter a word, it immediately begins to pick up things from other people. A word's meaning is infinite and a dictionary is merely a farce. Poets rub words together to hear what happens; they don't care about meaning.

"Metaphor is a kind of compression. It means, literally, translate or carry over. To carry something over from one area into another area, you have to look at one situation through another situation. Metaphors are the very gist of how we operate.

"Money is metaphor. If your buck pays for a haircut and a cab ride and a toothbrush, those are all variations of one man's work into another man's work. Transactions are metaphors. In management we use metaphor as a technique for brainstorming. Operations Research is systematically employed metaphor in which you select a problem as something to be perceived by everybody and they all turn their own forms of perception loose and each translates it through his perception processes and each comes up with a completely different set of metaphors or ideas on that problem."

How does it help to have McLuhan now calling "metaphor" what management was quite happily calling Operations Research?

"It's just like the advertisers who say, 'What did we do that time?' If they know what they are doing it saves a lot of work and an awful lot of energy.

"This Operations Research, by the way, is surely one of the big new patterns emerging in management. It's dialogue teaming and working on common problems in depth—instead of assigning fragmented problems to individual guys in the firm." And this again neatly supports his overall thesis of the change from lineal to oral approaches.

According to McLuhan, every time you put undue emphasis on one sense, the others all perform complicated readjustments. When sensory preferences change, the culture changes with them and the new electric age radically alters our sensory preferences. One task of his new communications institute at the University of Toronto is to measure such orders of sensory preference.

"Our sensory preferences are changing rapidly. A culture consists of an order of sensory preferences—how much lighting, how much sound, how much space, how much distance, how much color.

"It is the medium itself that alters our sensory preferences. The quick effect is on the young. It filters through to older people much less than it does to the four-year-old. If you know exactly what changes have occurred in sensory preferences as a result of TV conditioning, then you know how many years you've got before you've got to contend with that factor in the marketplace. You can pinpoint these things, put them right up on the wall where your product designers can see them. The new feeling for space in housing, for example, has come in since TV in a very hot potent way. . . ."

"In a highly visual society, people are all alienated. They are all outsiders looking in on the social scene. This sense of separation and analytic detachment resulted from print, and ends with the new electric technology. But we have built up and institutionalized all this alienation for a long time in forms of privacy and individualism. When suddenly it ends, the roof falls in.

"Now the speed with which these new technologies act on different groups or cultures can be pinpointed once you have adequate measurements of the existing order of sensory preferences."

He does offer one startling prediction.

Technologies, to McLuhan, are all extensions of man. Clothes and houses extend his skin. The wheel extends his legs. Electricity extends his entire nervous system; a TV camera extends his eye and a microphone his ear. And now computers extend some of the activity that previously only went on inside man's brain. "This is tantamount to an extension of consciousness. If you extend enough of it you have, in effect, pushed consciousness itself outside.

"I think we have a chance in our lifetime of broadcasting consciousness in the same way we now broadcast light. Now consciousness is an activity, it's not a content. It's like hearing or doing something: It's a form of action. So this will be another of those items in the 10 per cent area . . . ."

And on and on Marshall McLuhan goes, worrying at this new perception now like a dog at a slipper. It's a radical and exciting

idea and it will probably arrive because McLuhan is achieving
a pretty good track record for the accuracy of his vision.

But with a little luck, by the time Western man does learn to
broadcast his consciousness and thus starts another psychic-social-
economic upheaval, Marshall McLuhan of Toronto will have
pushed his studies and ponderings far enough along to be able to
plot its results in advance.

5 it is perhaps typical of very creative minds that they hit very large nails not quite on the head. —KENNETH E. BOULDING

If, as Marshall McLuhan repeats almost to the point of being repetitious, the medium is the message, there is really no way of reviewing these two extraordinary books* in a medium as linear,
visual, and nontactile as print. One might use a book as a weapon,
for, as McLuhan understands very well, a weapon is also a medium
and a message, in which case one would simply throw the book at
the reader. When I took my degree at Oxford I was literally struck
by the fact that the Vice-Chancellor, in conferring the degree, hit
the four kneeling candidates before him solemnly on the head with
a large Bible: "In nomine Patris (bang!) et Filii (bang!) et
Spiritus (bang!) Sancti (bang!)" Reading these books is a rather
similar experience. One is tempted to put the whole review into the
form of a comic strip with balloons simply saying "Pow!,"
"Zowie!," and so on. Or perhaps one could simply abandon the
alphabet and write a long line of asterisks, exclamation points, and
question marks, like this: ! * * ! * * * ! ! * ? * ? ! * *

---

* Editor's Note: *The Gutenberg Galaxy* and *Understanding Media*.

It is clear after reading these books that something which Mc-Luhan will not allow me to call an explosion but which I am damned if I will call an implosion is going on in Toronto, beneath the deceptive surface of what is often regarded as a plain and provincial, even Presbyterian, exterior. The knowledgeable, however, will nod sagely to each other and murmur a magic password, "Innis." The late Harold Innis, whose stature rises as we recede from him, was perhaps the first man to realize that communication was the key to social phenomena of all kinds. The all-too-select few who have read a remarkable little magazine called *Explorations*, which came out of Toronto some years ago, realized that the Innis ferment was working mightily. Again, to vary the medium and to mix the metaphor, the McLuhan books are the skyrocket that came out of this ferment, and one feels almost that if one lit them with a match they would soar up into the sky and explode into a thousand stars.

Let me, however, try to come down to earth and explain what the books are about. *The Gutenberg Galaxy*, in spite of the fact that convention compels it to be printed as a codex, is obviously designed to be printed on a Moebius strip. It has no real beginning or end, though it ostensibly begins with *King Lear* and ends with a significant reference to *Finnegans Wake*, which also has no beginning or end. It has no chapters, but is divided into about a hundred sections, each of which is headed by a chapter gloss, which summarizes but is also an integral part of the section. Each of these is pretty self-contained, and can be read almost at random in any order. The total effect is almost literally that of a galaxy or a great garden of jeweled aphorisms. I can perhaps best give the flavor of the book by quoting some of these, almost at random. For instance, page 18, "The interiorization of the technology of the phonetic alphabet translates man from the magical world of the ear to the neutral visual world"; 22, "Schizophrenia may be a necessary consequence of literacy"; 24, "Does the interiorization of media such as 'letters' alter the ratio among our senses and change mental processes?"; 26, "Civilization gives the barbarian or tribal man an eye for an ear and is now at odds with the electronic world"; 31, "The new electronic interdependence recreates the world in the image of a global village"; 124, "The invention of typography confirmed and extended the new visual stress of applied knowledge, providing the first uniformly repeatable 'commodity,' the first assembly-line, and the first mass-production"; 199, "Print, in turning the vernaculars into mass media, or closed systems, created the uniform, centralizing forces of modern nationalism"; 208, "The uniformity and repeatability of print created the 'political arithmetic' of the seventeenth century and the 'hedonistic calculus' of the eighteenth"; 239, "Nobody ever made a grammatical error in a nonliterate society"; 251, "Typography cracked the voices of silence."

Frankly, hopefully "gentle reader," how do you review a book like this? *Understanding Media* is somewhat more conventional in form, in that it has chapters, and does seem to have a beginning and an end. The crackling quality of the ideas and of the style, however, remains, and it is really the same book as *The Gutenberg Galaxy* in a slightly more conventional form, and applied more directly to the problems of the modern world. Even so, there is a new idea on almost every page, and the sheer density of new ideas is so great that at the end one has a distinct feeling of having been hit over the head. The publisher is reported to have said that nobody would read a book unless at least 90 per cent of it was familiar, and there is no doubt that a book of this kind, where 90 per cent of the ideas are unfamiliar to the average reader, is exhausting. It has long been a custom of mine to take notes of the books I read on the flyleaves at the back, and usually the page or two which the publisher thoughtfully provides, presumably for this purpose, is ample. I usually only jot down things which I think are somewhat new to me or significant. In McLuhan's case I find I have not only covered all the flyleaves provided, but my notes have spilled over onto an assortment of airline menus and hotel stationery, reflecting the synthesis of two means of communication, the airplane and the book.

Now, however, comes the sober and earthy work of appraisal. Is the *Galaxy* a firework, exploding into stars and descending as a stick, or is there something here that shines continuously as part of the structure of the social universe? What, in other words, happens to the McLuhan message after it has gone through the medium of the Boulding nervous system? I think my conclusion is that there are a good deal of fireworks, but in the middle of the fireworks there are some real bright and continuing stars, in the light of which the world will never be quite the same again. I will try to summarize in some chapter glosses of my own.

1. A social system is largely structured by the nature of the media in which communications are made, not by the content of these communications.

This, I take it, is the central message of McLuhan, and with this proposition I think I agree almost 99 per cent. It is the invention of spoken language that differentiated man from the beasts, and enabled him to create societies, social systems, and social evolution in the first place. The invention of writing is a major mutation. Without it, urban civilization would have been inconceivable, even though it is not the only precondition of civilization. Thus, we must have the domestication of plants and animals, that is, agriculture, before a sufficiently large and stable food surplus appears with which cities can be fed. Men must be fed before they can write. Once they start to write, however, a whole new fabric of social life is created, and man becomes conscious of time, and the social organization extends backward into the past and forward into the future in a way it could never do in a purely oral society. Societies with alphabets do differ from those with ideographs, though perhaps McLuhan overdoes this. All languages are really ideographic. The alphabet is merely a crutch toward learning the *gestalt* patterns of whole words and sentences, though it is undoubtedly convenient in writing dictionaries and developing lexicographical orderings. The relationship between literacy and violence forms a fascinating theme which recurs constantly in McLuhan. The letters of the alphabet are the dragon's teeth from which spring armed men. I am not sure that he is entirely right in this; I suspect rather that the alphabet and the armed men both spring from a more remote and fundamental cause, which is the rise of large-scale organization itself. The apparent peacefulness of the Neolithic village and the beastly violence of civilization may reflect merely the ability to organize violence, and even though literacy is part of the skills of organization, it is by no means the whole.

2. Media can be divided into "hot" media, which do not involve much participation on the part of the recipient, and "cool" media, in which the process of communication involves a great deal of participation on the part of the recipient. The effect of a medium on the structure of society depends very much on its temperature.

The terminology, I think, is unfortunate, but the idea is an important one, even if McLuhan runs it a little into the ground. Print is a hot medium. It is like a branding iron, imposing its own pattern on the page, if not on the mind. It is endlessly repeatable; it implies abstraction. It carries man away from intimate, complex relationships, from *Gemeinschaft* into *Gesellschaft*, from tribalism into nationhood, from feudalism into capitalism, from craftsmanship into mass production, from lore into science. It builds large-scale organizations because it develops abstract and simple human relationships, and permits the almost endless multiplication of messages and patterns. By contrast, speech is a cool medium, developing dialogue, response, feedback, complex and intricate patterns of personal relationships, family-centered societies, a familistic ethic, tribalism, and superstition. McLuhan argues that by far the most important thing that has happened in the twentieth century is the development of television, which is a cool medium of communication, involving a high level of participation on the part of the viewer, mainly, it would seem, because the television image is so imperfect.

It is clear that McLuhan has an enormously important idea here. On the other hand, it is not difficult to catch him out in inconsistencies, especially in his discussion of television, where he seems the least convincing. From one point of view, surely both radio and television are as hot media as print, in the sense that they do not really evoke dialogue or feedback between the recipient and the originator of messages. On the other hand, one feels that McLuhan is quite right in pointing out the enormous contrast between radio and TV. Hitler was a phenomenon of the brief radio age. On

TV he would have been as ridiculous as McCarthy was. There is no doubt that TV elected Kennedy, defeated Nixon, and destroyed McCarthy, and that radio was the secret of the power both of Hitler and of Roosevelt. But this has very little to do with the hot-cold continuum, as McLuhan describes it. The real difficulty here, and it is something which is likely to distract attention from the enormous importance of McLuhan's message, is that he has tried to squash into a single dimension properties of media which require at least three dimensions for their exposition. We have on the one hand the dimension of involvement of the recipient, which is the one on which McLuhan concentrates, and this is indeed important. It accounts for a great deal of the different effects of oral *versus* written communication, or the difference between the printed page and the picture, or the difference between Renaissance and modern painting, or the difference between Mozart and Strindberg. I would like to call this dimension the *demandingness* of the media. Some media are demanding, some are undemanding. On this dimension, I suspect that print is "cooler" than McLuhan thinks. Print is not imprinted on the mind the way it is on paper. In order to effect the transmission from the printed page to the nervous system of the reader, an enormous amount of involvement is required, and the pattern of the printed page has to be translated with the aid of an enormous memory bank into a totally different pattern in the nervous system. After all, there are no letters in the brain. Demandingness here is perhaps more a function of the context of the medium than the actual physical form of the medium itself, and McLuhan often makes the mistake of supposing that it is the physical form of the medium which is significant rather than its social context.

A second dimension which McLuhan tries to squash into his single continuum is the *range* of a medium. This is closely related to the ability of the medium to develop a system of feedback from the communicatee to the communicator. A conversation, even more a dialogue, is the medium with the smallest range. It exists for the most part only at a single point in time and space, even though there is a time dimension in individual memory. The invention of writing made it possible for the present to speak to the future, and to hear from the past. It also made it possible for one man to communicate with people far beyond the range of his voice. Printing merely introduced a quantitative change in this dimension. It merely had the effect of amplifying the effect of manuscript. It is significant, I think, that in the age of print between Gutenberg and Edison, a man could communicate in visual form to many more people than he could communicate with orally. Electronics changed all this. The phonograph and the tape did for the ear what writing and printing had done for the eye. It enabled us to hear people from the past and to speak to people in the future. It also increased the potential number of people who can hear one man to include the whole population of the earth. As communication increases in range, however, it tends to lose in feedback. With increase in range, dialogue passes into monologue.

A third dimension of media is their information *density*. McLuhan hints at this many times, but never quite seems to spell it out. The concept here is close to the information theorist's concept of capacity. The information intake of the human is limited by the capacity of his sense organs. The ear has a greater capacity than the skin, and the eye than the ear. The combination of all the senses has a greater capacity than any one of them taken singly. The problem is complicated by the fact that the capacity may not be a simple additive quantity. We are interested, furthermore, not merely in the amount of information which can be transmitted per unit of time, but in the total information which can be transmitted and processed during the life of a system. There is no point in having an enormous intake of information through the senses for five minutes if it takes us five days to digest and process the information we have received. It is probably the information-processing apparatus which is the real bottleneck, not the information-receiving apparatus. The failure to realize this occasionally leads McLuhan astray. I suspect, for instance, that he puts too much stress on "synaesthesia," or the combination of the senses, and not enough on the fact that it is the processing of information in the human nervous system which is the really crucial process in the social system. In this sense it *is* the message, not the medium, which is important. The message is not just another medium, as McLuhan is continually saying, for the message consists of the processing of information into knowledge, and not the mere transmission of information through a medium.

3. Print created an "explosion" resulting in the breakup of an old integrated order into individualistic, differentiated, atomistic, mechanical human particles, producing classical economics, Protestantism, and the assembly line. Electricity creates an "implosion" which unifies the nervous systems of all mankind into a single contemporaneous whole, bringing us back to the tribal village, this time on a world scale.

This exciting theme recurs constantly in McLuhan's work. It is one of those great flashes of light which make the surrounding world seem rather dim, and it seems almost sacrilegious to ask if this idea is true or can be tested. Print certainly had a lot to do with Protestantism and capitalism. On the other hand it also had a lot to do with the rise of the modern nation, the development of national literatures, and the breakup of the transnational order of the Middle Ages. It is true that a book (in manuscript) created medieval Europe, and another book created Islam, and with the coming of print these old unities fragmented. Is this the result of print, however, or is it simply the result of multiplication? Surely if Gutenberg had discovered an offset process by which manuscripts themselves could simply be reproduced cheaply and easily, the effect would have been exactly the same as the discovery of print. Here again I think we see McLuhan concentrating on one dimension of a medium to the exclusion of others. Similarly with the electric implosion. It is certainly true that the rise of large-scale organization is intimately connected with the development of the telephone and telegraph and instantaneous communication. These inventions have had an enormous effect in increasing the range of media, both in terms of the distance over which dialogue could be conducted, and also in terms of the number of people to which a single person can speak. On the other hand, I would argue that electricity in itself has not had much effect on either the demandingness or the density of media in general. It has raised some and lowered others. Consequently, I have doubts about the world village. It is true, I think, that an increase in the range of media, whether this is conversations or weapons, increases the optimum scale of organization, and that we have probably now got to the point where the optimum scale of political organization is the whole world. This does not mean, however, that we are going back to the tribal village. We are going on into something quite new and strange, and even though this newness and strangeness is highly conditioned by the nature of the media that produce it, it is by no means clear that McLuhan has caught the exact relationship. It is perhaps typical of very creative minds that they hit very large nails not quite on the head.

These criticisms in no way detract from the enormous importance of these works. They should provide hypotheses for social sciences to test for a hundred years to come. One would like to see them required reading in every university. There is indeed in these days an invisible college, as de Solla Price calls it, of people who have perceived the crucial role of information processes in social systems. I am not sure that I would appoint McLuhan president of this invisible college, but I would certainly welcome him as its dean.

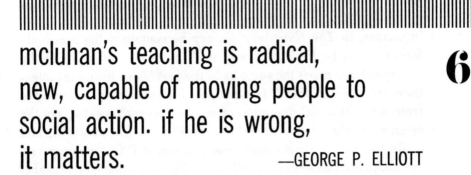

mcluhan's teaching is radical, new, capable of moving people to social action. if he is wrong, it matters.
—GEORGE P. ELLIOTT

6

Marshall McLuhan began as a literary scholar, an English professor, a free-roving speculative intellectual. His writings were to be found in the best intellectual quarterlies. The range of his erudition and the brilliance of his ideas were beyond cavil.

His first book, *The Mechanical Bride: Folklore of Industrial Man,* published in 1951, consists of fifty glosses on texts taken from the mass media, nearly all advertisements from magazines. The glosses are charged with intelligence, but also with moral outrage. "That man counts himself happy today whose school training wins him the privilege of getting at once into the technological meat grinder. That is what he went to school for. And what if he does have the consistency of hamburger after a few years? Isn't everybody else in the same shape? Hamburger is also more manageable than beef cuts." In 1962 he published *The Gutenberg Galaxy.* The book is the best of his three for several reasons. In it he contemplates such literary texts as *Don Quixote,* and the notions these texts stimulate in him are a good deal more interesting than the notions provoked by, say, the table of contents of *The Reader's Digest* for August, 1947 (one of the texts glossed in his first book). It employs his scholarship coherently; at least a fourth of it consists of quotations from other speculative scholarly intellectuals of the first order, so that you have the reassuring feeling that McLuhan is adding to a substantial body of intelligent opinion rather than exploding on his own. In it, he also cleared his prose of his earlier too easy tone of moral outrage. ("Value judgments have long been allowed to create a moral fog around technological change such as renders understanding impossible.") Perhaps most

important, in *The Gutenberg Galaxy* he contained the messianic
fervor which he later gave way to. The ideas (and a lot of the
examples) are much the same as in the first book; his moral intentions are unmistakable ("Is it not possible to emancipate ourselves
from the subliminal operation of our own technologies? Is not the
essence of education civil defense against media fallout?"), and
while his tone is often prophetically arrogant ("Cultures can rise
far above civilization artistically but without the phonetic alphabet
they remain tribal, as do the Chinese and Japanese."), what he
intends to accomplish in this book is still, for him, modest. "A few
decades hence it will be easy to describe the revolution in human
perception and motivation that resulted from beholding the new
mosaic mesh of the TV image. Today it is futile to discuss it at
all." (Two years, not two decades, later, in his next book he discusses this subject at great length.) One result of the relatively
calm qualities of *The Gutenberg Galaxy* is that, when he drops one
of his idea-bombs, it has a more or less rational context to qualify
it, to give it meaning, and it does not lose its distinctiveness by
being only one of dozens of blockbusters scattered about promis-
cuously. "The unconscious is a direct creation of print technology,
the ever-mounting slag-heap of rejected awareness." An idea like
that needs room to blow up in, lots of pages on both sides to
cushion its effect in the reader's mind. This idea is not given nearly
enough room, but it gets some; and anyway the book isn't booby-
trapped with so many loaded notions but what you can manage to
get through it in one piece, if you're lucky.

Then in 1964 came *Understanding Media: The Extensions of
Man.* Scholarship dwindled, messianism magnified, and the book
sells like crazy. Marshall McLuhan has become a power in the
land. There are a good many intellectual messiahs among us these
days, none of them very impressive; Norman O. Brown, for example, is faddish. But McLuhan is in my opinion much the most
powerful. Brown's nostalgia for Innocence (polymorphous perverse sexuality for everybody), free from the incursions of the
Devil (inhibition), is hardly worth mentioning except as one more
instance of Rousseauistic utopianism. That he has a following is
mildly interesting, but I doubt that his teachings will lead to anything much graver than programmatic fondling, than which we

have more disturbing prospects now before us; besides, it's good material for satire. McLuhan's teaching, however, is radical, new, animated by high intelligence, and capable of moving people to social action. If he is wrong, it matters.

It is not possible to give a rational summary of McLuhan's ideas, for two reasons: The attitude and tone of his writing are at least as important as the ideas themselves, and to systematize these ideas, even in outline, would be to falsify their nature and impact. His writing is deliberately anti-logical: circular, repetitious, unqualified, gnomic, outrageous. "It was thanks to the print that Dickens became a comic writer." Absurd! Still, maybe there's something to it? It's worth thinking about at least.—Good McLuhan.

Though his ideas do not compose a system, they are a recognizable complex. They are about the ways in which the media—a term he stretches until it includes language and technology—extend and alter our means of perception and communication and thereby affect our nature. In his earlier writings, he, the good English professor, was appalled by what he observed in the mass media. But gradually he came to believe that the vulgarity, immorality, and imbecility which characterize so very much of what the media (apparently) communicate to the masses are really of secondary importance. "The medium is the message." That is to say, what is communicated has much less effect on us than the means by which it is communicated. For example, he attributes to the introduction of movable type a "galaxy" of changes in Western man's consciousness, making it possible for us to act without reacting and thereby engendering extreme specialization of social function and a sort of cultural schizophrenia; his argument in support of this thesis is formidable, illuminating albeit extreme, and all his own. He attributes equally extensive changes to the electronic media, especially TV; in gauging the effect of TV on our nature, he says, the fact that TV images are made mosaically and simplify their subjects to cartoons is incomparably more important than whether the program content is intelligent or stupid, in good taste or bad, honest or meretricious. His TV argument is as brilliant and original as his movable-type argument, and it stirs one to thought about a subject which needs to be thought about. For this one is grateful to him, as one is grateful for many isolated insights. But one is not grateful for the argument as a whole; pretending to be a forecast based on solid fact, it is mostly a wishful prophecy deriving from apocalyptic vision.

Things are changing so fast, he says, that we must control the media right now, not a moment to lose, if they are not to destroy us:

> The mark of our time is its revulsion against imposed patterns. We are suddenly eager to have things and people declare their beings totally. There is a deep faith to be found in this new attitude—a faith that concerns the ultimate harmony of all being. Such is the faith in which this book has been written. It explores the contours of our own extended beings in our technologies, seeking the principle of intelligibility in each of them. In the full confidence that it is possible to win an understanding of these forms that will bring them into orderly service, I have looked at them anew, accepting very little of the conventional wisdom concerning them.

Exactly how these forms are to be brought into "orderly service" is never made clear. The omission of this *how* becomes enormously important: We are being altered by TV and the other electronic media; all we have to do is to control them (but *how?*) in order to achieve the wholeness we have long lacked.

It is easy to see why McLuhan is listened to so eagerly: With the highest of intellectual credentials, he sounds like a Future-salesman assuring us that there are great days ahead and that what seems to be so terrible now arises only from resistance to change. What if admen do use TV as a way to spread lies and distortions and idiocy? It doesn't matter much anyway: The medium is the message, and a medium is neither moral nor immoral. All in our culture are being changed by TV, those who don't watch as well as the addicts, so why not watch? Don't resist, don't be obsolete before your time, move with the age. In plain words, Progress, with Utopia in view. An electronic Chiliasm. The Millennium now.

In itself, McLuhan's vision matters little more than Norman O.

Brown's. It is not hard, really, to say, "I'm for civilization, grow-ing up, heterosexual lovemaking with and without orgasms, cities, and language," then shove those two mantics into their earthly paradises and lock the gates on them. But McLuhan is carefully listened to by admen (who never expected it would be an English professor that would justify them!), and he has followers in educa-tion, some of whom are influential. Two that I have met are Sister Jacqueline, president of Webster College in St. Louis, and Father Walter Ong, professor of English at the University of St. Louis, where McLuhan taught for seven years. Sister Jacqueline is a very active member of a committee which advises the Office of Educa-tion and the President. This committee is under the chairmanship of Jerrold Zacharias, the physicist in good part responsible for the reforms in the teaching of physics and mathematics in the schools, and it is now engaged in devising experiments for the improve-ment of every sort of teaching. One subcommittee consists of writer-teachers; it divided into conservatives like me who believe that the schools can and should primarily be concerned to teach writing and reading, and progressives who believe that the schools should build upon the children's own oral language, each child making a tradition of himself, and should use all possible electronic audio-visual aids. Two of the progressives are the novelists John Hawkes and Albert Guérard, Jr., who are presently engaged in an oral-tradition experiment at Stanford under a grant from the Office of Education. The conservatives proposed no experiments, certainly no electronic ones, but smaller classes and more teachers, extra training for the teachers, and better texts; they were shunted aside. There are a good many other progressivistic, Rousseauistic, Mc-Luhanite innovators in education now, churning out notions. We shall be hearing a lot from and about them. They accept, or agree with, McLuhan's view: "We are entering the new age of education that is programmed for discovery rather than instruction. . . . We would be foolish not to ease our transition from the fragmented visual world of the existing educational establishment by every possible means." This idea sounds fine, and it would be fine, if one could just ignore the complex of ideas which it is part of, and the narcosis which is their goal.

My contention is that McLuhan has become a double agent. He originally went out among tribalizing Media as a spy from civilization. (Spy is mine, but the tribal-civilization dichotomy is his, and useful.) But he stayed there too long; in Blake's words, which McLuhan tirelessly quotes: "We become what we behold." Now, in his last book and in his lectures since then, he continues to be an agent reporting back to civilized (literate, literary) people what the tribes are up to; but he also functions among us as an agent of the Media, proclaiming the destruction come and to come. To support this charge that he is a double agent, let me cite two statements he made before a meeting at the P.E.N. international conference in New York in June 1966. Challenged by the critic John Simon with having deserted literature for advertising and TV, he said that, on the contrary, he saw it as his mission to save literature from the media. He also said he did not believe a lot of the ideas he threw off; he was using them to "probe the environment." However, six months before, in the grand ballroom of the Waldorf, he addressed (for a star fee, I am told by a man who sells advertising and who was there) an assemblage of business and advertising executives. He did not tell them he was probing the environment or saving literature from the media. He told them pretty much what he had already said in *Understanding Media*. A sincere double agent: Both sides are right. He often speaks, quite plausibly, of "point of view" as being a result of print and of how he is true to the electronic age because he writes mosaically. No fixed point of view? Why shouldn't one be working for both sides at once? The only reason I can think of why one shouldn't is neither mechanical nor electronic but moral, and though McLuhan refuses to fog himself up with moral concerns, he can't stop me from applying moral criteria to him. I am civilized and maybe I'm foggy, but I don't want either myself or my world to be retribalized. Tribalization may be inevitable, as McLuhan says, though I doubt it. But whether it is inevitable or not, and whether he is sincere or not, I do not like defectors. He is not an open enemy. He is not even an ally who sneakily opens the gates of the city to that enemy. He is an ally who sets about to persuade *me* to open the gates, using the arguments that our common enemy is stronger than we and bound to win, that we have terrible faults which succumbing to our enemy may cure if we handle him right (but *how?*), and besides the enemy can't help being barbarous, it's the environment he lives in, he's bringing this environment with him, it's irresistible and will get us, no matter what.

I wish I could confound him with erudition, but since that would require an extensive knowledge of history (both political and cultural), economics, sociology, philosophy, literature, psychology, and anthropology, to say nothing of a really exhaustive knowledge of the history and practice of technology, and since I have nowhere near the scholarship for the task, I am perforce content to write a short essay instead of a monograph and to cite one instance of an error in a subject I know well, the one standing for the many. McLuhan writes:

> In Shakespeare's Troilus and Cressida, which is almost completely devoted to both a psychic and social study of communication, Shakespeare states his awareness that true social and political navigation depend upon anticipating the consequences of innovation.

The statement in the which-clause and the one in the main clause are both untrue as they stand, and by the time they had been modified into truth they would be unrecognizable. (It is obvious that I think his famous message, "the medium is the message," is only a partial truth; in the language media, at any rate, the message too is part of the message.) Not only is his interpretation of *Troilus and Cressida* untrue, but the five lines he quotes in support of his interpretation do not in fact support it.

> The providence that's in a watchful state
> Knows almost every grain of Plutus' gold;
> Finds bottom in th' uncomprehensive deeps;
> Keeps place with thought, and almost, like the gods
> Do thoughts unveil in their dumb cradles.

Of course, like other thinkers, McLuhan could have quarried Shakespeare for ideas and expressions of attitudes to offer in evidence for his own thesis. Instead, he inserts, with monomaniacal intrusiveness, his own idea into this play, attributes the idea to

Shakespeare, and claims that the whole play is about that idea. In this he is like a psychological nut who sees *Hamlet* as a study of the Oedipus complex or a linguistic nut who can't see the poetry for the morphemes. A few such extravagances in a book don't matter much, but *Understanding Media* offers an accumulation of errors —distortions, contradictions, projections, simplifications, limit-smashings—so considerable that finally one says, "No, I don't trust ideas which have this infirm a foundation." McLuhan-civilized used to offer evidence which supported his insights; but McLuhan-barbarian does not deign to answer critics who point out the errors which riddle his prophecies. The arrogance is the message.

I also wish I could confound him rationally, by refuting his complex of ideas. But the complex is repetitive, "mosaic," hortatory, apocalyptic, as impervious to the discriminations of logic and common sense as to the corrections of scholarship. Worst of all, it is self-justifying. If you apply logic to it, he disposes of you by saying that you are a print-formed mind who has been made obsolete by Hume and electricity. If you say man is being changed all right but not so drastically or so fast as he maintains, he counters by telling you to wake up, you are still in the nightmare of print-induced unconsciousness, "consciousness will come as a relief," and he quotes *Finnegans Wake* at you (*he* understands it, *you* don't), saying that he takes his prophecies from the "radar feedback" of great art since great art constitutes a sort of "early warning system" for society. If you judge his ideas morally, he says he is not prescribing but describing. This statement may be valid intellectually but it is not valid emotionally, and it is certainly not true of McLuhan's own practice. In *Understanding Media*, he describes less than he prophesies, and what he admonishes us to do manages to be at once vague, capitulatory, and appalling.

The last sentence of the book is an opinion—a valuable opinion —expressed as a truth: "Panic about automation as a threat of uniformity on a world scale is the projection into the future of mechanical standardization and specialism, which are now past." But the sentence before this one betrays the Reader's Digesty sentiment that *really* we are all creative and mass leisure will release our creativity: "The social and educational patterns latent in automation are those of self-employment and artistic autonomy." Pardner, when you say that, laugh. He substitutes, and his rhetoric urges us to substitute, electricity for divine grace: ". . . since with electricity we extend our central nervous system globally, instantly interrelating every human experience. . . . We can now, by computer, deal with complex social needs with the same architectural certainty that we previously attempted in private housing." Finally, having put his trust in consciousness, he makes it clear, at the end of the chapter on "The Spoken Word," what the new, electronically expanded consciousness is good for:

> Electric technology does not need words any more than the
> digital computer needs numbers. Electricity points the way to
> an extension of the process of consciousness itself, on a
> world scale, and without any verbalization whatever. . . . Today
> computers hold out the promise of a means of instant translation
> of any code or language into any other code or language.
> The computer, in short, promises by technology a Pentecostal
> condition of universal understanding and unity. The next logical
> step would seem to be, not to translate, but to by-pass
> languages in favor of a general cosmic consciousness which
> might be very like the collective unconsciousness dreamt of by
> Bergson. The condition of "weightlessness," that biologists say
> promises a physical immortality, may be paralleled by the
> condition of speechlessness that could confer a perpetuity
> of collective harmony and peace.

Maybe this is one of those idea-clusters he doesn't really mean; maybe he is just probing the environment with it. Well, as part of the environment, let me respond: I don't like the idea (I don't like being probed with it either). The electronic heaven-on-earth of his vision is a world village of mute mindlessness, a parody of harmony and peace because the possibilities of disharmony and conflict have been lobotomized. He wants, and wants us to want, to turn most of the work of our minds over to the computers. I know—even with my foggy, unexpanded consciousness I know—that there are disadvantages to being human. But at least it's interesting, it's various. I'm for going on with it.

Editor's Note: See Part 6, p. 283 for McLuhan's comments.

The Honeymoon of the

2

Mechanical Bride

suppose crime did pay? is it an accident that the narcissistic heroes like tarzan, superman, cowboys, and sleuths are weak on social life? is bogart america's shropshire lad?

—MC LUHAN

McLuhan's first book, *The Mechanical Bride: Folklore of Industrial Man,* appeared in 1951. A brilliant *tour de force,* it explores the extent to which public opinion is manipulated even in a democratic society by industry and advertising, and is profusely illustrated by examples of mass culture. The book abounds in puns, which McLuhan uses in a Joycean manner as "crossroads of meaning":

Say it with tanks.

The more the burier, said Digby O'Dell.

The Ballet Luce?

Nothing recedes like success.

Do you want your social woe to show?

Do it the (Emily) Post Way.

Can you see through his adnoise?

Love at first flight?

The Bold Look—The face that launched a thousand hips?

How Not to Offend—A message for all thinking and/or stinking people?

The book met a generally approving if limited reception. One of the most interesting critiques was by John S. Black, who jointly reviewed *The Mechanical Bride* and C. Wright Mills's *White Collar* for the Jesuit magazine *America.* Black found a decided parallelism in the viewpoints of the two writers: Both were concerned with the effects of industrial power—on values (McLuhan) and class control (Mills); both cried out for awareness to "unmask and smash the stereotypes of vision and intellect with which modern communications swamp us" (Mills); but neither, Black complained, showed any concern for "man's final destiny."

Rudolph E. Morris (7) is Professor of Sociology at Marquette University. His rather somber but substantial précis of *The Mechanical Bride* was published in *Renascence,* a Catholic journal where McLuhan's occasional pieces have appeared over the years.

Walter Ong, S.J. (8), a former student of McLuhan's, is Professor of Literature at St. Louis University. His own book, *Ramus: Method and the Decay of Dialogue,* was crucial in the shaping of the central thesis of *The Gutenberg Galaxy.* Ong finds "particularly intriguing theologically" some of McLuhan's ideas on modern sensibility, although he tends to dissociate himself from his teacher's Thomistic preferences. The review—in some ways a teleological sermon—contains one of the earliest expositions of the influence of Pierre Teilhard de Chardin on contemporary American Catholic thinking and is a vital key to the understanding of McLuhan's intellectual development after 1951. In the next decade McLuhan was to increase his scope of awareness, and the liturgical imperatives implied by his first book were to be dealt with in a much more detached and balanced way.

"The Picture on Your Mind" (9), like the Gossage (1) and Culkin (3) essays in Part 1, is an early example of McLuhan applied. The piece appeared in *Ammunition,* the trade paper of a C.I.O. automobile workers' union.

7 how refreshing to see a critique of a period and of its morals avoiding moral indignation! —RUDOLPH E. MORRIS

It is almost a paradox in this era of specialization that we can come to an understanding of our world only through a simultaneous approach from all possible starting points. A combined effort of philosophy, literary criticism, and sociological analysis is needed; and even this is not enough if the synthetic attack is not carried by a strong conviction of what the end of man is, and by a no less decisive will to reopen an adequate space in our society to the genuine values of human existence. Several writers have recently tried to bring out the meaning and trend of modern mass society through a universal survey. But no one has done it with so much verve and in so original a way as Herbert Marshall McLuhan.

Mechanization, technical developments in means of communication, and modern psychology today make full control over the human mind possible. Public opinion can be manipulated. And it is not only in the totalitarian state that this enormous power is used (or rather, abused) to get command over man. *The Mechanical Bride* shows to what an extent also in our democratic society the individual is subjugated to the iron rule of the collective mind; even to those to whom this fact was well known Mr. McLuhan's profusely illustrated book comes as a revelation. It is to the author's credit that we are thunderstruck and overwhelmed by his presentation of things we "know." His ingenious method produces this effect which may make us stop and think before it is too late. His idea is to use the devices of "commercial education," by which the public is being made helpless, for the purpose of the public's enlightenment. Hence, he guides the reader through the nightmarish thicket of advertisements, comic strips, newspaper front pages which impress themselves upon us daily and hourly. He shows us what they mean and brings to light correlations and connections between them and other currents of thought, sentiment, and ideas we would never dream of. He attempts "to set the reader at the center of the revolving picture created by these affairs where he may observe the action that is in progress and in which everybody is involved. From the analysis of that action, it is hoped, many individual strategies may suggest themselves." I would go further and hope that even group strategies may be evoked by the stimulating thoughts of our author.

Going through this book with the unusual title, the highly unconventional illustrations, the problem-summarizing questions at the beginning of each chapter which challenge us with their biting wit, one is tempted to classify *The Mechanical Bride* as a magnificent satire of our industrial society. But when one reads the text one is surprised at the elaborate analysis and philosophical profundity which lead the discussion into a dimension different from the satirical approach. The book itself can be called scientific, in spite of much unorthodoxy in presentation, form, and content. But the effect certainly is that of a satire.

We would not realize the full implication of industrialization on the human person and the life of mind and spirit if the author did not force us into seeing the paradoxical contradictions of our present ways of life. He goes through with it to the end of the rope. For instance, in the case where the "rope" is an expensive bracelet (in an advertisement of a famous jeweler), he refers to Tawney's *Religion and the Rise of Capitalism* and to a thought of Bergson's who, in his studies of time and mind, makes it clear that if all the motion in the universe were doubled in speed, including the passing of our own lives, we would recognize it through the impoverishment of our minds thus produced.

The chapter whose heading was chosen as the title for the whole book centers around two female legs on a pedestal (the advertisement of a hosiery manufacturer). Mr. McLuhan considers these isolated legs as a facet of our "replaceable parts" cultural dynamics, and he develops this idea to its last consequences. There is today this strange dissociation of sex not only from the human person but even from the unity of the body. The mechanization of our whole life makes us believe that the application of some external medicament or piece of clothing or perfume to each single part of

our body will make us glamorous or successful. This conception
of human life, body and mind, as a mechanical unit is a by-product
of a way of thinking that derives from our theoretical and practical
intercourse with the machine. Business has then taken hold of this
pattern of analytical thinking and exploited it for commercial purposes. How many more products can be invented and sold if each
part of our body requires a special remedy? The commercializa-
tion of this trend toward mechanization, on its part, has then led
to the current glamor campaigns. Mr. McLuhan now makes it clear
that this current emphasis on glamor and sex does not at all indicate "new heights of a man-woman madness."

> **Sex weariness and sex sluggishness are, in measure at least,
> both the cause and increasingly the outcome of these cam-
> paigns. No sensitivity of response could long survive such a
> barrage. What does survive is the view of the human body as
> a sort of love-machine capable merely of specific thrills. . . .
> It makes inevitable both the divorce between physical pleasure
> and reproduction and also the case for homosexuality. In the
> era of thinking machines, it would be surprising, indeed, if the
> love-machine were not thought of as well.**

I believe that for people actively interested in a Catholic renascence nothing can be more important than to search and discover the causes for the attitudes, so much prevailing in our present
society, which paralyze life and prevent us from achieving unity of
body and mind and soul. There is scarcely an author who has analyzed the situation so forcefully as Herbert Marshall McLuhan. In
this book he is a sociologist with the additional wisdom of a generally educated man. His findings can certainly be used as much
for an interpretation of contemporary literature and of the climate
in which it lives, as far as better understanding is concerned of the
complex matters which are causing marriage problems, individual
unhappiness, and the indifference toward the higher things in life
so often observed and blamed but so little seen as an unavoidable
consequence of the age of industrialization.

    In this connection the chapter "Horse Opera and Soap Opera" is
also very enlightening; for again the split between business and

society, between action and feeling, office and home, man and woman is presented to us with a rich mass of literary references. I hope that many courses in contemporary literature will become more attractive to the students for the teachers' having gone through this book.

This review would be incomplete if mention were not made of the most pertinent remarks of Mr. McLuhan's in regard to privacy. Naturally an ad for Lysol in a chapter called "How Not to Offend" is the occasion. "The privacy that was once the refreshment of the mind and spirit is now associated only with those 'shameful' and strenuous tasks by which the body is made fit for contact with other bodies." With reference to observations made by Margaret Mead (who is often quoted) our author says: "The bathroom has been elevated to the very stratosphere of industrial folklore, it being the gleam, the larger hope, which we are appointed to follow."

There is no doubt that the separation of things which belong together and the loss of privacy (among our youth also a loss of a desire for it, this loss mainly conditioned by our educational system, especially on the college level) are the main factors of human life in industrial society. It is the essence of *The Mechanical Bride* to bring these facts again and again to our attention, each time in a new and stimulating facet.

There are some valuations in the book with which one has not to agree. The author is unenthusiastic about the *New Yorker* or James Thurber or Ogden Nash, but he approves of Li'l Abner and its creator, Al Capp. He seems one-sided in his chapter on public opinion polls, entitled "The Galluputians": he emphasizes the negative elements of polls, inducing the individual to replace convictions by vague opinions and to give up his identity, but he forgets that public opinion surveys also strengthen the role of the individual in society because they make him realize that the voice of the "little man" counts.

In general, however, Mr. McLuhan is not at all negativistic. Comparing himself with the sailor in Poe's *A Descent into the Maelstrom,* he quotes the sailor as saying that he even sought amusement in speculating upon the velocities of the happenings in the whirlpool.

It was this amusement born of his rational detachment as a
spectator of his own situation that gave him the thread which
led him out of the Labyrinth. And it is in the same spirit that
this book is offered as an amusement. Many who are accustomed to the note of moral indignation will mistake this
amusement for mere indifference. But the time for anger and
protest is in the early stages of a new process. The present
stage is extremely advanced. Moreover, it is full, not only of
destructiveness but also of promises of rich new developments
to which moral indignation is a very poor guide.

How refreshing to see a critique of a period and of its morals
avoiding moral indignation!

8 in a way, the angels have a greater
social problem than even industrialized
man.   —WALTER ONG, S.J.

The symbolism with which industrial man has surrounded himself
—the symbolism of his advertising, his clothes, comic strips,
corpse literature, etiquette manuals, "great books," cowboys and
Hollywood dream walkers or "somnambules" (the Ingrid Bergman
type), chum-tone news reporting, electric brains, picnics, Gallup
polls, tommy-gun gossip columns, radio ventriloquists, Boy Scout-
ing, mannequins—all this is a language which he both understands
and does not understand. The present book, which treats of these
things and others like them, is not intended to be either alarmist or
coddling. It simply proposes enlarging the area of understanding.

A collection of advertising or other printed displays with accompanying discussions, the book can be dipped into anywhere. Its
assorted-goods technique of presentation is employed because, at

present, and perhaps for good, it is impossible to provide a neat summary of the symbolism involved in industrial living which does not suppress many points worth making. Besides, as the author explains (page v), this technique reproduces the whirling phantasmagoria which is being analyzed and accustoms the reader to a sense of motion. You may as well get acclimated to doing your thinking on the industrial merry-go-round, because you can't get off this side of death, and even at death the mortuary industry will put you back on for a while.

Professor McLuhan considers the awareness which his book seeks to cultivate not merely as a means of understanding the contemporary world, but as a condition of understanding anything adequately, including the remotest past. "The quality of anybody's relations with the mind of the past is exactly and necessarily determined by the quality of his contemporary insights" (page 44). This is a thesis with which it is hard to disagree. All the concepts by which we deal with anything are founded directly not on the past but on our contemporary sensory experience in the world we know. The philosopher who understands St. Thomas in terms of the "levels" of abstraction in St. Thomas' philosophical "system" is understanding St. Thomas' thought in terms of two analogies which never occurred to St. Thomas but which float readily enough to the surface of minds conditioned as ours are. It is impossible to uncondition ourselves. And it is not necessary. A better possibility and necessity is open to us: *to understand our own conditioning*—in the instance given (not Professor McLuhan's), to understand how the "level" and "system" come into our consciousness and what they mean there.

There is resistance to an understanding based on continued dispassionate surveillance of our interior possessions. It is disconcerting to be reminded, for example, that the things which we find ourselves doing for recreation will reveal our secret ambitions and fears. Prying into such deep-seated psychological symbols as Blondie or Dagwood or Emily Post (at this symbolic level, fictitious and real personalities are indistinguishable) is regarded with suspicion by the mind convinced, in Professor McLuhan's words, "that we are as we are and only a cheap sneak would ask any questions." One persuasion at work here seems to be the most insidious of anti-intellectualisms: If we know too much about the processes at work in life as we live it, life won't be fun any more—a thing Professor McLuhan is certainly not convinced of, for his work is as amusing as it is upsetting.

If the author's whirligig of insights does not admit of reduction to one or two heads, it does turn on two pivots indicated by his title, *The Mechanical Bride: Folklore of Industrial Man*. Mechanics and sex, Professor McLuhan maintains, are the predominant themes in the general "public consciousness" and in operations upon it. Of these, perhaps mechanics is the more significant, for the sexual theme has always been present in mythologies and folklore and acquires its present tonality when it is disinfected of its natural symbolic force and given a present mechanical orientation (some would say materialistic, but *mechanical* seems more accurate, since sex is necessarily materialistic in the sense that its bipolarity is a kind of refraction of the composite structure of material beings). The Greeks had Eros, who was not above reproach but nevertheless touched chords which can be heard, modulated, in the Canticle of Canticles. But instead of Eros, or even Aphrodite, Dr. Kinsey has his "sexual outlets," which make for graphs and psychological engineering and provide mathematical averages as absolute standards for measurement. A third pivotal point, death, which the author adds to the other two (page 101), is inevitably associated with sex, as we know from mythology and psychoanalysis and metaphysics (sex and death are both corollaries of material existence), and can be regarded as simply enlarging the view here.

The myths which the author finds employing these twin themes and others as well are not myths in the sense that they are stories or definitely stated beliefs turned loose within the public mind by those who are out to exploit it. They exist in the minds of the exploiters as well as in the minds of the exploited, and, generally speaking, are as little understood by the one as by the other. They are simply present as a result of the conditions in which reality is engaged today. Industrial society is a turtle, and these myths are the shell which he has grown on his back and which he has to get

outside himself to see. Most members of the National Association
of Manufacturers are quite unaware that an entirely run-of-the-
mill Buick advertisement crosses the mechanical and sex motifs to
show the automobile establishing itself deep in American consciousness as a surrogate for woman and all that woman means—
thus, incidentally, throwing light on some radical adjustment problems in the modern home. (Among other things, the whole world of
"comfort," classically associated with the mother, is transferred to
the automobile, the home-feeling put on wheels.)

Of the other myths and symbolizations touched on here only
some can be mentioned. The all-but-exact parallel between the way
the front page of a newspaper is organized and the painting technique of a Picasso, the literary technique of a Joyce. The "Ballet
Luce" of *Life, Time,* and *Fortune,* with newsmen posed as the great
romantics. "Know-how" as a marketable item. The consumer-goods
mentality: achievement symbolized in power to buy what will keep
you from being different from anybody else. Coeducation as neuter
education in a technologically reduced world. The personal hy-
giene hysteria and the human organism as a chemical factory. Al
Capp as the sole robust satirical force in the popular consciousness
because of the genuine irony in his feel for "the full beat of the big
phony heart of a public which craves massive self-deception." This
against the essentially uneasy sentimentalism of Chic Young's
Blondie. Daddy Warbucks, the "war profiteer of transcendent virtue." The voice of the lab (newspaper headline: "Scientists Await
Cow's Death to Solve Mathematics Problem"). Woman trained to
sense herself as an object rather than as a person. The Humphrey
Bogart tough as a symbol of industrial man's loneliness. The "freedom" literature. The tonality of the Coca-Cola ad. *Polyanna Digest.*
Horse and soap opera.

* * *

This treatment of industrial man can have particular relevance
on the American Catholic intellectual front today. In the United
States, the Church is in a curious position with relation to the general industrial culture. Here she has made more of an adjustment
to this culture at the practical level than she has anywhere else in

the world. American Catholicism means, to both Americans and Europeans, a Catholicism which is living out this adjustment with the intensity the American environment demands. And yet, when we are taken as a group, our understanding of what we are doing so instinctively, and of America in general, is very slight indeed.

Despite a well-grounded and enviable notion of the obligations of patriotism in theory, the Catholic-trained mind is likely to approach the American scene as such with a wild emotional loyalty which makes for chauvinism and gives Catholics as a group a bad name in intellectual circles, and which may have as its odd intellectual complement a purely negative technique of denunciation founded on the vague and second-hand notion that America is materialistic and that only those particles of American civilization which can be hooked directly to pre-Reformation Catholicity or to the Catholic protagonists in post-Reformation controversy merit our explicit attention.

The tendency toward self-centeredness here is, of course, understandable in terms of the Church's history as a minority group in the United States, tolerated, but only just. Still, the fact remains that, with some notable exceptions, such as the excellent work of Father John Courtney Murray, there is no theology of Catholicism in America, such as Brownson or Hecker envisioned generations ago, although there is promise of development. Hitherto we have combed theology manuals and analyzed papal encyclicals—excellent and indispensable sources both, but not only incapable of supplying a direct intellectual attack on the reality with which we are surrounded but actually crying for this attack as a necessary complement to what they supply. Blanshard's diatribes against the Church, whatever their unfortunate result among non-Catholics, are likely under Providence to occasion good fruit within the Church itself by sensitizing us more to the points at which we must work hard to find out for the Church what American culture really is and what her relation to it can or must be.

What happens when the Church engages itself with the institutions generated by our industrial milieu—with radio advertising? Comic strips? Mass production techniques—for example, in schools which we like to style educational "plants"? The crowd emotions exploited by sports? Ideologies which result in family budgets and envelope systems? At present are we in the position of the commercial advertiser and of Hollywood, who exploit popular art without even knowing how to make the effort to lay hold of the solid human foundations of its symbolism?

The position of the liturgy in contemporary society perhaps best highlights the situation. Why is the gap between the tonality of life in general and that of the liturgy greater today than it was in the Middle Ages when the Catholic laity, and most certainly the clergy, were on the whole far more ignorant of their catechism and their theology than they are now? The answer is to be sought in the complete reorientation of the symbolic world today. Whereas ancient man had felt the world of nature as the dominant pressure on his life and had let his symbolism grow out into and back from this world, today the machine—at present, with its arch-symbol the atom bomb, but for some centuries now with considerable control of our vocabulary and its most forceful metaphors—has largely replaced nature in this function within our consciousness, and a new kind of symbolism, not so much a replacement as a complication, has taken hold. The situation is reminiscent of that when the Church first faced the pagan world and not only transfused it with her sacraments, which were part of her original equipment and gave her immediate symbolic entry, but, more particularly, transposed and transformed it with the sacramentals which she drew right out of it—from the armory of her enemy.

It is not impossible to find things in the industrial world today capable of liturgical transposition and transformation. There is the ideal of service, a genuinely new force as it exists in society today, redolent of "service" stations and of economic competition, but, it would seem, perhaps, unpredictably fecund in a Church whose head on earth calls himself *Servus servorum Dei* (the Servant of the Servants of God) and whose Founder said He had come not to be served but to serve.

There is American optimism, obviously of a piece with the positive note struck by Catholicism in American culture and at strange variance with the negative Protestant note—behind Blanshard's attack on American Catholicism lies his great fear that such typically American phenomena (which, to his great embarrassment, his whole negative approach rules out of his own thought for good) will prove more viable in the Catholic Church than anywhere else. Yet, as a group, the knowledge we exhibit of the history of American optimism and its psychological valence in our lives is pretty close to zero. Unlike Europeans, we fall back on this optimism a-plenty. We are exploiting it. Sentimentally, we are close to it— but in ways we don't understand, for intellectually we have hardly looked at it at all.

It might be argued that sentimental nearness is sufficient. The Church, after all, transformed an ugly medieval cult of courtly love into chivalric ideals and what not without ever having a theory of what she was doing. Yes, but co-operative thinking was not so possible in an age without printing presses or any communication much faster than walking. The Church did not have the means of understanding strewn about her as we do today. Perhaps that is why she did not succeed better and why the part of the tradition she didn't succeed with remains with us today as a slightly altered but permanent ulcer in Hollywood's conception of the romantic.

Again, capable of transposition or redemption is the ideal of personal austerity in the otherwise somewhat comical get-up of the American go-getter. Are we to limit our intellectual approach here to decrying the Puritan background of this austerity or are we to admit that it is part of *our* lives and to try to transform it? Catholics once transformed—not without change, to be sure—a whole family of pagan "virtues" which they found, with a far more suspect heredity, in the pagan Aristotle.

In our glib denunciations of "materialisms," have we overlooked important facts? There is the fact pointed out by the author of the present book (page 112) that American materialism is not only in some ways more materialistic than other materialisms, but in other ways much less materialistic. The American sense of abundance encourages us to let our material goods lie rather loosely about us—Europeans know that in daily life (not only when our national best interests dictate the policy), we are more prone than they to give things away or even to destroy them. There is no sentimental cult of materialism in the United States in the way there is in England or in Russia. We are incorrigible sentimentalists, but material*ism* isn't one of the things we thus venerate.

Professor McLuhan does not treat explicitly of dogmatic or liturgical implications, but he leaves open a hundred doors here into every area of Catholic life. Knowing him as a former member of the English faculty at St. Louis University and as present professor of English at St. Michael's College in the University of Toronto, we are aware that he does this quite deliberately.

His observations regarding the possible nature of overall readjustment in the modern sensibility are particularly intriguing theologically. On several occasions, (pages 34, 50, 97) he returns to the notion that the conception of fusing human arts, interests, and pursuits in a functional biological unit—a conception grown largely out of the interests of the last few centuries and echoing in the terms "social organism," "organization" and their correlates— should perhaps yield in the present world to a conception of *orchestrating* these things. This notion of orchestration, borrowed from A. N. Whitehead, provides for a possible theory not only of continuity but expressly of discontinuity as well. Thus, its connections with the atom and with relativity physics are plain. The concept would presumably enable us to make allowance for obvious and seemingly inevitable discontinuities in industrial society just as modern physical theory countenances expressly the discontinuity of the atom.

The theological connections of "orchestration," which Professor McLuhan does not touch on, are teasing enough: the "choirs" of angels, the ancient harmony of the spheres (conceived of as ruled by the angels or "separated spirits"), the hymns of creation, the popular concept of heaven with its banal but quite explainable harps, not to mention Dante's concept of heaven. The connection between harmony and discontinuity theory is not fanciful here. When the harmony symbolism asserts itself in terms of the angels, it does so precisely to provide what Whitehead, in another context, styles a "theory of discontinuous existence,"—the angels it will be recalled, are not only separated from matter but are, as a necessary corollary, so discontinuous from one another that many, if not most, theologians today are unwilling to admit that there can be more than one in any one species. In a way, the angels have a greater social problem than even industrialized man. The spheres were equally discontinuous in the old Aristotelian cosmology—so that, if the cosmology had been right, which of course it wasn't, the notion of harmony or orchestration was an understandable one. The depth of this kind of background is suggested when it is brought to bear on our understanding of the angelic singing which on the first Christmas accompanied the announcement of a new unity for the human race: The singing becomes more than incidental accompaniment.

Is the deposit of faith to reveal new riches when we approach it with concepts associated with atom physics, as it did when St. Thomas approached it with concepts salvaged from Aristotle or when the nineteenth-century theologians approached it with the biological orientation which on the one side produced evolution theory but in their case flowered in the theology of the Mystical Body? Is renewed interest in angelology to be the next stage in relating the Mystical Body to the industrial world?

It should be observed that the discovery of new riches does not mean the renouncing of the old ones, though it may mean a readjustment in our attitude toward them. St. Thomas did not throw away St. Augustine. As you read the Einstein and Infeld account of the origins of relativity and field physics, you realize that Einstein did not exactly throw away Newtonian physics. Even in the nontheological context, it would be impossible simply to discard "organism" as outmoded and put "orchestration" in its place. The concept "organism" stands in a permanent relation to reality. "Orchestration" would provide an additional grasp of reality which would enable us to refine our notion of what the relation of "organism" is—as the notion of "relation" itself refined and further oriented the notions of Father, Son, and Holy Spirit in theological history.

For some time now in France, a favorite way of conceiving the earth engages it in spheres once more. There was first the earth's surface, a "geosphere," a surface devoid of life, unified by mere continuity. Then this was slowly infiltrated by a self-perpetuating network of living organisms, with an interlaced dependence on one another, to form a more highly unified surface than before, the "biosphere." In a third stage, with growing rapidity, man, bearer of intelligence, has made his way over the surface of the earth into all its parts, and now in our own day—with the whole world alerted simultaneously every day to goings-on in Washington, Paris, London, Rio de Janeiro, Rome, and (with reservations) Moscow— human consciousness has succeeded in enveloping the entire globe in a third and still more perfect kind of sphere, the sphere of intelligence, the "noosphere," as it has been styled by Father Pierre Teilhard de Chardin, S.J. Begun in the noosphere before it was the complete envelope it is today, the work of Redemption continues in this same noosphere through it involving all lower creation, for the "spheres" interpenetrate and react on one another.

The concept of orchestration may prove to be not precisely the concept we need for use in modern industrial society, but enough has perhaps been said to show that horizons are large when, by the use of some such terms, we regard our industrial civilization, however crudely, in a cosmic and religious context. To do justice to the horizons, we shall have to know much more than we do about the conditions of the immediate world in which we live, we shall have to be better alerted to our own consciousness.

Despite its hop-skip-and-jump approach—or rather because of it —the present book is an excellent introduction to the mass of literature which can help to a general awareness of American culture in its contemporary phase, and thus of ourselves. The juxtaposition of advertisements and text makes for shortcuts into the relevant portions of this literature.

But this manner of presentation here can lead to a false impression of "popularization." Despite the fact that much here will attract intelligent high-schoolers, it is hardly correct to say that this is a "popular" presentation for the reason that it contests the whole mentality which we have learned to style "popular." The impression of popularization, which close reading of the text will partly dispel, is due to the fact that Professor McLuhan, by every instinct in his being as well as by deliberate choice, is a teacher, an expositor, an opener-upper of things.

Besides, he has learned just about all there is to learn from the advertisers at whose method he cocks so critical an eye. His little blurbs introducing each section ("Latch onto our big idea index for deep consolation," "Let us make you over into a bulldozer") are a sort of meta-journalism, which practice in one dimension what they dissect in another—the difference being that here the author is frankly aware of what he is practicing and wants you to be aware.

We cannot escape our past or our present, and Professor Mc-Luhan lays no claim to complete freedom of the habits and techniques he is inspecting. Faced with these techniques, he observes (page 144), everyone finds that "the price of total resistance, like that of total surrender, is still too high. Consequently, in practice, everyone is intellectually and emotionally a patchwork quilt of occupied and unoccupied territory. And there are no accepted standards of submission or resistance to commercially sponsored appeals either in reading or living habits. All the more, then, is it urgent to foster habits of inspection until workable standards of securely civilized judgments emerge from these habits."

The situation holds not a threat, but a challenge (page 3): "It would be a mistake to join the chorus of voices which wails without intermission that 'Discontinuity is chaos come again. It is irrationalism. It is the end.' Quantum and relativity physics are not a fad. They have provided new facts about the world, new intelligibility, new insights into the universal fabric. Practically speaking, they mean that henceforth this planet is a single city. Far from making for irrationalism, these discoveries make irrationalism intolerable for the intelligent person. They demand much greater exertions. . . ."

the girl may be sweet and innocent and harmless, but coca-cola isn't. the next time you get a tooth knocked out, put it in a glass of coca-cola and watch it dissolve in a day or so.

9

—AMMUNITION (C.I.O.)

". . . the propaganda value of this simultaneous audiovisual impression (movies) is very high, for it standardizes thought by supplying the spectator with a ready-made visual image before he has time to conjure up an interpretation of his own."—Marshall McLuhan

Death House

The illustration: A picture of the front page of the *New York Times*.

The ideal: The front page of any newspaper is a design—a modern design which represents how complicated the world is. How necessary it is for the people of the world to reach out for a deep sense of solidarity with each other.

But despite the significance of events, the newspapers have laid a cheaper, more sensational meaning over the design.

Quoting a news item: Two men condemned to death allow a motion picture to be made of them. Then they see the motion picture on television. They die, thrilled that they have seen themselves on television. Other people, seeing the same television show, are thrilled at being right in the death house on the inside of an execution.

Drug

The illustration: The front page of a Hearst paper.

The idea: Hearst papers and other papers, too, try to turn each front page into an excitement (exploiting sex, fear, desire) because the promise of cheap satisfaction is easy to sell aroused people.

93

But people who are continually excited, drugged, don't go back, ever, to a sober view of the world.

Snotty People

The illustration: An advertisement of *Time* magazine, which shows a newspaperman of twenty-five years ago, with the caption: a nose for news and a stomach for whiskey.

The idea: The *Time* formula is to turn the news into an inside dope report from one snob to another snob (*Time* readers are superior people: The news in *Time* looks down on the people in the news).

The *Life* formula is pictures of girls in girdles, plus articles on the wonders of science, plus religious art wrapped in the suggestion that by looking at these pictures slowly week after week, you will eventually become cultured—like *Life* itself.

Death and Sex

The illustration: An ad in which a handsome gal looking at the rain takes deep consolation in the fact that someone dear to her is protected against water in the ground by a Clark metal grave vault.

The idea: Even death has been sexualized in the advertisements.

Revolt by Television

The illustration: Edgar Bergen and Charlie McCarthy.

The idea: Factory workers resent the overlordship of the factory in their lives. Consumers, whether consciously or not, resent the way they are manipulated, and lied to, and exploited. People do get rebellious when they think of the cement of corporation control hardening on them.

So a program like Bergen and McCarthy allows everyone with any rebelliousness at all to be rebellious briefly and harmlessly by identifying with Charlie McCarthy.

For a while you laugh your head off at Charlie (the rank and file) talking back to Bergen (the authority). But then the announcer

reads the commercial, tells you exactly what to buy. Dutifully you
go out, hynotized, and buy it. The rebelliousness has been laughed
out of you.

Winchell and Slime

The illustration: An item in Walter Winchell's column.

The idea: Winchell (editor's note: the smell of slime you get
when you hear Winchell broadcast is real. Despite all his mouth-
ings about democracy, he sat by silently while a Negro singer was
publicly humiliated just because she was a Negro in a New York
saloon. Then, instead of hiding, or exhibiting a decent embarrassment, he used his column to abuse the woman whose humiliation he
condoned). Winchell's style on the air, the machine gun sound,
suggests a cheap killer with a machine gun. That is the pleasure in
listening to him. You hear a vicious, cruel person abusing (assassi-
nating) people with vicious bullet-like gossip. . . . Listen, Mr. and
Mrs. North America, and all the ships at sea, let's go to press.
Imitation gangster. . . .

Money Molds the Man

The illustration: An RCA advertisement of a family listening to
radio to illustrate the notion that Americans have freedom to
listen and to look.

The idea: The president of RCA said before a Congressional
committee, ". . . 'he who controls the pocketbook controls the man.'
Business control means complete control, and there is no use arguing to the contrary."

Suppose you had government radio instead of business radio,
would things be any better?

Are schools any better because they are run by the city or the
school board instead of by business?

The falsification of standards—money is everything. Money
acquits you of all crimes. The worst crime is to work for a living.
Cooperation is either criminal or Communism. If you have money
in your pocket, you deserve what you can buy with it. If you starve
to death or die from lack of medical care, it's your own criminal
fault, and you're lucky not to be sent to jail for disorderly conduct.

"Whatever fosters mere passivity and submission is the enemy of (freedom)."

Suppose Crime Did Pay

The illustration: The cover of a comic magazine, Crime Does Not Pay.

The idea: Suppose crime did pay (as it obviously does in many cases, the men with the highest incomes in the country by evasion and avoidance make their antisocial behavior pay off to the tune of $6 billion a year), would that make crime okay?

Aren't there reasons for acting decently and morally, and for not committing evil acts that do not pay off in cash?

In the ads, over television, over the radio, in the schools, the answer is, No.

Know How to Be Sick in the Stomach

The illustration: An ad for an ironer captioned "how to iron shirts without hating your husband."

The idea: Know-how in the ads is know how to keep your clothes ten times whiter. Know how to end unpleasant breath. Know how to get married or to be happy or meet new men or be charming. There is not only a machine (a gadget) that will do anything. But with the right know-how, you, too, can be a machine that will be charming, successful, a railway mail clerk, play the piano.

Great Books

The illustration: A photograph from *Life* of a group of young men and women in a charade of the Great Books, the discussion program sponsored by the University of Chicago.

The idea: The amount of education in a Great Book discussion or in a classroom, is fractional compared to the flood of miseducation that washes over every human being every day of his life in the U.S. Better than Great Books would be education aimed at getting people to understand the cheapness of the ads, the dishonesty of the movies and television, the fraud in the newspapers and the magazines.

Go With/Against the Crowd?

The illustration: The advertisement that features the slogan for the one man in seven who shaves daily.

The idea: Ads and opinion polls put together a trap that looks like a quandary. For one, they encourage people not to be eccentric, not to be different, to have opinions, clothes, behavior like other people. But at the same time, they also urge you to be a man of distinction, not like your fellows, but better than they, different from them. What should you do, get on the bandwagon or be a man of distinction?

Orphan Anybody

The illustration: Little Orphan Annie.

The idea: Why is Orphan Annie so successful a comic strip despite the unpopularity of the Republican politics she preaches? Reduced to a kind of child-mindedness by the whole weight of propaganda, people tend to identify themselves with Orphan Annie in the mood you have when you feel your parents don't love you and you are all alone in the world. Little Orphan Annie is you going out in the world all alone and succeeding. The Republican propaganda is grafted on.

Home at the Waldorf

The illustration: An International Sterling advertisement headed "First Breakfast at Home"—a girl in a $250 negligee, Hollywood glamour type, her husband in a $200 suit, kissing across the breakfast table with five hundred bucks worth of silverware to hold the coffee, the sugar, and the cream.

The point: Home was never like this, except it is always like that in the ads. "An ad like this is a machine for taking spectators for a ride." It loads you with desires that take you way out of the

way of where you should be going (where should you be going—
nobody can know but you—and you can't know either until you are
drained of the poison that has been put in you). It puts you in a
spin from which you never emerge. The people who are excluded
from these ads, you come to believe, don't belong there. The people
who have, deserve what they have.

Oh, Innocent Knockout Drops

The illustration: A Coca-Cola ad with a cool, sweet, innocent,
beautiful girl.

The idea: The girl's sweetness and innocence suggest the sweet
refreshing, cool harmlessness of Coca-Cola. The girl may be sweet
and innocent and harmless, but Coca-Cola isn't. The next time you
get a tooth knocked out, put it in a glass of Coca-Cola and watch it
dissolve in a day or so.

Sides

The illustration: An ad of the electric light companies showing
the umpire in a football game carrying the ball. The caption,
"What goes on here."

The idea: The electric light companies give themselves away.
People (people who accept the rules in sports) admit the umpire
would be wrong to take sides. But in the game the electric power
companies play, what sides are there?

Two sides, the companies and the people.

If the government, playing umpire, picks up the ball and runs
with it, who gains, who loses?

Obviously in this giveaway ad, the companies lose, but the people gain.

In this game the umpire should be playing on the side of the
people.

Looking Critically

McLuhan's method is to look at an ad, a comic strip, a newspaper page, a newspaper story the way a critic might look at a

painting, or a movie, or a play, or a book. Or the way you might look at a fellow you know in an attempt to understand what kind of person he is.

Try it yourself. Look at an ad. Any ad. Is it honest? What kind of appeal does it make? Does it have overtones or undertones that stimulate notions that the product can't possibly fulfill? Is it designed to lead you on to understanding, or to block off understanding by some lie? Does it have an economic interest? Does it suggest some people are better than others?

You might even try making ad analysis into a game for your family.

Try an ad analysis at the dinner table sometime.

Explorations in the NEW WORLD

3

why have the effects of media, whether speech, writing, photography or radio, been overlooked by social observers through the past 3500 years of the western world?
—MC LUHAN

At a Paris café in 1920, Marcel Duchamps, André Breton, François Picabia, and other leading Dadaists exhibited works of art and protest. Picabia displayed a chalk drawing on a blackboard, invited criticism, and then abruptly erased his sketch. He defended this willful act of destruction using pure Dadaist logic: The drawing was no longer valid; it had an aesthetic life of only two hours. . . .

The functional life of the journal *Explorations: Studies in Culture and Communication* was expressed in eight issues, published from 1953–1957. Edited by Marshall McLuhan and Edmund Carpenter* and supported by the Ford Foundation, *Explorations* was the direct medium for papers and seminars presented at what eventually became the Centre for Culture and Technology at the University of Toronto. "The grammars of such languages as print, the newspaper format and television" were its main concerns, and it argued, as its editors have written:

> **that the revolution in the packaging and distribution of ideas and feelings modified not only human relations but also sensibilities. It further argued that we are largely ignorant of literacy's role in shaping Western man, and equally unaware of the role of electronic man in shaping modern values.****

The publication had a limited circulation† and was most un-

---

* Carpenter edited and wrote *Explorations #9*, but it was primarily a graphic study of Eskimo culture. In format and principle, it has an identity quite distinct from the earlier issues of the magazine.

** Edmund Carpenter and Marshall McLuhan, eds., *Explorations in Communication* (Boston: The Beacon Press, 1960), p. lx.

† The editors printed about 1,000 copies of each issue. Numbers 7 and 8 are collector's items.

orthodox in design. Each issue was planned by Harley Parker as a work of art. The typography reflected a Dadaist or Futurist irrationalism clearly at war with Newtonian gravity and Gutenberg uniformity—words were set in nonlinear, floating arrangements, pages were unnumbered, etc. The contributors, however, were respected scholars. David Riesman wrote on "The Oral and Written Traditions" and the modifying effects of media analysis on his study of American character, *The Lonely Crowd*: "If oral communication keeps people together, print is the isolating medium *par excellence*." Siegfried Giedion, in "Space Conception in Prehistoric Art," related prehistoric art to contemporary art in terms of abstraction, transparency, and symbolization. H. S. Chaytor discussed "the acoustic image" of the printed word.

Both the editorial and typographic styles of *Explorations* owed much to Wyndham Lewis' pre-World-War-One journal, *Blast,* in which Lewis issued manifestoes on life and art and set them in headline case, creating staccato rhythms of anger. But where Lewis engaged his adversaries, the "enemies" of art:

> **EVERYWHERE**
> **LIFE IS SAID**
> **Instead of**
> **ART**

McLuhan addressed media:

WHY DID MARX MISS THE COMMUNICATIONS BUS?

WE ARE RAPIDLY RE-CREATING ON AN ENORMOUS GLOBAL SCALE THE PRE-INDUSTRIAL WORLD OF THE BE-SPOKE TAILOR

ORAL MAN idolizes the literary
LITERARY MAN dreams of oral conquests

THE NEW ORGANIZATION MAN IS AN ORAL MAN WITH A HEART OF TYPE

In 1954, McLuhan privately printed a pamphlet, *Counterblast,* which best expresses his ambivalent attitude toward Lewis. *Explo-*

rations may be seen, I believe, as a working out of this ambivalence in McLuhan's mind, permitting him ultimately to accept Lewis' style while rejecting his "message" or content.

Although the intention of *Explorations* was to study *all* media and their cultural consequences, studies in book and print culture were stressed. By 1958, McLuhan himself, as well as other editors, had moved away from this emphasis and the journal was no longer functional. Nonetheless, McLuhan followed through in *The Gutenberg Galaxy* many of the ideas first expressed in successive issues of *Explorations,* although his second book did not appear until 1962.

Since there has been very little critical writing about this important period in McLuhan's development—in the middle and late 1950's—most of the material that I have chosen for this section to illustrate the evolution of what by now must be termed a "system" is by McLuhan himself.

*   *   *

In "Verbi-Voco-Visual" (10), which appeared in *Explorations* #8 in 1957, McLuhan deals with the concept of the auditory imagination. The application of mass media to education is discussed in "Classroom Without Walls" (11), another *Explorations* piece. The Manifesto section of #8 was designed and set by Harley Parker, to be viewed as well as read, an *aesthetic* as well as a *literary* event.

William Blissett (12), a professor of English at the University of Toronto, writes a parody-critique of *Explorations*, pointing out the journal's paradoxical attitude to its self-chosen medium, the printed word.

"Joyce, Mallarmé, and the Press" (13) appeared in 1954 and is included here to show the transition in emphasis in McLuhan's work that becomes apparent toward the middle of the decade. No longer concerned exclusively with literary phenomena, McLuhan now begins to superimpose upon his critical assumptions a grammar of communications.

A telecast by **Marshall McLuhan, Harley Parker,** and **Robert**

Shafer (14) in 1960 distinctly anticipates much of the material that appeared two years later in *The Gutenberg Galaxy.*

"Report on Project on Understanding New Media" (15), from which I have chosen excerpts, was prepared by McLuhan in 1960 for the National Association of Educational Broadcasters on a grant from the Office of Education, United States Department of Health, Education, and Walfare. The Report is an attempt to answer the various questions about media McLuhan poses—at that time he considered media only in terms of the traditional forms of communication. In *Understanding Media: The Extensions of Man,* the definition of *medium* was expanded to include clothing, weapons, games, etc.

10 where the hand of man never set foot.
—MARSHALL MC LUHAN

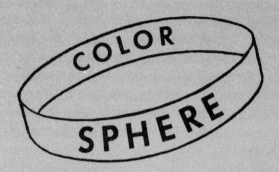

The age-old conflict between the Eastern integrity of the interval and the Western integrity of the object is being resolved in oral culture.

Pound's *Treatise on Harmony* states:

A sound of any pitch, or any combination of such sounds, may be followed by a sound of any other pitch, or any combination of such sounds, providing the time interval between them is properly gauged; and this is true for any series of sounds, chords or arpeggios.

This is a physical fact in color and in design as well.

A superimposed metronomic time or space pattern is intolerable today in verse, in town planning or in music.

Bartok sought new musical order in the rhythms and patterns of folk speech.

The interval is the means of epiphany or revelation.

It is the release which Hopkins called Sprung Rhythm.

It is the instrument of anological intuition of Being.

It is the dynamic symmetry of tensions among proportions which yields the Golden Section in space or time.

The Munsell Color Sphere does not take us into the inclusive auditory world its form implies. The spectator is left outside with one facet of color at a time.

True color experience derives from involvement of all the senses at once—synesthesia.

Man lives in such a sphere of jazzed up rag-time sensuous be-bop.

To bring order into this jangled sphere man must find its center.

A valid color sphere would have the spectator in the center.

Sensation of pure color is only possible through the acoustics of the word.

In actual visual experience of color, perception changes constantly because of factors of background and eye fatigue.

Therefore symmetrical balance and harmony are possible only when man is at the center of the sphere.

In the model sphere colors of strong hue and chroma
will be at the center of the sphere, retreating colors further away.

Today our engineering and town planning permit the extension of such model spheres to every area of physical experience at ground level or from the air.

The color sphere or modulor is cued in with the auditory space of our oral, electronic culture.

THE CITY

no longer exists, except as a cultural ghost for tourists. Any highway eatery with its TV set, newspaper, and magazine is as cosmopolitan as New York or Paris.

The METROPOLIS today is a classroom; the ads are its teachers. The classroom is an obsolete detention home, a feudal dungeon.

The metropolis is OBSOLETE

ASK THE ARMY

The handwriting is on the celluloid walls of Hollywood; the Age of Writing has passed. We must invent a NEW METAPHOR, restructure our thoughts and feelings. The new media are not bridges between man and nature: they are nature.

Gutenberg made all history SIMULTANEOUS: the transportable book brought the world of the dead into the space of the gentleman's library; the telegraph brought the entire world of the living to the workman's breakfast table.

NOBODY yet knows the language inherent in the new technological culture; we are all deaf-blind mutes in terms of the new situation. Our most impressive words and thoughts betray us by referring to the previously existent, not to the present.

WE ARE BACK IN ACOUSTIC SPACE

We begin again to structure the primordial feelings and emotions from which 3000 years of literacy divorced us.

Counterblast, 1954

POETIC IMAGERY

ONLY a part of an author's imagery comes from his reading. It comes from the whole of his sensitive life since early childhood. Why, for all of us, out of all that we have heard, seen, felt, in a lifetime, do certain images recur, charged with emotion, rather than others? . . .

AUDITORY

IMAGINATION

What I call the "auditory imagination" is the feeling for syllable and rhythm, penetrating far below the conscious levels of thought and feeling, invigorating every word; sinking to the most primitive and forgotten, returning to the origin and bringing something back, seeking the beginning and the end. It works through meanings, certainly or not without meanings in the ordinary sense, and fuses the old and obliterated and the trite, the current, and the new and surprising, the most ancient and the most civilized mentality.

T. S. ELIOT (From *The Use of Poetry and the Use of Criticism*, 1933)

today we're beginning to realize that
the new media aren't just mechanical
gimmicks for creating worlds of illusion,
but new languages with new and
unique powers of expression.

11

—MARSHALL MC LUHAN

It's natural today to speak
of "audio and visual aids" to teaching,
for we still think of the book as norm,
of other media as incidental.
We also think of the new media
—press, radio, movies, TV—
as MASS MEDIA
& think of the book
as an individualistic form.

Individualistic because it
isolated the reader in silence &
helped create the Western "I."
Yet it was the first product of
mass production.

With it everybody could have
the same books.
It was impossible
in medieval times for
different students, different institutions,
to have copies of the same book.
Manuscripts, commentaries, were dictated.
Students memorized.

Instruction was almost entirely oral,
done in groups.
Solitary study was reserved for
the advanced scholar.
The first printed books were
"visual aids" to oral instruction.

Before the printing press,
the young learned by
listening, watching, doing.
So, until recently, our own
rural children learned the
language & skills of their elders.
Learning took place
outside the classroom.
Only those aiming at professional careers
went to school at all.

Today in our cities,
most learning occurs outside the classroom.
The sheer quantity of information conveyed by
press-mags-film-TV-radio
far exceeds
the quantity of information conveyed by
school instruction & texts.
This challenge has destroyed
the monopoly of the book as a teaching aid
& cracked the very walls of the classroom,
so suddenly,
we're confused, baffled.

In this violently upsetting social situation,
many teachers naturally view
the offerings of the new media
as entertainment,
rather than education.
But this view carries
no conviction to the student.

Find a classic
which wasn't first regarded
as light entertainment.
Nearly all vernacular works
were so regarded until the 19th century.

Many movies are obviously handled
with a degree of insight & maturity
at least equal to the level permitted
in today's textbooks.
Olivier's Henry V *&* Richard III
assemble a wealth of
scholarly & artistic skill
which reveal Shakespeare at a very high level,
yet in a way easy
for the young to enjoy.

The movie is to dramatic representation
what the book was to the manuscript.
It makes available
to many & at many times & places
what otherwise would be restricted
to a few at few times & places.
The movie, like the book,
is a ditto device.
TV shows to 50,000,000 simultaneously.
Some feel that the value
of experiencing a book
is diminished by being extended
to many minds.
This notion is always implicit
in the phrases "mass media," "mass entertainment"—
useless phrases obscuring the fact THAT
English itself
is a mass medium.
Today we're beginning to realize
that the new media aren't just

mechanical gimmicks
for creating worlds of illusion,
but new languages
with new & unique powers of expression.
Historically, the resources of English
have been shaped & expressed in
constantly new & changing ways.
The printing press changed,
not only the quantity of writing,
but the character of language
& the relations between author & public.
Radio, film, TV pushed
written English towards
the spontaneous shifts & freedom of
the spoken idiom.
They aided us in the recovery
of intense awareness of
facial language & bodily gesture.
If these "mass media"
should serve only
to weaken or corrupt
previously achieved levels of
verbal & pictorial culture,
it won't be because
there's anything inherently wrong with them.
It will be because we've failed
to master them as new languages in time
to assimilate them to
our total cultural heritage.

These new developments,
under quiet analytic survey,
point to a basic strategy of culture
for the classroom.
When the printed book first appeared,
it threatened

the oral procedures of teaching, and
created
the classroom as we now know it.
Instead of making
his own text, his own dictionary, his own grammar,
the student started out with these tools.
He could study, not one,
but several languages.
Today these new media
threaten, instead of merely reinforce,
the procedures of this traditional classroom.
It's customary to answer this threat
with denunciations of
the unfortunate character & effect
of movies & TV,
just as the comicbook
was feared & scorned & rejected
from the classroom.
Its good & bad features
in form & content,
when carefully set beside
other kinds of art & narrative,
could have become a major
asset to the teacher.

Where student interest is already
intensely focused
is the natural point
at which to be
in the elucidation of
other problems & interests.
The educational task
is not only
to provide
basic tools
of perception,

**but to develop
judgement & discrimination
with ordinary social experience.**

*Few students ever acquire skill
in analysis of newspapers.
Fewer have any ability to discuss
a movie intelligently.*
To be articulate & discriminating
about ordinary affairs & information
is the mark of an educated man.
It's misleading to suppose
*there's any basic difference between
education & entertainment.*
This distinction merely relieves people
*of the responsibility of
looking into the matter.*
It's like setting up a distinction between
*didactic & lyric poetry
on the ground that one
teaches, the other pleases.*
However, it's always been true
*that whatever pleases
teaches more effectively.*

bless explorations (careful: there's cordite mixed with the popcorn). bless its editors and contributors, eminent products of book-culture, determined to get their notions down in print where we can square up to them. —WILLIAM BLISSETT

12

NEITHER FAITH IN MACHINERY NOR FEAR OF MACHINERY

EXPLORATIONS follows Matthew Arnold here. Three times a year it advances culture by allowing, by provoking, a free play of mind over stock opinions and prejudices. That is one reason (not the only) that it is so irritating—quite the most irritating thing in current print. The average intelligent man fights shy of being made more intelligent in any unfamiliar, unexpected way.

A BOOK IS THE DEATH OF A TREE

Even in Canada, where trees are many and books are few, that saying of St-John Perse stops me cold. However, I'll let EXPLORATIONS have it for their next raid on book culture if they will ponder the question, What is a TV program the death of?

COFFINED THOUGHTS AROUND ME

What has become of the six-times reiterated epigraph about EXPLORATIONS not being a reference journal where truth is embalmed for posterity, now that the early issues are reported worth their weight in hen's teeth?

O.K. NAMES ALL MARSHALLED

So the Makers of Modern Literature are more willing than the professoriate to concede the mass media as "here to stay," "whether we like them or not"? Wait a minute: are they all happy paddlers in the wave of the future?

> Faun's flesh is not to us,
> Nor the saint's vision.
> We have the Press for wafer;
> Franchise for circumcision.

Baudelaire felt himself contaminated by the touch of newsprint; he made no objection to the book as an object.

Stéphane Mallarmé (like Stephen Dedalus) "read the book of himself": for him THE BOOK could stand as the symbol of total truth, and in its cause he made a hit-and-run raid on newspaper layout as the symbol of chaos, the

H A P H
A Z A R D

The advertising tout in *Ulysses* is L. Boom. ("Machines—smash a man"). The hero of the book is someone else.

Picasso, unlike *Paris-Soir*, does not advertise *Paris-Soir* or endorse its views in his collages.

Trying to tell me that sleepwalkers with *Finnegan* cut their ear-teeth on the *Toronto Telegram* or the *$64,000 Question*, not products of the professoriate, like EXPLORATIONS?

SCAT   BRAIN   ING
TER   STORM

"So long as there is a question of amusing, touching, or seducing men's minds one might agree, at a pinch, that broadcasting would be adequate. But science and philosophy demand quite another rhythm of thought than reading aloud could allow, or, rather, they impose an absence of rhythm. Reflection stops or breaks its impulsion every second, it introduces uneven tempos, returns, and detours which demand the physical presence of a text and the possibility of handling it at leisure."
—Paul Valéry, *Reflections on the World Today*, tr. Francis Scarfe.

THOUGHT CONSTITUTES THE GREATNESS OF MAN
Gimmicks are not thoughts.

DISTRACTED FROM DISTRACTION BY DISTRACTION
"Publicity, which is one of the greatest evils of our age, insults our eyes, falsifies every epithet, destroys landscapes, corrupts all standards and all criticism, exploits trees, rocks, and monuments, and on pages which are spewed out by machines, confuses the assassin with the victim, the hero, today's centenarian and the martyred child." Valéry.

WHAT'S THE RUSH?
"Writing that will be less interesting tomorrow than it is today." Gide on journalism.

Non-poetry eats poetry, turning it into cliché and slogan.

Poetry, like the moon, does not advertise anything. (March, 1958).

BOOKS ARE OBSOLETE? SO IS HOMO SAPIENS
"Soon we shall be obliged to build ourselves strictly isolated cloisters where neither the radio waves nor the newspapers can penetrate and in which our ignorance of all politics can be preserved and cultivated.

Their inhabitants will despise speed, numbers, the effects produced by mass by surprise by contrast by repetition, by novelty, and by credulity. People will go there from time to time, in order to look through the bars at a few specimens of *free men.*" Valéry.

IT'S DRAUGHTY WITH ALL THE WALLS DOWN
If automation is to bring an age of idleness, it may curtail the mass-media and encourage the rebuilding of walls, the proliferation of minority audiences with a taste for limited editions, horseback riding, heraldry.

O SAY CAN YOU HEAR?

The Chinese ideogram has only a ghost of a vocal or auditory dimension. You must SEE THE TEXT. Musical setting is an added attraction. China was the last word in book culture. Even its painting was written. It is now becoming a wall-newspaper culture.

HOW ORAL IS ORAL?

"A little lowly hermitage it was . . ."

"For God's sake, hold your tongue and let me love . . ."

Spenser soft and dreamy, Donne a naked speaking voice? Perhaps, but try reading aloud several stanzas of Spenser, several poems of Donne. I heard it tried on the radio, with all the understanding and finesse that either poet could desire. Spenser, for all his archaism, came across; Donne, for all his colloquialism, did not. Spenser is consecutive as sound and song, Donne is interrupted as print and talk. Donne appeals to a sophisticated literacy indifferent to the qualities of "smooth song" that Spenser shares with popular poetry. "Strong lines" are lines of print: Donne's text must be seen.

SUMMIT TALK ON MAGIC MOUNTAIN

Settembrini, the liberal chatterbox rhetorician, has a horror of "analphabetic darkness." Naptha, the Jewish-Marxist-Jesuit dialectician scorns "that bogey." Settembrini loses the argument. So does Naptha.

CONTROLLED EXPERIMENT

Give one group of students printed time-tables; instruct others by public-address system (vocal emptiness echoing within marble doom) on how to get from B'llv'll to Gwoff via Tra'a. See who gets where.

BLAST "here to stay": BLAST "whether you like it or not"—
the hectoring bullyragging buddybuttonholing style, Madison

Avenue's middlebrow answer to the middlebrow Marxists of the 30's. And, while we're about it, BLAST BLAST.

BLESS EXPLORATIONS (Careful: there's cordite mixed with the popcorn). BLESS its editors and contributors, eminent products of book-culture, determined to get their notions down in print where we can square up to them.

THE SOUND OF ONE HAND CLAPPING
EXPLORATIONS a monologue of epigrams and gags with standard articles (some of them distinguished) thrown in as filler. Time for a dialogue?

Editor's Note: See Part 6, p. 270–271 for McLuhan's comments.

it is strange that the popular press as an art form has often attracted the enthusiastic attention of poets and aesthetes while rousing the gloomiest apprehensions in the academic mind.

13

—MARSHALL MC LUHAN

Declining to write for the *Revue Européenne* in 1831, Lamartine said to its editor:

> **Do not perceive in these words a superb disdain for what is termed journalism. Far from it; I have too intimate a knowledge of my epoch to repeat this absurd nonsense, this impertinent**

inanity against the Periodical Press. I know too well the work
Providence has committed to it. Before this century shall run
out journalism will be the whole press—the whole human
thought. Since that prodigious multiplication which art has given
to speech—multiplication to be multiplied a thousandfold
yet—mankind will write their books day by day, hour by hour,
page by page. Thought will be spread abroad in the world with
the rapidity of light; instantly conceived, instantly written,
instantly understood at the extremities of the earth—it will
spread from pole to pole. Sudden, instant, burning with the
fervor of soul which made it burst forth, it will be the reign of
the human soul in all its plenitude. It will not have time
to ripen—to accumulate in a book; the book will arrive too late.
The only book possible from today is a newspaper.

It is strange that the popular press as an art form has often attracted the enthusiastic attention of poets and aesthetes while rous-
ing the gloomiest apprehensions in the academic mind. The same
division of opinion can be traced in the sixteenth century concerning the printed book. Two thousand years of manuscript culture
were abruptly dissolved by the printing press. Failure to understand this arises from various overriding assumptions about the
universal benefits of print. But today when technology has con-
ferred ascendancy on pictorial and radio communication it is easy
to detect the peculiar limitations and bias of the four-century span
of book-culture which is coming to a close.

In her recent study of George Herbert, Rosamund Tuve stressed
the extent to which metaphysical conceits were direct translations
into verbal terms of popular pictorial imagery of the late Middle
Ages. She was able to show that the characteristic conceits of Herbert and others arose from the meeting of the old manuscript culture (with its marginal pictures) and the new printed medium. In
the same way, many others have argued that the peculiar richness
of effect of Elizabethan and Jacobean language was the result of a
meeting of the oral tradition and the new printed culture. Mere
literature doesn't begin until the oral tradition was entirely sub-
ordinated to the silent and private studies of the bookman. It was
the life-long claim of W. B. Yeats that in Ireland this conquest over

the spoken word was less complete than elsewhere in Anglo-Saxony.

So, if the metaphysicals owe much to their adaptation of medieval pictographs to the printed medium, it could be suggested that modern poetry with its elaborate mental landscapes owes much to the new pictorial technology which fascinated Poe and Baudelaire and on which Rimbaud and Mallarmé built much of their aesthetics. If the Jacobeans were receding from a pictographic culture toward the printed page, may we not meet them at the point where we are receding from the printed word under the impetus of pictorial technology? Manuscript technology fostered a constellation of mental attitudes and skills of which the modern world has no memory. Plato foresaw some of them with alarm in the *Phaedrus:*

> The specific which you have discovered is an aid not to memory,
> but to reminiscence, and you give your disciples not truth but
> only the semblance of truth; they will be hearers of many
> things and will have learned nothing; they will appear omniscient
> and will generally know nothing; they will be tiresome
> company, having the show of wisdom without the reality.

Plato is speaking for the oral tradition before it was modified by literacy. He saw writing as a mainly destructive revolution. Since then we have been through enough revolutions to know that every medium of communication is a unique art form which gives salience to one set of human possibilities at the expense of another set. Each medium of expression profoundly modifies human sensibility in mainly unconscious and unpredictable ways. Alphabetic communication brings about an inevitable psychic withdrawal, as E. J. Chaytor showed in *From Script to Print*, with a train of personal and social maladjustments. But it secures a host of advantages. Psychic withdrawal is automatic because the process of literacy is the process of setting up the interior monologue. It is the problem of translation of the auditory into the visual and back again, which is the process of writing and reading, that brings the interior monologue into existence, as can be observed in the study of pre-literate cultures today. This introversion with its consequent weakening of sense perception also creates inattention to the speech

of others and sets up mechanisms which interfere with verbal recall. Exact verbal recall is scarcely a problem for pre-literate
cultures.

Throughout *Finnegans Wake* Joyce plays some of his major
variations on this theme of "ABCEDmindedness" in "those pagan
ironed times of the first city . . . when a frond was a friend." His
"verbivocovisual" presentation of an "all nights newsery reel" is
the first dramatization of the very media of communication as both
form and vehicle of the flux of human cultures. Most of the problems of reading the *Wake* dissolve when it is seen that he is using
the media themselves as art forms as in a "phantom city phaked of
philm pholk." The lights go up in his "Feenichts Playhouse" as
the sun dips at the end of the Anna Livia section, and he is ready
to mime the war of light and dark, of Michael, the Devil, and the
maggies in a zodiacal dance of the witches ("monthage") "with
nightly redistribution of parts and players by the puppetry pro-
ducer."

Throughout the *Wake* this interior "tubloid" or tale of a tub is
linked both to the cabbalistic significance of the letters of the alphabet and to the psychological effect of literacy in creating a general
"ABCEDmindedness" in human society.

But the arrest of the flux of thought and speech which is the written page permits that prolonged analysis of thought processes from
which arise the structures of science. Pictographic Chinese culture,
for example, would seem to stand midway between the extremes of
our abstract written tradition and the plenary oral tradition with
its stress on speech as gesture and gesture as "phatic communion."
And it is perhaps this medial position between the noncommunicating extremes of print and pictorial technology which attracts us
today to the Chinese ideogram.

A principal feature of manuscript culture was its relative unity.
The rarity and inaccessibility of manuscript books fostered a habit
of encyclopedism. And where scholars were not numerous there
were additional reasons for each of them to be acquainted with the
entire range of authors. Moreover, manuscripts were studied slowly
and aloud. Silent reading was impossible until the presses created
the macadamized highways of print. The handwritten book was a

broken road which was traveled slowly and infrequently. It kept the reader close to the dimensions of oral discourse. The publication of a poem consisted in reading or reciting it to a small audience. The promulgation of ideas was by public disputation.

Print multiplied scholars, but it also diminished their social and political importance. And it did the same for books. Unexpectedly, print fostered nationalism and broke down international communication because publishers found that the vernacular audience was larger and more profitable. As H. A. Innis·has shown in *The Bias of Communication*, the printed word has been a major cause of international disturbance and misunderstanding since the sixteenth century. But pictorial communication is relatively international and hard to manipulate for purposes of national rivalry. H. A. Innis has been the great pioneer in opening up the study of the economic and social consequences of the various media of communication; so that today any student of letters is necessarily indebted to him for insight into changing attitudes to time and space which result from shifting media. In particular his studies of the newspaper as a major branch of the technology of print are relevant to the study of modern literature. Beginning as an economic historian, Innis was gradually impelled to consider not just the external trade-routes of the world but also the great trade-routes of the mind. He became aware that the modern world, having solved the problem of commodities, had turned its technology to the packaging of information and ideas.

If the manuscript tradition encouraged encyclopedism, book culture naturally tended to specialism. There were enough books to make reading a full-time occupation and to ensure an entirely withdrawn and private existence for the whole class of bookmen. Eventually there were enough books to splinter the reading public into dozens of noncommunicating groups. This has meant a large degree of unawareness in our culture of the meaning and drift of its most obvious developments. The bookman as such is not easily interested even in the technology and art of the book form of communication. And as this form has been modified by the popular press, and later developments, the exponents of book culture have registered various emotions but little curiosity. It is not, therefore, incongruous that real understanding of the changes in modern communication should have come mainly from the resourceful technicians among modern poets and painters.

Much of the novelty of the *Portrait, Ulysses,* and the *Wake* is an illusion resulting from inattention to technical developments in the arts since Newton. That manipulation of a continuous parallel between modern Dublin and ancient Ithaca, which Mr. Eliot has noted as the major resource of *Ulysses,* was a transfer to the time dimension of a "double-plot," a technique which had been the staple of all picturesque art for two hundred years. De Gourmont observed that one achievement of Flaubert had been the transfer of Chateaubriand's panoramic art from nature and history to the industrial metropolis. And Baudelaire had matched Flaubert in this witty reversal of the role of picturesque landscape. But English landscape art in painting, poetry, and the novel was decades in advance of France and Europe, a fact which was inseparable from English industrial experiment and scientific speculation. In her fascinating book *Newton Demands the Muse,* Marjorie Nicolson records the impact of Newtonian optics on the themes of the poets. But the techniques of rendering experience were equally modified in the direction of an inclusive image of society and consciousness. The new vision of space and light as outer phenomena which were precisely correlative to our inner faculties gave a new meaning and impetus to the juxtaposition of images and experiences. The taste for the discontinuities of Gothic art was one with the new interest in the juxtaposition of various social classes in the novels of the road (Fielding, Smollett, Mackenzie) and in the juxtaposition of historical epochs as well as primitive and sophisticated experience in Scott and Byron. More subtle was the juxtaposition of various states of the same mind in *Tristram Shandy* and the sleuth-like quest for the origins of such states on the part of Sterne and later of Wordsworth.

But the parallel development of the arts of spatial manipulation of mental states which was occurring in the popular press has been given no attention. Innis has shown how the new global landscapes of the press were not only geared to industry but were themselves the means of paying for new roads, for railway and telegraph and cable. The physical landscape of the earth was changed very quickly by the landscapes of the newspaper, even though the political scene has not yet caught up. The networks of news, trade, and transport were one. And newspapermen like Dickens who had no stake in established literary decorum were quick to adapt the technology of print to art and entertainment. Well before the French impressionists and symbolists had discovered the bearings for art of modern technology, Dickens had switched the picturesque perspectives of the eighteenth-century novel to the representation of the new industrial slums. Neurotic eccentricity in the subworld of the metropolis he proved to be a much richer source for the rendering of mania and manic states of mind than the crofters of Scott or the yokels of Wordsworth. And Dostoevski mined from Dickens freely, as G. B. Shaw did later still. But just how valid were the impressionist techniques of the picturesque kind familiar to the news reporter appears in the notable essay of Eisenstein in *Film Form* where he shows the impact of Dickens on the art of D. W. Griffiths.

How deeply English artists had understood the principles of picturesque art by 1780 appears from the invention of cinema at that time. In 1781 De Loutherbourg, the theatrical scene-painter, contrived in London a panorama which he called the "Eidophusikon" so as "to realize pictures in all four dimensions." His "Various Imitations of Natural Phenomena, Represented by Moving Pictures" were advertised in these words and caused a sensation. Gainsborough, we are told by a contemporary, "was so delighted that for a time he thought of nothing else, talked of nothing else, and passed his evenings at the exhibition in long succession." He even made one of these machines for himself capable of showing sunrise and moonrise as well as storms and ships at sea. Gainsborough through this cinema was experiencing the novelty of cubism with "lo spettatore nel centro del quadro."

Another familiar instance of the abrupt newspaper juxtaposition of events in "picturesque perspective" is *The Ring and the Book*, an explicitly newspaperish crime report given as a series of "inside stories," each one contained within another like Chinese boxes. But it was Mallarmé who formulated the lessons of the press as a guide

for the new impersonal poetry of suggestion and implication. He
saw that the scale of modern reportage and of the mechanical
multiplication of messages made personal rhetoric impossible.
Now was the time for the artist to intervene in a new way and to
manipulate the new media of communication by a precise and delicate adjustment of the relations of words, things, and events. His
task had become not self-expression but the release of the life in
things. *Un Coup de Dés* illustrates the road he took in the exploitation of all things as gestures of the mind, magically adjusted to the
secret powers of being. As a vacuum tube is used to shape and control vast reservoirs of electric power, the artist can manipulate the
low current of casual words, rhythms, and resonances to evoke the
primal harmonies of existence or to recall the dead. But the price
he must pay is total self-abnegation.

The existentialist metaphysic latent in Mallarmé's aesthetics was
stated in 1924 in *In Praise of Newspapers* by Karel Capek:

> The newspaper world like that of the wild beasts exists solely
> in the present; Press consciousness (if one can speak of
> consciousness) is circumscribed by simple present time
> extending from the morning on to the evening edition, or the
> other way round. If you read a paper a week old you feel as if
> you were turning the pages of Dalimil's chronicle: no longer
> is it a newspaper but a memorial. The ontological system of
> newspapers is actualized realism: what is just now exists . . .
> literature is the expression of old things in eternally new
> forms, while newspapers are eternally expressing new realities
> in a stabilized and unchangeable form.

By extending the technique of reporting the coexistence of events
in China and Peru from global space to the dimension of time,
Joyce achieved the actualized realism of a continuous present for
events past, present, and future. In reverse, it is only necessary to
remove the date-line from any newspaper to obtain a similar if less
satisfactory model of the universe. That is what R. L. Stevenson
meant when he said he could make an epic of a newspaper if he
knew what to leave out. Joyce knew what to leave out.

For that school of thought for which the external world is an opaque prison, art can never be regarded as a source of knowledge but only as a moral discipline and a study of endurance. The artist is not a reader of radiant signatures on *materia signata* but the signer of a forged check on our hopes and sympathies. This school has supported the idea of the function of art as catharsis which, as G. R. Levy shows in *The Gate of Horn,* was a preparation for the lesser Greek mysteries. But if the world is not opaque and if the mind is not of the earth earthy, then this moral view of art should yield to the cognitive view. However that may be, the cathartic, ethical view of art has led to a doctrinaire hostility to the use of discontinuity in art (the theme of Arnold's preface to *Poems,* 1853) and indifference to all popular art. And in the past century with every technological device advancing the discontinuous character of communication the stand taken by the cathartic and ethical school has enveloped the entire world of popular culture in a haze of esoteric nescience, disguised, however, as a profound moral concern with the wider hope and the higher things. Joyce had a phrase for this anticognitive attitude, "the cultic twalette."

Moral and aesthetic horror at the ignobility of the popular scene gave way to an opposite attitude in the symbolists, and Mallarmé is, before Joyce, the best spokesman of the new approach. In his *Shop Windows* (*Étalages*), while analyzing the aesthetics of commercial layout, he considers the relations between poetry and the press.

A shop window full of new books prompts his reflection that the function of the ordinary run of books is merely to express the average degree of human boredom and incompetence, to reduce to a written form the horizon of the human scene in all its abounding banality. Instead of deploring this fact as literary men tend to do, the artist should exploit it: "The vague, the commonplace, the smudged and defaced, not banishment of these, occupation rather! Apply them as to a patrimony."

Only by a conquest and occupation of these vast territories of stupefaction can the artist fulfill his culturally heroic function of purifying the dialect of the tribe, the Herculean labor of cleaning the Augean stables of speech, of thought, and feeling. Turning directly to the press, Mallarmé designates it as "a traffic, an epitomization of enormous and elementary interests . . . employing print for the propagation of opinions, the recital of divers facts, made plausible, in the Press, which is devoted to publicity, by the omission, it would seem, of any art." He delights in the dramatic significance of the fact that in the French press, at least, the literary and critical features form a section at the base of the first page. And even more delightful:

> Fiction properly so called, or the imaginative tale, frolics across the average daily paper, enjoying the most prominent spots even to the top of the page, dislodging the financial feature and pushing actuality into second place. Here, too, is the suggestion and even the lesson of a certain beauty: that today is not only the supplanter of yesterday or the presager of tomorrow but issues from time, in general, with an integrity bathed and fresh. The vulgar placard, bawled . . . at the street corner thus sustains this reflection . . . on the political text. Such experience leaves some people cold because they imagine that while there may be a little more or less of the sublime in these pleasures tasted by the people, the situation as regards that which alone is precious and immeasurably lofty, and which is known by the name of Poetry, that this situation remains unchanged. Poetry (they suppose) will always be exclusive and the best of its pinions will never approach those pages of the newspaper where it is parodied, nor are they pleased by the spread of wings in our hands of those vast improvised sheets of the daily paper.

Mallarmé is laughing at these finicky and unperceptive people for whom the press appears as a threat to "real culture"; and continues:

> To gauge by the extraordinary, actual superproduction, through which the Press intelligently yields its average, the notion prevails, nonetheless, of something very decisive which is elaborating itself: a prelude to an era, a competition for the foundation of the popular modern Poem, at the very least of innumerable Thousand and One Nights: by which the majority of readers will be astonished at the sudden invention. You are

assisting at a celebration, all of you, right now, amidst
the contingencies of this lightning achievement!

The author of *Ulysses* was the only person to grasp the full artistic
implications of this radically democratic aesthetic elaborated by
the fabulous artificer, the modern Daedalus, Stéphane Mallarmé.
But Joyce was certainly assisted by Flaubert's *Sentimental Education* and *Bouvard and Pécuchet* in adapting Mallarmé's insights to
his own artistic purposes. A very little reflection on the scrupu-
lously banal character of Flaubert's epics about industrial man
illuminates much of the procedure in *Ulysses* and the *Wake*.

Crise de Vers, *Étalages*, and *Le Livre, Instrument Spirituel* all
belong to the last few years of Mallarmé's life, representing his
ultimate insights (1892–1896). And in each of these essays he is
probing the aesthetic consequences and possibilities of the popular
arts of industrial man. In *Le Livre* he turns to scrutinize the press
once more, opening with the proposition, self-evident to him, that
the whole world exists in order to result in a book. This is a matter
of metaphysical fact, that all existence cries out to be raised to the
level of scientific or poetic intelligibility. In this sense "the book"
confers on things and persons another mode of existence which
helps to perfect them. And it is plain that Mallarmé regarded the
press as this ultimate encyclopedic book in its most rudimentary
form. The almost super-human range of awareness of the press now
awaits only the full analogical sense of exact orchestration to perfect its present juxtaposition of items and themes. And this implies
the complete self-effacement of the writer, for "this book does not
admit of any signature." The job of the artist is not to sign but to
read signatures. Existence must speak for itself. It is already richly
and radiantly signed. The artist has merely to reveal, not to forge
the signatures of existence. But he can only put these in order by
discovering the orchestral analogies in things themselves. The result will be "the hymn, harmony, and joy, as a pure ensemble ordered in the sharpest and most vivid circumstance of their inter-
relations. Man charged with divine vision has no other mode of
expression save the parallelism of pages as a means of expressing
the links, the whims, the limpidity on which he gazes."

All those pseudo-rationalisms, the forged links and fraudulent intelligibility which official literature has imposed on existence must be abandoned. And this initial step the press has already taken in its style of impersonal juxtaposition which conveys such riches to the writer. This work of "popular enchantment" which is the daily paper is not lacking in moral edification, for the hubbub of appetites and protests to be found among the advertisements and announcements proclaims each day the "original servitude" of man and the confusion of tongues of the tower of Babel. But the very format of the press resembles "a retracted wing which is ready to spread itself," awaiting only the "intervention of folding or of rhythm" in order to rid us of all that passes for "literature."

Mallarmé sees this impersonal art of juxtaposition as revolutionary and democratic also in the sense that it enables each reader to be an artist: "Reading becomes a solitary, tacit concert given to itself by the mind which recaptures significance from the least sonorities." It is the rhyming and orchestrating of things themselves which releases the maximum intelligibility and attunes the ears of men once more to the music of the spheres. We are finished, he says, with that custom of an official literary decorum by which poets sang in chorus, obliterating with their personal forgeries the actual signatures of things. In fact, the new poet will take as much care to avoid a style that is not in things themselves as literary men have in the past sought to achieve and impose one.

In approaching the structure of *Ulysses* as a newspaper landscape it is well to call to mind a favorite book of Joyce's, *The Purple Island* of Phineas Fletcher, the author's name suggesting Finn the arrow-maker. Fletcher presents the anatomy and labyrinths of the human body in terms of an enchanted Spenserian landscape. Many have pointed out the importance of the human form of the sleeping giant, the collective consciousness, as the structure of the *Wake*. And Joyce was careful to instruct his readers in the relation between the episodes of *Ulysses* and our bodily organs. (In 1844 the American press greeted the telegraph as "the first definite pulsation of the real nervous system of the world.") In *Ulysses* in episode seven we find ourselves in a newspaper office in "the heart of the Hibernian metropolis." For Joyce the press was indeed a "microchasm" of the world of man, its columns unchanging monuments to the age-old passions and interests of all men, and its production and distribution a drama involving the hands and organs of the entire "body politic." With its date line June 16, 1904, *Ulysses* is, newspaperwise, an abridgment of all space in a brief segment of time, as the *Wake* is a condensation of all time in the brief space of "Howth castle and environs."

The date line of *Ulysses*, the day of the end of the drought in the land of "The Dead," the day of the meeting of Joyce and Nora Barnacle, was the day that Joyce was to preserve in exile as Aeneas carried to New Troy the ashes and hut-urn of his ancestors (Fustel de Coulanges' *The Ancient City* is a useful introduction to this aspect of Joyce's filial piety). But whereas the techniques of the *Wake* are "telekinetic" and are explicitly specified as those of radio, television, newsreel, and the stuttering verbal gestures of H. C. E., it is the newspaper as seen by Mallarmé that provides most of the symbolist landscapes of *Ulysses*. As a daily cross-section of the activities and impulses of the race the press is an inclusive image affording possibilities of varied orchestration. A passage in *Stephen Hero* (page 186) suggests the direction in which Joyce has modified the superficial cross-section of the popular press:

> The modern spirit is vivisective. Vivisection itself is the most modern process one can conceive. . . . All modern political and religious criticism dispenses with presumptive states. . . . It examines the entire community in action and reconstructs the spectacle of redemption. If you were an esthetic philosopher you would take note of all my vagaries because here you have the spectacle of the esthetic instinct in action. The philosophic college should spare a detective for me.

The key terms here, vivisection, community in action, reconstruction, detection, are related to every phase of Joyce's aesthetic. In *Modern Painters* Ruskin discusses the discontinuous picturesque techniques in medieval and modern art under the term "grotesque," noting it as the avenue by which popular and democratic expression enters the serious levels of art:

A fine grotesque is the expression, in a moment, by a series of
symbols thrown together in bold and fearless connection of
truths which it would have taken a long time to express in any
verbal way, and of which the connection is left for the beholder
to work out for himself, the gaps, left or overleaped by the
haste of the imagination, forming the grotesque character. . . .
Hence it is an infinite good to mankind when there is a full
acceptance of the grotesque . . . an enormous amount of
intellectual power is turned to use, which in this present
century of ours, evaporates in street gibing. . . . It is with a
view to the reopening of this great field of human intelligence,
long entirely closed, that I am striving to introduce Gothic
architecture . . . and to revive the art of illumination . . .
the distinctive difference between illumination and painting
proper, being, that illumination admits no shadows,
but only gradations of pure colour.

Ruskin in describing the grotesque gives the very formula for
"vivisection" or the community in action, though he hadn't the
faintest idea of how to adapt this ideal to contemporary art. It was
not misleading on Joyce's part, therefore, when he spoke of his
work as a Gothic cathedral or of the *Wake* as an activated page of
the Book of Kells. In presenting "history as her is harped," Joyce
concludes: "And so the triptych vision passes out of a hillside into
a hillside. Fairshee fading. Again am I deliciated by the pica-
resqueness of your irmages." (*Wake*, page 486). It is the Mallar-
méan method of orchestration of the qualities of ordinary speech
and experience that recurs, again, and again in the *Wake*:

and inform to the old sniggering publicking press and its nation
of sheepcopers about the whole plighty troth between them,
malady of milady made melody of malodi, she, the lalage of
lyonesses, and him, her knave errant . . . for all
within crystal range.

The last "crystal" image gives the typical translation of the auditory into the visual, music into color, the harp of Aeolus into the
harp of Memnon, time into space, which is the kind of metamorphosis which is going on everywhere in the *Wake*.

But the world of *Ulysses,* being primarily a modulation of space, is relatively static and newspaperish in its landscapes. It stands as inferno to the purgatorio of the *Wake.* However, in the Aeolus section of *Ulysses,* which is governed specifically by the organ "lungs" and the art of rhetoric, "everything," as Bloom says, "speaks for itself." The sheets of the newspaper become the tree harp for the wind of rhetoric. And the tree harp of the newspaper office is appropriately located beside the rock pillar of the hero:

> Before Nelson's Pillar, trams glowed, shunted, changed trolley, started for Blackrock.

The trams with their rows of cast steel provide a parallel network to the linotype machines and the rows of printed matter. But if the tree and pillar provide the true image of a hero cult, the rhetoric that blows through the leaves of this tree is that of an alien speech. Much is made of this contretemps throughout the episode, and the climax brings this dramatic conflict to an issue. J. J. O'Malloy recites John F. Taylor's defense of the Gaelic revival, the theme of which is the Mosaic refusal to accept the gods and cult of the dominant Egyptians, a refusal which made possible his descent from Sinai "bearing in his arms the tables of the law graven in the image of the outlaw." This passage, the only one Joyce seems to have recorded from *Ulysses,* has an obvious bearing on the relation of his own art to English culture.

In his *Dialogue de l'Arbre* Valéry expounds the Aeolian cosmology of trees, roots, trunks, branches, leaves:

> Chacun dit son nom. . . . O langage confus, langage qui t'agites, je veux foudre toutes tes voix. Cent mille feuilles mues font ce que le rêveur murmure aux puissances du songe.

And he proceeds to contemplate the tree as a labyrinth merging with river and sea yet remaining a giant. In the same way the Aeolian tree music of the press "reamalgemerges" with the Mosaic eloquence of Sinai and the mountain, just as Anna Livia is also ALP (and Aeolus was a volcano spirit, that is, a cyclopean or mountain figure. He was the reputed father of Ulysses and hence of Bloom). The cyclopean aspect of Aeolus and the press provides an important motif, that of crime detection and the private eye. The press man as a "Shaun the cop" or cyclops type ("though he might have been more humble there's no police like Holmes") is presented in this episode as a parody or ape of the artist. Editor Myles Crawford, soliciting the services of Stephen, boasts of the sleuthing feats of "we'll paralyze Europe" Ignatius Gallaher. Gallaher's idea of scare journalism is paralysis as opposed to the artist's idea of awakening. Gallaher reconstructed the pattern of the Phoenix Park murders to paralyze Europe; the artist reconstructs the crime of history as a means of awakening the dead. As "bullock-befriending bard," Stephen is the threader of that labyrinth described by Virgil in the fourth Georgic, the fable of the ox and of the bees of poetic inspiration.

Nevertheless Joyce is not questioning the parallel between journalism and art in respect to the retracing process. The very conditions of journalism fostered insight into artistic production, because daily or periodic publication led to a great deal of serial composition. This in turn compelled authors to write their stories backward. Edgar Poe, a journalist, in "The Philosophy of Composition," begins:

Charles Dickens, in a note now lying before me, alluding to an examination I once made of the mechanism of Barnaby Rudge, says—"By the way, are you aware that Godwin wrote his Caleb Williams backwards?"

Poe then develops the familiar symbolist doctrine of poem as an art situation which is the formula for a particular effect. The same method of composition in reverse enabled Poe to pioneer the detective story. There is nothing accidental, therefore, about the Aeolus episode being crammed with instances of reversal and reconstruction. Applying the same principle to language yields, in the *Wake*, a reconstruction of all the layers of culture and existence embedded in the present forms of words and speech gesture.

It was natural that eighteenth-century writers should have been attracted to the retracing and reconstruction principle of art, which made Horace Walpole say of *Tristram Shandy* that it was the first book which consists "in the whole narrative going backwards." A little later Dr. Thomas Brown of Edinburgh argued that the poet's imagination differed from the ordinary man's by the power of reversing the direction of association. Once picturesque art, following the spectroscope, had broken up the continuum of linear art and narrative the possibility of cinematic montage emerged at once. And montage has to be arranged forward or backward. Forward it yields narrative. Backward it is reconstruction of events. Arrested it consists of the static landscape of the press, the coexistence of all aspects of community life. This is the image of the city presented in *Ulysses*.

i wonder whether the rebellion of children today in classrooms and against the book has anything to do with the new electronic age we live in?

—MARSHALL MC LUHAN

14

McLUHAN: Today the globe has shrunk in the wash with speeded-up information movement from all directions. We have come, as it were, to live in a global village. Our information comes at high speed, electronic speed from all quarters. We would seem to be living, almost under ear conditions, of a small village world. I'm Marshall McLuhan. With me, Robert Shafer and Harley Parker are going to attempt a voyage through the recent centuries—five centuries—of Gutenberg culture: the Gutenberg Galaxy.

Before us are two utterly incongruous objects: a South Sea mask representative of primitive culture and pre-literate man; and a television set, representative of post-literate, electronic man. Between these two extremes exists the Gutenberg Galaxy, five centuries of print resulting from a thousand years of phonetic alphabet.

But there are very interesting similarities between this mask at one end and the television set at the other. The mask is sculptural, and I believe that the TV image is also sculptural—in the sense that it demands from us certain fill-ins (a tactile quality) for all of our senses, just as the mask came from a world in which all the senses were simultaneous.

PARKER: The ear-man lived in a world of all the senses, information from all quarters and through all senses at once. . . .

SHAFER: All of this is really packaged into the television set today.

McLUHAN: But the eye-man of the West would seem to have lived in a very abstract dimension of sight rather than of all the other senses, the way the ear-man lived. How did we make the transition from this echoing auditory world? How did we ever get from that ear world to the eye world that we so much take for granted?

PARKER: It was an ear world certainly to the Eskimo. He wouldn't live very many minutes unless he were tuned in in such a way with all his senses so that he knew what was going around him all the time, simultaneously.

McLUHAN: Isn't the Egyptian scribe one of the key figures in creating the transition from the ear world to the eye world?

PARKER: Absolutely, because he is dealing in hieroglyphics, pictorial messages.

McLUHAN: The medieval scribe simply carried on the world of the visual, the phonetic structure, the Egyptian and Greek culture. Translation of sound into sight, isn't it, because the stylus on the clay tablet and the quill on the scroll are ways of getting sound into sight?

PARKER: That is the really crucial point. Man makes a squiggle and it is a sound.

McLUHAN: This is a tremendous technology which enables them to translate all the other ear cultures into their own visual culture . . . and to control it. The same thing is going on at the present time in China; we're still translating Chinese tactile-auditory culture into our phonetic alphabet.

PARKER: I know a Japanese editor who told me the story of production on a Japanese newspaper, in which they deal with 41 phonetic symbols and 20,000 Chinese ideograms. I asked him how they could possibly produce a newspaper under such conditions, and he told me that they did it with a staff perhaps 35 times as big as our own newspaper staff. One man for instance will have maybe 500 to 1000 of these little wooden blocks in which the ideogram is engraved, and if somebody wants "woman washing pot," the appropriate man comes up with the little ideogram for that particular thing.

SHAFER: They are undergoing a transition from the older ear world to the eye world by this means. . . .

PARKER: After Gutenberg, we have a thing that is very, very different indeed from the Japanese or the Chinese 20,000 ideograms. We have replaceable units, uniform parts put together to make words—millions of words—in a variety of languages. We put them together in a way that has parallels to our assembly-line systems, and it's really a long, long line of words.

SHAFER: It ended the handicraft world, set up the mechanical world. . . .

McLUHAN: Absolutely. It created a totally new world of producer-consumer relationships . . . gave us a kind of assembly-line. . . . We move at that point into the world of numbers, which are also moveable. (The world and language of numbers is parallel to the world and language of letters. The latter created the visual, Euclidean world of uniform space. Number provided us with the means of translating the visual Euclidean world back into the space of touch and sound, of tactile measurability.) The mechanization of writing took place by means of the segmenting of the old handicraft motions and actions into static types, which has its parallel in Number. The same sort of thing extended to numbers. That is, letters revolutionized math.

How did Gutenberg bring about that strange Renaissance fact of individualism and nationalism? You can see how print would create an individual person, inner-directed, a kind of person highly self-centered and very much self-analytical.

PARKER: One of the most fascinating sides of the Renaissance was the way in which it took its print culture as a system of aesthetics. Leonardo da Vinci, as a matter of fact, was the type of man who could move from a work of art to a siege gun. He was capable of seeing the aesthetics of all mechanical production, and working with them.

McLUHAN: What about self-expression? It is strange that print technology should have fostered the habit of self-expression and self-analysis. That whole effort itself—portraiture and self-analysis, and the whole drive toward self-expression and self-investigation —this is characteristic of the Renaissance. Well, portraiture of a unique individual is typically Renaissance. There were very few portraits before self-portraits.

PARKER: Portraits of any kind—individualized portraits—are scarcely seen before the Renaissance. Here in this Rembrandt we have a picture which is Rembrandt looking into a mirror, and painting himself in the mirror. You get the visual echo effect, as it were.

McLUHAN: Perhaps the same kind of echo effect that we could see in the infinity sign? And perhaps the same sort of thing that we associate with the old Aunt Jemima type advertisement?

PARKER: This was one in which Aunt Jemima held a package, showing a picture of Aunt Jemima holding a package, and so on.

McLUHAN: This is the perfect expression, isn't it, of uniform repeatable type converging upon zero. Infinity? We are saying here that the infinity sign as we know it was really impossible before print, really didn't happen before Gutenberg. The sonneteers were very, very much concerned with that same form of repetition:

> Like as the waves make towards the pebbled shore,
> So do our minutes hasten to their end;
> Each changing place with that which goes before,
> In sequent toil all forwards do contend.

Shakespeare's concern with time as segmented is seemingly an exact repeat of the pattern of the Gutenberg types.

PARKER: The exact antithesis to the earlier world of fill-in, lack of line.

McLUHAN: Yes, you can see the tie-in between self-expression, self-analysis, point of view, perspective—an amazing complex there of formal overlay. There is another use of the same form in *Macbeth*:

> To-morrow and to-morrow and to-morrow
> Creeps in this petty pace from day to day . . .

Shakespeare seems to have been obsessed with the aesthetics of print in a way quite different from Leonardo, but we've more familiar with this repeatable uniformity, receiving form into infinity, in space rather than in time. Like telephone poles. . . .

PARKER: Or like the trans-Siberian railroad we used to see in our geography books, which carries on the idea of a recession into infinity.

McLUHAN: This is the exact visual equivalent of "Tomorrow and tomorrow and tomorrow." The idea of the segmenting and of space and time. With the Gutenberg achievement of mechanization of handicraft, we seem to have moved almost into a kind of world the Egyptians thought of.

PARKER: I remember the story of Thoth, the Egyptian god of writing, who was believed by the Egyptians to have been the instigator of all the sciences, and all the other arts.

MCLUHAN: Aren't we saying merely that the Gutenberg effect was to pattern in new form all the arts and sciences—mathematics, physics as well as painting, poetry—changing the concepts of time, the concepts of space, for an entire age and an entire culture.

SHAFER: The idea of a repeatable experiment is important here. An experiment which you can repeat over and over and over is scientific, isn't it?

PARKER: Like Aunt Jemima.

MCLUHAN: These infinity signs are present in our culture in a variety of ways. One tremendous consequence, of course, of Gutenberg printing, as compared with the manuscript, was the speed-up of the information movement. With exactly uniform materials that could be distributed from the central source, you could move by roads—and roads were soon built to carry this uniform material— you could move anywhere, you could organize whole communities at a distance. What we might call homogeneity of citizenship. By similar training and uniform educational patterns you could create a kind of manpower pool of almost uniform replaceable products.

SHAFER: If you can mass-produce print in the vernacular of a particular country, you can give everyone the same thing to read in that country at the same time.

MCLUHAN: You create the boundaries of that nation at the same time you do this. As soon as people could see their own language in print form, they began to develop a sense of national unity, and also of national markets. This is a tremendous leap, isn't it, from the Egyptian scribe's world of merely translating ear into eye. Here you have eye taking over totally the organization of all knowledge.

SHAFER: Publication is possible, here for the first time, perhaps in a mass way. By repetition you could publish yourself anywhere.

McLUHAN: In the scribe's world, publication would be to read his manuscript aloud to probably no more than thirty people at a time.

SHAFER: This was publication for Chaucer. It wouldn't have given him a very grandiose view of himself, would it, if publication only consisted of reaching a few dozen people? The print man must have felt an enormous extension and growth of his ego by means of print. He must have felt an access of power, when his image could be multiplied so many times exactly in uniform pattern for so many unseen people. This must have created a vast dimension of Renaissance megalomania. The whole idea at that point of his fame lasting forever is, of course, so much a part of that. This was true of the Renaissance man in many ways, in his exploration and his colonization, his conquest of space.

McLUHAN: Also the idea of the establishment of an empire as a permanent structure. No accident that Columbus and print coincide.

SHAFER: Before Gutenberg, people had relatively little incentive to become egotistically projected onto a whole civilization.

McLUHAN: What we've been saying here really is that print in the advent of the Gutenberg era had a rather tremendous effect on human sensibility and perception in some of the ways that we have seen. I suppose that today with the speed-up of information by electric means we're in an even greater revolution than Gutenberg produced in the Renaissance?

PARKER: Only today we're going in the opposite direction perhaps, aren't we?

McLUHAN: You think that perhaps we're driving back toward the ear world from which Egyptian scribes translated us. This is, I think, the message of our television set and our primitive mask. This is apparent in our contemporary art. Many people would regard this as a pessimistic view of development, wouldn't they, of just retrograde metamorphosis?

SHAFER: Well, we don't mean here that print is going to vanish at all, do we?

PARKER: No, we certainly don't mean that.

McLUHAN: I mean that there occurs a different ratio of the senses. After all, man lives by extending his sensibilities into the world and understanding it in that way. During the Gutenberg period you had almost complete eye orientation. Now we are moving back to what I would like to think perhaps a better orientation.

SHAFER: Let's consider for a moment a little more closely the effects of the Gutenberg thing on organizing a society. That is, for example, if you have these uniform repeatable means of delivering messages, you also have a uniform repeatable method of training citizens. You can then begin to develop a homogeneity, a sameness in the society, which gives you access to tremendous power. Teaching of reading becomes standardized, what the reader reads is standardized.

Methods, techniques of communication, do formulate our modes of thinking, our ways of thinking. Everything we attack, we attack in a certain way which is a result of this technology.

McLUHAN: We associate the uniform modular structure of the printed page with the classroom itself, with the seating plan—the grid system.

SHAFER: A teacher and a class with seats bolted to the floor is a very good example of this idea of uniform interchangeable parts.

PARKER: Children all studying the same subject at the same time.

McLUHAN: Visually, the classroom is the exact counterpart of the book page, with the teacher like the page heading, and the lines underneath . . . the movable types being the students.

SHAFER: Well, they're not particularly movable; the students are only slightly movable.

McLUHAN: I wonder whether the rebellion of children today in classrooms and against the book has anything to do with the new electronic age we live in?

SHAFER: I would think that the breakup of the grid system in the classroom may be leading to the breakup of uniformity in other aspects of our society as we move along to different kinds of patterns. The whole progressive education movement, we might say, was a kind of rebellion against lineality and grid structure.

McLUHAN: But that's been going on for a long time—the Romantic poets were violently opposed to lineal structure too, just as much as Rousseau; but this same structure has appeared in our novels, our movies—it's in almost every organized experience we are accustomed to deal with.

SHAFER: The interesting thing is that change never takes place completely and arbitrarily. We have several modes present simultaneously. We still have classrooms with desks bolted to the floor, and we have classrooms where they are not; and we have uniformity present in a variety of ways in our society, and we have many places where uniformity is breaking up.

McLUHAN: Apparently, education is now facing a tremendous problem of transition between two worlds. In fact, they both coexist. Making a transition from one vast embracing technology to another would seem to call for the utmost attention, offering the utmost challenge to human understanding. This entire global village that we see before us suggests that we are moving educationally into a set of challenges and opportunities which are quite fantastic. Whether people are prepared to meet these things or not, I don't know, but I think that we are doing something about it right here.

15 is it natural that one medium should appropriate and exploit another?
—MARSHALL MC LUHAN

Why have the effects of media, whether speech, writing, photography or radio, been overlooked by social observers through the past 3500 years of the Western world? The answer to that question, we shall see, is in the power of the media themselves to impose their own assumptions upon our modes of perception. Our media have always constituted the parameters and the framework for the objectives of our Western world. But the assumptions and parameters projected by the structures of the media on and through our sensibilities have long constituted the overall patterns of private and group association in the West. The same structuring of the forms of human association by various media is also true of the non-Western world, and of the lives of pre-literate and archaic man as well. The difference is that in the West our media technologies from script to print, and from Gutenberg to Marconi, have been highly specialized. Specialism creates not stability and equilibrium, but change and trauma, as one segment of experience usurps and overlays the others in aggressive, brawling sequence and cycle.

All that ends now in the electronic age, whose media substitute all-at-onceness for one-thing-at-a-timeness. The movement of information at approximately the speed of light has become by far the largest industry of the world. The consumption of this information has become correspondingly the largest consumer function in the world. The globe has become on one hand a community of learning, and at the same time, with regard to the tightness of its inter-relationships, the globe has become a tiny village. Patterns of human association based on slower media have become overnight not only irrelevant and obsolete, but a threat to continued existence and to sanity. In these circumstances understanding media must mean the understanding of the *effects* of media. The objectives of new media have tended, fatally, to be set in terms of the parameters and frames of older media. All media testing has been done within the parameters of older media—especially of speech and print.

Today in top-management study and planning, assumptions and objectives are recognized to be distinct entities. Let me quote from a Westinghouse "Long Range Planning" brief of August 3, 1960:

> Now it is imperative that whenever there is a change so that
> actual developments do not coincide with your assumptions,
> you must change your assumptions and you must change any
> plans that were based on the assumption that has now
> turned out to be erroneous. . . . It is absolutely imperative that
> you must know what your assumptions are, and that you must
> recognize that things are not going to develop in the future
> in accordance with your assumptions. . . . Now, the primary
> difference between an assumption and an objective is that an
> assumption pertains to things that are beyond your control,
> and an objective pertains to things that are achieved
> through your own effort.

What the writer of this brief does not know is that assumptions can also come within the range of prediction and control just as soon as it is recognized that the new media of communication in any age, as they penetrate and transform the older media, are the source of new assumptions and consequently the causes of change in our objectives.

The study of media constituents and content can never reveal the dynamics of media *effects*. Media study has lagged behind all other fields in this century, even behind economics, as the following quotation from W. W. Rostow's *The Stages of Economic Growth* (Boston: Cambridge University Press, 1960, page 90) will show:

> The argument of this book has been that once man conceived of his physical environment as subject to knowable, consistent laws, he began to manipulate it to his economic advantage; and once it was demonstrated that growth was possible, the consequences of growth and modernization, notably its military consequences, unhinged one traditional society after another, pushed it into the treacherous period of preconditions, from which many, but not all of the world's societies have now emerged into self-sustained growth through the take-off mechanism. . . .

Media study has not begun to approach the awareness of this "take-off mechanism" of social change involved in the shaping and speeding of information for eye and for ear and for touch and kinetics.

Our project set out to bring media study within the range of the expanding awareness here indicated by Rostow in economics. My assumptions, then, were:

(a) that nothing had yet been done to bring understanding to the effects of media in patterning human association,

(b) that such understanding was quite possible; media assumptions do not have to remain subliminal,

(c) that the absence of such understanding was eloquent testimony to the power of media to anesthetize those very modes of awareness in which they were most operative.

My objectives were:

(a) to explain the character of a dozen media, illustrating the dynamic symmetries of their operation on man and society,

(b) to do this in a syllabus usable in secondary schools. (Secondary schools were chosen as offering students who had not in their own lives become aware of any vested interest in acquired knowledge. They have very great experience of media, but no habits of observation or critical awareness.

Yet they are the best teachers of media to teachers, who are otherwise unreachable.)

Writing

1. What would be the problems of introducing the phonetic alphabet today into Japan and China?
2. Would the consequences of introducing the phonetic alphabet into China today be as drastic as when the Romans introduced the same alphabet to Gaul?
3. Will the ideogram survive in some new roles in the same way that the printed book finds new work to do in the electronic age?
4. What are some of the advantages of the ideogram over our alphabet?
5. Does a form of writing which involves complex situations at a single glance favor cultural continuity and stability?
6. By contrast, does a form of writing that favors attention to one-thing-at-a-time foster instability and change?
7. In other words, is the man of the ear a conservative, and the man of the eye a liberal?
8. Why should writing weaken the human memory? Pre-literate man, amazed at the efforts of the white man to write down his thoughts and sayings, asks: "Why do you write; can you not remember?"
9. Why should a pre-literate people have no concept of words as referring to things, but only of words as being things?
10. Is the "content" of writing the medium of speech? Is it possible for any medium to have a content except it be another medium?
11. Is the medium the message?
12. Is it possible for a mathematical proposition or demonstration to have content?

Print

1. Let us try to discover any area of human action or knowledge unaffected by the forms and pressures of print during the past five centuries.

2. If the forms of print have shaped all the levels of action and organization in the Western world up until the advent of nuclear technology, does this explain and justify the type of stress which we allow to our printed forms in the educational establishment?

3. If a nuclear technology is now succeeding the mechanical print technology of the past five centuries, what problems does such a transition present to the educator? To the political establishment? To the legal establishment?

4. What would happen to the society that did not recognize or identify these problems at all?

5. What happened to medieval education when it failed to understand the nature of print?

6. Consider why anthropology with its pre-literate concerns should have so much in common with post-literate and nuclear forms of communication?

7. How did the uniformity and repeatability of the print production process affect human arrangements in time and in space?

8. Why should the speeding of information flow for the print reader create historical perspective and background? Why should the much slower information flow of the manuscript make such background impossible?

9. Why should the electronic speed of information flow eliminate historical background in favor of "you are there?"

10. Why is homogeneity of space and time arrangement natural under print conditions of learning?

11. Why was it revolutionary for Columbus to assume that he could keep moving in a straight line, in one direction? Why are there no straight lines in medieval maps? Why was it unthinkable for them that space should be continuous and homogeneous?

12. Why should the Columbus pursuit of the straight line in navigation have been necessary in order to discover the round earth?

13. Are the flat-earthers on strong ground in terms of our Western devotion to Euclidean space?

14. In garment-making and hence in clothing styles, the straight seam was impossible before the sewing machine. Trace some of the implications of the straight line and of mechanism in one or more other fields of human organization.

15. How much is our notion of "content" affected in the case of printing by the blank page as filled with movable type?

Press

1. Does the aspect of newspaper as inclusive image of the community commit the newspaper to the job of exposing private manipulation of the communal thing? Is there an inevitable clash between the public nature and function of a newspaper and the private points of view of many of the interests in a community?

2. Consider the same news story as handled on radio and television, and in the newspaper. Do you think any one of these ways of handling the news especially adapted to any particular kind of news? Does world news, for example, seem most appropriate in headline form? Does local news find its most appropriate form on the radio?

3. Which medium—press, radio, or television—is most effective in gaining the participation of the viewer? Does the newspaper reader tend to be a mere spectator of events? Is the radio listener more closely involved? Is the television viewer most challenged to participate in action?

4. Does the newspaper typically create the outlook of the sidewalk superintendent in all community matters?

5. Is the job of the newspaper to dramatize the issues within a community?

6. How did the news photograph alter the nature of the newspaper and the news story?

7. How had the print affected the nature of news coverage prior to the photograph? (See Ivins' *Print and Visual Communication.*)

8. Has the influence of radio and television been to encourage newspapers to a more editorial attitude to the news? If news

can be given by radio and television, does the newspaper see its unique advantage to consist in background to the news?

9. Why should the newspaper find so little sympathy with historical perspective on any matter? (See *Time* magazine as a newspaper trying to achieve historical perspective.)

10. What devices does a newspaper employ to provide a sense of continuity from day to day for its readership?

11. Why should the newspaper, in processing opinion in such ways as to produce homogeneous emotions and attitudes, be a major means of mobilizing the manpower resources of a nation?

Telephone

1. How would a speed-up of information movement to telephone dimension affect the pattern of authority and of decision-making?

2. Ask your friends and parents how the telephone shapes their business and social lives.

3. What, for example, is the effect of the telephone in medical practice? In political life?

4. What has been the role of the telephone in the newspaper world?

5. Consider the way in which the telephone is used in Broadway plays, or in Hollywood movies, as indication of its real force and character.

6. What qualities of drama and action come to mind in relating the telephone to stage and movie and novel?

7. Is it natural that one medium should appropriate and exploit another?

8. Is the use one medium makes of another the clearest testimony to its nature?

9. Why is the telephone so irresistibly intrusive?

10. Why do Europeans and especially English people particularly resent the telephone?

11. Why does an Englishman prefer to manage his appointments by telegraph and postcard rather than person-to-person telephone calls?

12. Why is it difficult to exercise delegated authority in a world supplied with telephones?
13. Is the telephone extremely demanding of individual attention?
14. Is it abrupt, intrusive, and indifferent to human concerns?
15. How does the telephone affect the typewriter? Does it enormously speed up and increase the role of the typewriter? Check this question with the book *Parkinson's Law* by C. Northcote Parkinson.

Movies

1. In view of the various cultural backgrounds of England, France, America, Russia, India, and Japan, what qualities would you expect to appear most in the movies made in these countries?
2. In his *Film As Art*, Rudolph Arnheim for example says that the American film-maker excels in the single shot; the Russian in montage. Why should this be?
3. Why should the European and the Russian and the Japanese have regarded the film as an art form from the first? Why should the English-speaking world have such difficulty in seeing popular forms of entertainment as art forms whether the movie, the comic strip, or the common advertisement?
4. How did movies sell the American way of life to the backward countries of the globe? Consider the role of uniformity and repeatability as indispensable to competition and rivalry. How could competition thrive where unique expression and achievement are stressed?
5. Was the picture story borrowed from the cartoon world?
6. Is there any hook-up between magazine picture stories and silent movies? If so, is it in the isolation of one emotion at a time?
7. Magazines like the *Saturday Evening Post* have discovered that idea articles, written like movie scenarios shot by shot, sell better than short stories. Check the technique of such articles.

Radio

1. What was the effect of the radio on movies? On newspapers? On magazines? On language? On the concept of time?
2. How do P.A. systems relate to radio?
3. Does the P.A. system affect the visual as well?
4. What changes occurred in radio listening and programming after television?
5. Why is radio so intensely visual in effect?
6. What was the relation of radio to the rise of Fascism, politically and psychologically?
7. Why should radio exert such force among the pre-literate and the semi-literate?
8. What was the overall effect of radio among highly literate people?
9. Why does the twelve-year-old tend to turn from the television set to radio?

Television

1. Engineers claim that a thousand-line television image would provide almost as high definition as the present movie image. Supposing that an equally high definition of retinal impression were achieved for television, what would be the effect of its multi-point mosaic structure over and above the retinal impression?
2. Why should the broken line of the television mosaic emphasize the sculptural contours of objects?
3. Why has sculpture traditionally been spoken of as the voice of silence? Does this mean that the sculptural object exists on the frontier between sight and sound?
4. Is there any possible line of investigation suggested by the fact that sound waves become visible on the fuselage of jet planes just before they break the sound barrier? Does this suggest that the various human senses are translatable one into the other at various intensities?
5. If sculpture exists on the frontier between sight and sound,

does this mean that beyond that frontier is writing and architecture and enclosed or pictorial space? In a word, must the nuclear age civilize those primitive dimensions from which we emerged by means of writing and the visual organization of experience? Can this be done without mere destruction both of the primitive and of the civilized achievement?

6. Consider the power of any medium to impose its own spatial assumptions and structures. Extend your observations to discriminate and distinguish between the kinds of space evoked and constituted by the film on one hand, television on the other.

Recommendations

Communication, creativity, and growth occur together or they do not occur at all. New technology creating new basic assumptions at all levels for all enterprises is wholly destructive if new objectives are not orchestrated with the new technological motifs.

Dr. James E. Russell, of the National Education Association's Educational Policies Committee, commenting on my paper "The New Media and the New Education," felt that I had not included consideration of the computer's effect:

> What I had in mind is the new dimension forced on education
> by the existence of computers and teaching machines. This runs
> at a much deeper level than the distinction between print
> and nonprint communications. It has to do with a new concept
> of the nature of thought. . . . All rational propositions can
> be reduced to binomial terms.

As Tobias Dantzig revealed in his book on *Number*, primitive, pre-digital counting was binomial. Post-digital computation returns to the pre-digital just as post-literate education returns to the dialogue. However, what the computer means in education is this. As information movement speeds up, information levels rise in all areas of mind and society, and the result is that any subject of knowledge becomes substitutable for any other subject. That is to say, any and all curricula are obsolete with regard to subject matter. All that remains to study are the media themselves, *as forms*, as modes ever creating new assumptions and hence new objectives.

This basic change has already occurred in science and industry. Almost any natural resource has, with the rise in information levels, become substitutable for any other. In the order of knowledge this fact has given rise to Operations Research, in which any kind of problem can be tackled by nonspecialists. The technique is to work backward from effect or result to cause, not from cause to effect. This situation resulting from instantaneous information movement was referred to by A. N. Whitehead in *Science and the Modern World*, when he pointed out that the great discovery of the later nineteenth century was not the invention of this or that, but the discovery of the technique of discovery. We can discover anything we decide to discover.

In education this means the end of the one-way passing along of knowledge to students. For they already live in a "field" of knowledge created by new media which, though different in kind, is yet far richer and more complex than any ever taught via traditional curricula. The situation is comparable to the difference between the complexity of a language versus the crudities of traditional grammars used to bring languages under the rule of written forms. Until we have mastered the multiple grammars of the new nonwritten media, we shall have no curriculum relevant to the new languages of knowledge and communication which have come into existence via the new media. These new languages are known to most people but their grammars are not known at all. We have "read" these new languages in the light of the old. The result has been distortion of their character and blindness to their meaning and effects.

Non-Euclidean space, and the dissolution of our entire Western fabric of perception, results from electric modes of moving information. This revolution involves us willy-nilly in the study of modes and media as forms that shape and reshape our perceptions. That is what I have meant all along by saying the "medium is the message," for the medium determines the modes of perception and the matrix of assumptions within which objectives are set.

All of my recommendations, therefore, can be reduced to this one: Study the modes of the media, in order to hoick all assumptions out of the subliminal, nonverbal realm for scrutiny and for prediction and control of human purposes.

Such a program can most readily be instituted today at the level of secondary education.

The GALAXY reconsidered

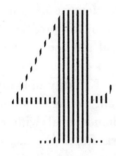

schizophrenia may be a necessary consequence of literacy. —MC LUHAN

The Gutenberg Galaxy, which appeared in 1962, is essentially a summary of McLuhan's earlier conceptualizations about media and has a perhaps overly indulgent concern with the cultural effects of the printed word. It found a more esoteric audience than *Understanding Media.* In fact, academic critics even now seem to prefer it to the more recent book.

Although the *Galaxy* has a rather conservative format, McLuhan gave it an organization similar to that of his late journal, *Explorations*: The arrangement of statements or manifestos was more or less arbitrary, and each element of opinion formed part of a mosaic or field approach. In his preface, McLuhan writes: "The reader may find the end of the book, 'The Galaxy Reconfigured,' the best prologue."

There is a curious note of finality in many reviewers' comments. They assume that McLuhan, having disposed of the BOOK, will let other, more competent hands deal with electronic media. John Simon, writing in the *New Republic,* accused McLuhan of "playing the history-of-ideas game and playing it none too well." McLuhan, however, had concluded the *Galaxy* with a question he intended to pursue: "What will be the new configurations of mechanisms and of literacy as these older forms of perception and judgment are interpenetrated by the new electric age?"

*   *   *

John Freund (16) teachers English at the University of Western Michigan. His review provides a crisp introduction to the *Galaxy.*

Patrick D. Hazard (17) of Beaver College is concerned with the problems of communication theory as they relate to the teaching of

English. His somewhat argumentative review makes a distinction between the McLuhan of the *Bride* and the McLuhan of the *Galaxy*.

Dell Hymes (18) is a specialist in anthropological linguistics at the University of Pennsylvania, and his critique reflects his own particular scholarly discipline. McLuhan replies to Hymes in Part 6, also entering there some additional remarks by E. S. Carpenter.

Frank Kermode (19), professor of English at Bristol University and formerly co-editor of *Encounter*, did much with his review to establish McLuhan as an important contemporary thinker. Some of Kermode's ideas are reflected in Dwight Macdonald's essay in Part 5.

A. Alvarez (20), a prominent English critic, writes frequently for the *New Statesman*. Alvarez and Christopher Ricks (Part 5) express similar views of McLuhan's Catholic bias.

Dan M. Davin (21) is Secretary to the Society of Fellows of the Clarendon Press, Oxford.

Raymond Williams (22), a literary historian and fellow of Churchill College, Cambridge, is troubled, like Kermode, by McLuhan's method of analysis and presentation, but nonetheless considers the *Galaxy* "a wholly indispensable work."

16 the gutenberg galaxy...strikes us as a hybrid species, disquieting rather than beautiful. —JOHN FREUND

> The error of our eye directs our mind:
> What error leads, must err; O, then conclude,
> Minds sway'd by eyes are full of turpitude.
> *Troilus and Cressida*

Cressida's lament, as she forsakes Troilus for Diomed, states the central theme of *The Gutenberg Galaxy*: the mind of Western man has been swayed by his eye since the invention of printing. It is ironic that Cressida alone among the characters of Shakespeare's drama should recognize the fatal visual bias that is afflicting not only herself but the entire Greek expedition. It would be a more than tragic irony if Marshall McLuhan's identical diagnosis of Western man's difficulties over the past five hundred years should fall only upon the deafened ears of Ulysses' and Thersites' modern counterparts; for *The Gutenberg Galaxy* is as important a book as it is daring, representing the beginning of a breakthrough into complete consciousness for modern man.

The Gutenberg Galaxy is a unique book in two ways. It renders explicit certain insights hitherto confined to poetic expression, and it subjects scholarly style to the discipline of "formal" arrangement—a discipline similarly confined hitherto to poets and other artists. Remarks of this kind might lead a reader to expect a highly polished, "literary" essay, but the effect of the book is quite the contrary. It strikes us as a hybrid species, disquieting rather than beautiful, and as we do with almost every pioneer effort, we tend to note its departures from the ways of the past without discerning the new path it is pursuing. But of all who may read *The Gutenberg Galaxy* (and its insights are pertinent to many fields), those with a background in English studies will enjoy a special advantage. To be sure, the novelty of Professor McLuhan's ideas and his "mosaic" approach to his data will present difficulties. Nevertheless, English scholars are familiar with the mosaic approach already in the "organic" shape of many modern poems; and as for the ideas, we have encountered them before—in Shakespeare, Blake, Yeats, or James Joyce, to name but a few.

Indeed, *Finnegans Wake*, from which Professor McLuhan frequently quotes, contains the implicit statement of almost all that *The Gutenberg Galaxy* makes explicit. For example, Professor McLuhan dwells upon the effects of one or another of our five senses splitting away from the total sensorium and becoming dominant—the auditory in primitive and the visual in modern man. Joyce throughout the *Wake* contrasts the functions of the eye and the ear, both in such characters as Shem and Shaun and in his mode of expression which everywhere presents certain meanings to the eye and others to the ear. But perhaps the most important parallel between the two works is the concern each author has with the effects of man's technologies upon his attitudes, values, and preceptions, each conceiving of history as a continual interaction between man's uttered, or "outered," creations and his inner awareness.

It is not necessary to read *Finnegans Wake*, fortunately, to understand *The Gutenberg Galaxy*. Professor McLuhan deals with "ABCEDminded man," as we have noted, explicitly, and though he does not present his data and quotations in the customary (since Gutenberg) manner, the reader will have no great difficulty understanding the thesis. As it is impossible, however, to summarize Professor McLuhan's ideas without severe distortion, I will only attempt to describe this central thesis in broad outline and a few of its more important ramifications.

I have already noted that the main theme of the book is that Western man's eye has swayed his mind since the invention of printing. More exactly, the wide use of the print medium in the centuries after Gutenberg tremendously reinforced the visual bias that the adoption of the phonetic alphabet had given to man's perceptions. As a result, Western society drastically reorganized its values and modes of social behavior around the new visual patterns fostered both directly and indirectly by the new medium. Let it be immediately clear that it is not in the *content* of the books coming off the early presses that Professor McLuhan finds the force for such profound social change. This remained essentially medieval for two centuries after the invention of printing. Rather it is in the medium itself that we are to detect the operative cause: linear organization of uniform, repeatable type began to move information at unheard-of speeds and placed such unheard-of demands upon the visual sense that the eye assumed a dominance in the sensorium that it is only recently beginning to lose. Professor McLuhan's concern throughout his book is to display the manner in which this revolution in man's sensorium occurred and the consequences it has had for every facet of our culture. Our concern at the moment shall be to discover how Professor McLuhan can attribute such immense power to an aspect of communication that most of us consider relatively inert: the medium.

To begin with, Professor McLuhan would assert that man's technologies, which include the customary media of communication, are actually extensions of his senses: As man utters his thoughts, regardless of what medium he uses, he "outers" them. In "outering" through one medium, however, whether it be speech, sculpture, print, or architecture, he gives dominance to the sense organ corresponding to that medium in the following way. The medium itself is a closed system; that is, it is a self-contained system which follows its own rules. It is normally incapable of mixing with or translating itself into another. Thus the vitally important work of translating one medium into another devolves upon man. For instance, geometry and architecture are related as systems only through the intervention of man's mind. We *discover* relationships. Could the two systems interact directly, they would not be closed systems.

Man is by nature quite well fitted for the task of relating his various technologies to each other, for his sensory system functions normally in a state of synesthesia. Thus, faced with his own technologies, man interiorizes them and reintroduces them into the open system of his full sensorium for the purpose of translating and understanding them.

So far so good. Man can be viewed in this fashion as a creature perpetually involved in "outering" his senses in the form of various technologies or media and "innering" these new creations in order to maintain balance and harmony between them. The rub comes when man discovers a particularly powerful medium. Let us consider speech as a typical instance. Organizing so much of his experience for him vocally, speech makes tremendous demands upon the auditory field of the human sensorium when it is interiorized. In fact, so pervasive is the auditory impact of vocal speech that the ear tends to monopolize the functions of the other senses and to become the central translating device for all sensory phenomena. Thus it was with primitive man. As he witnessed his own speech translating all of his experience into an auditory framework—as he literally heard himself speaking—his other senses began to adapt themselves to the auditory mode and to organize their operations according to the patterns of auditory awareness. Furthermore, as man's sense ratio slowly altered in this manner, man became less and less able to discern the effect of the medium upon him, literally hypnotized by the dilation of one of his senses.

Professor McLuhan begins his investigation at this point: primitive man imprisoned in the auditory field of his sensorium through the effects upon him of his most important discovery, speech. *Homo loquens*, by the relentless pressure to translate the auditory phenomena of speech into the patterns of his other senses, and, even more important, through his endeavors to translate his other sense impressions into speech patterns, had slowly rendered his total sensory field into a closed system, governed almost exclusively by the ear. What freed man from this servitude? Or rather, what led him to abandon his auditory prison for a visual one? This is what *The Gutenberg Galaxy* sets out to show.

Of the many influential factors in the rise of visual awareness that Professor McLuhan notes, certainly the initial one is most important: the adoption of the phonetic alphabet. The phonetic alphabet is essentially different from any other written code in that its use demands that the very sounds of speech be made visible symbolically. The effects of such a transformation are shattering to the world of the ear, for acoustical patterns are basically different from optical patterns. What the ear patterns temporally in depth, the eye must pattern spatially on a surface. Phonetic literacy, thus, imposes a dualistic splitting of the sensory world upon whatever culture may adopt it, as it did upon the ancient Greeks.

But phonetic literacy alone cannot completely dislodge the ear from its position of power. Indeed, Professor McLuhan devotes a good third of his book to describing a multitude of other factors, each in a subtle way furthering the rise of visual organization from the time of the ancient Greeks to the invention of the printing press in the fifteenth century. Two important indirect influences perhaps should be noted here, for they indicate the complexity of formal causality, a complexity which Professor McLuhan takes great pains to present without distortion by means of his "mosaic" method of organization. The first is the powerful impetus that Rome gave to the notions of repeatability and uniformity in the organization of the Roman Empire—notably by means of its magnificent system of roads. The second is the pressure apparent in the later Middle Ages to process greater and greater volumes of information. Thus even before Gutenberg, in a scribal culture tending in other ways to stimulate auditory modes of awareness, tendencies toward visual patterning become increasingly apparent.

It was not, however, until the impact of print that the galaxy of print-related values, assumptions, and perceptual biases took definite form. But at this point the forces for closure became immense, and the swift acceleration of the process swept all before it. The eye replaced the ear as the central mode of perception; the auditory reign at last was ended, and the error of men's eyes now directed their minds.

What made up the Gutenberg galaxy? Perhaps it will not be too confusing if I simply enumerate a few of the more important effects of print in no particular order. I see no other way of suggesting the scope of the study, and I cannot show here, as Professor McLuhan does in his book, the complex ways in which they are related: the rise of perspective in painting; the development of nationalism in government; the drive toward unity of tone in prose style; the principle of the assembly line in manufacturing; the divorce of science and art in learning; the notion of "content" as it is found both in consumer goods and in communication—all of these, Professor McLuhan shows, derive from the new emphasis given to phonetic literacy by the homogenizing power of the line of print.

Stated in this bald fashion, the daring theme of *The Gutenberg Galaxy* may strike us as an oversimplification. Professor McLuhan, however, takes as many pains as are consonant with the scope of his study to avoid oversimplifying his theme. For instance, in several short but carefully composed passages he describes the different ways in which differing cultures responded to the print influence —the Spanish, the French, and the English. In short, the simplification that results from Professor McLuhan's study is genuine.

The Gutenberg Galaxy closes with a section entitled, "The Galaxy Reconfigured." Here Professor McLuhan concentrates on a theme which he has alluded to throughout the work but which he will develop more fully in a later book, *Understanding Media*: The Gutenberg galaxy has encountered another powerful galaxy in modern times, one which he calls the Marconi galaxy in order to suggest its electronic nature. We who are living through this encounter are being subjected to the terrific stresses engendered by the intermingling of two such giant systems. The collision need not be catastrophic, however; indeed, the situation affords a unique opportunity for modern man. He can at last awake from "single vision and Newton's sleep" into complete consciousness. Twentieth-century technologies are no longer closed systems; interaction between different media is now a possibility. Modern man can take active responsibility for bringing about a harmonious interaction among his technologies and thereby restore balance to his own sensorium. Not only is this a possibility today; as our technologies take on the characteristics of an open system, an organic whole, it becomes a necessity. But it is a necessity which leads to greater freedom. Professor McLuhan is especially eloquent when he urges this effort upon us (page 247):

> The point is, rather, how do we become aware of the effects of alphabet or print or telegraph in shaping our behavior? For it is absurd and ignoble to be shaped by such means. Knowledge does not extend but restricts the areas of determinism. And the influence of unexamined assumptions derived from tech-

nology leads quite unnecessarily to maximal determinism in
human life. Emancipation from that trap is the goal
of all education.

There is danger, however, in our situation today as well. The
new media of the electronic age are reawakening the long dormant
patterns of auditory awareness. If we passively allow ourselves to
be shaped by our media, we may find ourselves suddenly caught
up in a new tribalism. Indeed, there are those today who are unwittingly urging us toward this goal as they decry all of the Gutenberg values as profane and advocate a retreat from the rational life
into a more intense, "primitive" existence. Professor McLuhan is
not among those who are attracted by what he calls the "dominant
cliché" of our age, the "claque of the big battalions, as they move
in regimented grooves of sensibility" (page 71). Instead he urges
rationality, conscious selection of the kind of world we wish to live
in, a selection which certainly would not reject *all* of the values
which stemmed from phonetic literacy.

Marshall McLuhan is a professor of English. Perhaps it is his
experience in this least specialized of all academic fields which
enabled him to encompass the wide variety of specialized knowledge in the arts and sciences that was necessary to his undertaking.
At any rate, his synthesis is an extraordinary achievement; but
fully as extraordinary is the humanistic poise which he maintains
throughout the book. His attitude toward issues which divide the
world today remains descriptive rather than valuative, his tone
moderate.

The long history of the "error of the eye," the advent of which
Shakespeare perceived so clearly, is coming to an end. Facing us
now in its place is Lewis Carroll's looking-glass world. This world,
whose irrational absurdities so amused Victorian children, frequently terrifies the modern child, who sees—perhaps more clearly
than most adults—the terrifying tribalism of the "ear" world it
depicts in much of the world around him. Between these two
worlds, equally terrifying in different ways, Marshall McLuhan
suggests there is the possibility of another; but his plea is only for
sane choice among our alternatives.

the analogy between print and electronic media history means nothing when looked at closely. —PATRICK D. HAZARD

McLuhan's *The Mechanical Bride: Folklore of Industrial Man* suggested a striking way of using the strategies of *explication de texte* for the analysis of popular culture. For many impressed young English instructors, McLuhan's imagination had discovered a way of using high culture to exorcise the devils of mass- and midculture. McLuhan explains that his anthropological approach to American popular culture almost forced itself upon him when he found himself teaching Midwesterners Freshman English after finishing a Ph.D. dissertation on the medieval liberal arts curriculum in England. McLuhan, in effect, found himself in a "strange country" whose language he did not understand. He did his field work among *homo boobiensis* brilliantly, and *The Mechanical Bride* holds up solidly today despite McLuhan's disavowal of it as the product of "a victim of print culture." Indeed, *The Mechanical Bride* seems to me to provide the way to retain the achieved values of the Gutenberg revolution much more persuasively than *The Gutenberg Galaxy*. In fact, one must confess an increasing incomprehension of McLuhan's work, beginning with the later issues of *Explorations*, the now-terminated magazine on media problems, which was supported by the Ford Foundation.

Some supporters of McLuhan defend his unique approach by describing him as "prophetic." He is the intellectual frontiersman who blazes a trail for less sure-footed mortals who will then make a roadbed broad and level enough to carry the freight of civilization's institutions. The trouble with this defense of McLuhan is that he blazes away at every tree in the forest—and even the most dedicated road-builder refuses to macadamize in circles. Still one has learned so much from McLuhan that one tries to follow the leader far beyond the point of too much exasperation. Pre-literate man communicates by speech in a world of acoustic space. Simultaneity

and interdependence characterize this richly resonant tribal society. Writing, which follows the end of nomadism, and printing—
to a much greater extent—transform the spherical "ear and now"
of pre-literate man to the linear "eye am" of Cartesian and Newtonian man. McLuhan's fearless symmetry now suggests a world
returning to a retribalized global society based on electronics. This
eerie cosmos of rock and roll and Telstar is "the early part of an
age for which the meaning of print culture is becoming as alien as
the meaning of manuscript culture was to the eighteenth" (page
135). Granted, but what, as C. S. Peirce might ask, do the differences mean for intelligent action? McLuhan promises another
volume, *Understanding Media*,* which perhaps will get down to
cases. One hopes it will be more responsible than this one. For Mc-
Luhan's reading is so catholic, one needs to be a polymath to know
when he is making sense and when not. But inevitably he mentions
a book one *has* read as carefully as he expects his to be—and the
result is shocking.

Television in the Lives of Our Children, by Wilbur Schramm
and associates, is much too complex and solid a book to be dis-
missed contemptuously—and on the shaky grounds of McLuhan's
own incredibly speculative theory of the television image as made
by "light through" instead of "light on" its surface. "When we see
the reason for the *total failure* [reviewer's italics] of this book to
get in touch with its announced theme, we can understand [Mc-
Luhan argues apodictically] why in the sixteenth century men had
no clue to the nature and effects of the printed word" (page 145).
No one who has any acquaintance with the Schramm canon—and
no one should presume to write on communications who does not
have a thorough familiarity with it—can pretend that he is insensi-
tive to media differences or to the history of communications. To
so refuse to come to honest grips with Schramm's sociological
mode of understanding media change is to subvert the conditions
of academic discourse—and, incidentally, to put the whole "mosaic" theory of media comprehension in a strange light.

When McLuhan makes a hypothesis a minute and gives scarcely

---

* Editor's Note: This essay was written in 1964, a few months before the publication
of *Understanding Media*.

a shred of evidence—either his own or in the long quotations which constitute better than a third of the book—it is impossible to check out all his wild surmises. But when he touches an area where the reader is informed, belief unwillingly suspends itself. So when McLuhan speculates in a fast aside—"as today, the insatiable needs of TV have brought down upon us the backlog of the old movies, so the needs of the new presses could only be met by the old manuscripts" (page 142)—one wants to remind him that he is comparing the expedient of the *American* television industry with the way *parts* of western Europe responded in their various ways to the Renaissance and Reformation. More prudent industry policy which understood America's real needs would have greatly increased the coverage of local reality on American television, leaving the competing movie, with its groaning archives of once-expended fantasy, unknown on television. Cuban television features four-hour harangues; Italian television instructs illiterates; French television teaches groups of farmers. The analogy between print and electronic media history, then, means nothing when looked at closely.

It is a pity that McLuhan has chosen to grandstand with chapter titles ("glosses"). For example: "Heidegger surf-boards along on the electronic wave as triumphantly as Descartes rode the mechanical wave." To extend his metaphor, he forgets how hard the coral reefs that make surfing possible are on one's "sense ratio"—and that a pearl-diving surfboard is no fun even to the "audile-tactile" man. One suspects something like self-justification in one of his many asides, this one on his intellectual ancestor, Harold Innis: "There is nothing willful or arbitrary about the Innis mode of expression. Were it to be translated into perspective prose, it would not only require huge space, but the insight into the modes of interplay among forms of organization would be lost. Innis sacrificed point of view and prestige to his sense of urgent need for insight. A point of view can be a dangerous luxury when substituted for insight and understanding" (page 216). Perhaps so, but why, then, does McLuhan so often cite the strictly linear—and brilliantly insightful—purpose of Chaytor, Diringer, Dudek, Goldschmidt, Hadas, Jones, Kenyon, Lowenthal, and Wilson? Almost a third of "his" mosaic is their linearity. Indeed, for the student of media history, their various texts—and McLuhan's bibliography—are useful, even indispensable.

18 the author's mode of reasoning is such that <u>involvement</u> and <u>importance</u> (particularly of print) is transformed into <u>primary characteristic</u> and <u>determinant</u>.
                                                              —DELL HYMES

Mr. McLuhan describes his book as developing a mosaic or field approach to its problems. "Such a mosaic image of numerous data and quotations in evidence offers the only practical means of revealing causal operations in history."

It is a stimulating book. It is good to see the importance of alternative channels (speech, print) stressed and analyzed. It is to the author's credit that he does not stop with obvious, and superficial, contrasts between dominant use of oral communication and dominant use of printed writing, but carries the problem into a concern for general modes of perception, on the one hand, and for possible pervasive, yet unexpected, general social consequences, on the other. Moreover, the book is rich in pertinent materials and observations.

The book, however, cannot be trusted as more than stimulation. The oversimplified view of types of society and character gets facts wrong. It is not the case, for example, as stated in the book and highlighted in the "Index of Chapter Glosses," that "Print . . . made 'bad grammar' possible" and that "Nobody ever made a grammatical error in a non-literate society" (see Bloomfield,

"Literate and Non-Literate Speech," *American Speech* 2:432–439, 1927). The contrast between oral and typographic communication is carried to ludicrous extremes, as a vehicle of cultural criticism and historical explanation. It can no more stand against an adequate view of human history than any other single-minded exegesis known to us. The author's mode of reasoning is such that *involvement* and *importance* (particularly of print) is transformed into *primary characteristic* and *determinant,* sometimes with a footing in the evidence, sometimes by sheer assertion.

As a survey of the present scene, and prophecy, the book takes no account of the serious and empirical sociolinguistic work now accumulating from various parts of the world (by Ferguson, Gumperz, Weinreich, and others). Such work, concerned to delineate the role of alternative channels among other factors of communication, within definite and described social contexts, can hope to offer us more as a basis for understanding and action than can a mixture of passionate concern for the quality of human life (admirable), and a two-term view of its entire content and evolution (deplorable).

It is good to see how attractively the book makes use of typographic resources.

Editor's Note: See Part 6, pp. 272–274 for McLuhan's reply.

mc luhan substitutes the printing press for genesis and the dissociation of sensibility for the fall. —FRANK KERMODE   19

In Kipling's story, "The Eye of Allah," a clever man invents a microscope and Roger Bacon is delighted; but a wise man destroys it, calculating that the benefits it promises will be outweighed by the disorders it may produce in men's lives. When the microscope

eventually got invented even the best observers continued for a
while to see in it precisely what they expected to see (in every
spermatozoon a crouched homunculus), but this phase passed, and
man's newly microscopic eye created its own uncompromising expectations, as all technological extension of the sensorium tends to
do; and this held scientists up in the early days of our own era.
Mr. McLuhan may well believe that some sage missed a great
chance of preventing the nastiness of the typographical epoch by
omitting to break up Gutenberg's press; but he has to treat of
things as they are, and so he explains that there was a period when
we went on behaving as if our culture was still oral or anyway
manuscript, but soon our ways of looking and thinking became
typographical, that is, visual, linear, successive, instead of oral and
simultaneous. By now we have got to the point where we are so far
under the influence of a new electric technology that we can see
how arbitrary the typographical conventions were, but we have still
not liberated ourselves from them. McLuhan uses a cosmological
figure to illustrate this: He says the Gutenberg galaxy is now being
penetrated by the electric, and implores us to understand this
cosmic interfusion, so that we shall know how to live in an oral-
electric future. At present we are about as far into the electric era
as the Elizabethans were into the typographical.

In this book and in its successor (which is already written) Mr.
McLuhan has an insoluble problem of method. Typography has
made us incapable of knowing and discoursing otherwise than by a
"metamorphosis of situations into a fixed point of view"; that is,
we reduce everything to the linear and successive, as computers
reduce everything to a series of either-ors. And since he himself is
unable to proceed by any other method, he cannot avoid falsifying
the facts his book sets out to establish. Perhaps this difficulty is
more fairly put in a letter Mr. McLuhan was good enough to write
me, and which I take the liberty of quoting: He says the ideal form
of his book would be an ideogram. Or perhaps it could be a film;
but otherwise he can find no way "of creating an inconclusive
image that is lineal and sequential." Now this is, in a way, everybody's problem when he writes a book; the original idea has somehow to be got into linear form and it often changes surprisingly in

the process. Not necessarily for the worse, I think; though this is just what Shelley had in mind when he lamented that we never feel "the original purity and force" of a poem because "when composition begins, inspiration is already on the decline." The notion that poems begin with Usener's "momentary deity" and are diluted by sophisticated language (verbs, conjunctions) has, in various forms, been very influential in the later typographical era, and, as I say, it must have occurred, in humbler formulations, to everybody who has written a book. But McLuhan's problem is more acute, simply because his subject is precisely that distortion of consciousness which prevents our books being about their original subjects, the cries of their particular occasion. The more linear clarity he gives his book, the more obviously he himself becomes the victim of typographical distortion. His book tells us not to believe it. He fights against this by making each chapter-heading a sort of verbal ideograph; if you read them all quickly you get a sort of strip-cartoon puzzle-summary of the book. It seems to me that long books ought, on McLuhan's arguments, to follow long poems into oblivion; however, he has compromised and written a long, serious book.

Its theme is the overdevelopment, since Gutenberg, of the visual function, both in language and in other fields, with consequent disturbances in the whole organism. Typographical man is individualist and has a fixed point of view; he also has an idea of time and space which is arbitrary, though it seems to him instinctive; it is based on the invention, early in the typographical era, of perspective. Type carried on the work of the phonetic alphabet, which, with its de-tribalizing power, had created open societies and Euclidean geometry. Our sense of causation is shaped by our visual apprehension of spatio-temporal relations. We suffer, as Nietzsche says Socrates suffered, from a split between mind and heart, whereas tribal man is oral and perpetually "entranced"; thus we shall find ourselves at a serious disadvantage in the new electric technology because the emergent countries have not this incapacitating backlog of literacy and mechanistic techniques. We shall be like the Greeks; the invention of the phonetic alphabet enabled them to surge forward, but they soon settled into the limiting stereotypes the system imposed. We must be aware of the dangers of making permanent a similar sensory distortion. This isn't merely a matter of aesthetics; the Russians, and the Chinese especially, are much more oral than we are, and the Chinese are moving late into the Gutenberg visual technology, which puts a premium on nationalistic aggressiveness.

Since no aspect of modern life is unaffected by the rise and fall of visual technology, McLuhan has to work in very diverse fields. He does this by making a florilegium of extracts from specialists in anthropology, physics, spelling reform, art, liturgiology, theology, and most other subjects. His authorities stretch from Opie to Giedion, Heisenberg to Chaytor, Ong (a specially heavy debt, this) to Panofsky. Some of the authorities are unknown to me even by name, and I daresay specialists might find the book partial in its treatment of their interest, as I myself found it very odd on Shakespeare. But these bundles of miscellaneous learning add a lot to the interest of the book, and they are brought to bear on the central theme. McLuhan is enormously well-read, and one learns a lot from him. Yet he reminds me a little of the Ice Age hunters who come into the argument at one point, and are said to have discovered in the natural contours of the rock the image of the animal they sought. "A few lines, a little carving, or some color, are enough to bring the animal into view." Thus, perhaps, does McLuhan do his reading.

Obviously there will be times when the reader happens to have looked into the same cave and seen a different image. For example: McLuhan illustrates his key theory, "The auditory field is simultaneous, the visual mode is successive," by referring to the oral mode of scholasticism and St. Thomas' insistence that the literal includes the mystical sense. I object that pre-typographical Bible commentary indicates a highly *successive* approach to the text (and doesn't the word *literal* imply this anyway?). Reading a manuscript, even if this usually meant reading it aloud even to oneself, involved a degree of pausing upon single words which is far in excess of anything the literate reader of print, reading words in groups, will allow himself. Here is a single instance I happen to remember: Luke IV:13, "And when the whole temptation was finished (*consummata omni tentatione*) the devil left him. . . ." The commentators dwelt on one word nobody would now, presumably, think worth it, *omni,* and out of it got a theory that the temptation in the desert was a model of all temptation a man might possibly undergo. Print readers understand it simply: "When it was all over. . . ." Manuscript-oral men stop at each word, ignoring the syntactic whole. And, for that matter, what could be more successive than a Dominican disputation? What is that but a metamorphosis of situation into linear formulae?

All the same, it seems undeniable that the printing press changed our notions of time. As Ian Watt has argued, we might well think it significant that Fielding, planning the action of *Tom Jones,* made use of an almanac for the relevant year (1745)—an almanac being "a symbol of the diffusion of an objective sense of time by the printing press." It also altered our concept of space and of antiquity. (Curiously, McLuhan has nothing to say about the anthropological retribalization of Greece that has taken place in this century.) That print also brought on the Reformation, as McLuhan argues, seems much more dubious, though of course that event has been related to the development of *homo economicus,* and he wasn't possible (according to this thesis) without the individualizing, quantifying agency of print. It seems possible on the Gutenberg thesis to trace most of the disagreeable elements of life in this epoch to movable type; and what can't be so explained can be attributed to its forerunners. Thus McLuhan says that print destroyed monodic song and substituted polyphony; and if you argue that pre-typographical popes sometimes had to act in order to save the words of the Mass from melismatic encroachment, the answer would probably be that, with literate-manuscript men, the coming event cast its shadow before. I suppose there could be a very considerable list of objections to specific elements in the book, where the author's eye for "contour" leads him into positions of this kind.

It is now time to enter more general objections. The antithesis between oral and visual cultures seems to be too strongly asserted. Searching for evidence that the "ratio of the senses" was once less distorted by the supremacy of the visual, we cannot in the nature of the case get much farther back than the beginning of written records; you can argue that the damage was done by then, but this weakens the case for its having been caused largely by printing. For the senses always seem to have been thought of as existing in a hierarchy, usually with sight at the head of it. For Plato as for Shakespeare, sight was the "most pure spirit of sense": For Plato, as for typographic man, touch was the lowest of the senses. If we have reversed the position and put "tactility" at the top, we are returning—if anywhere—to pre-literacy, to the primitive. Everybody from Socrates on—perhaps from Cadmus on—is what Mc-Luhan calls a "literacy victim." It's no use blaming it on Gutenberg that all our knowledge is translation into visually dominated stereotypes, those bad substitutes for some tense, explosive ideogram.

Furthermore, there is an aspect of post-Gutenberg man almost too obvious to mention, but one has to, since the author also finds it so. This is the strong anti-typographical countercurrent in our culture. Antiquity viewed in perspective may be an achievement of typographic man; but so is the creation of a civilization heavily dependent upon, and imitative of, that remote world. The typographic men of the sixteenth and seventeenth centuries revered the oral rhetoric and the recited epic of Rome; the eighteenth century made a hero of the bard Homer. Typographic man invented counterpoint and bar-measures; but he also fought counterpoint, imitated ancient monody, and made possible modern opera. The poets have gone on insisting that theirs is an oral art. The first poem to take full account of the invention of printing was *Un Coup de Dès;* and even for Valéry, who was deeply impressed by this work, a poem remained "an abstraction, a piece of writing that stands waiting, a law that lives only in the human mouth." Prose writers may imitate Cicero or the somewhat less oral Tacitus; but the very survival of the notion of "prose style" implies a strongly oral element, not only for example in Joyce, where it suits McLuhan's book, but also in Dr. Johnson. We typographic men have certainly paid our respects to oral culture.

McLuhan might well answer that this merely shows how men of high sensibility react naturally against the typographical attempt to reduce their sensoria, and hanker after the original state of

nature, oral, tactile, simultaneous. But Tharmas fell; or, to use a
Blake reference employed by McLuhan, God was unable to keep
us "from single vision and Newton's sleep." Blake was thinking of
the eighteenth-century reduction of the universe to the typographic-
visual: "If Perceptive organs vary, Objects of Perception seem to
vary." And, far back, he postulates, as McLuhan does, a primitive
sensibility dissociated by something: in this case the alphabet and,
ultimately, print.

Mr. McLuhan never uses the expression "dissociation of sensibility," but he is always talking about it and in a very literal way;
no one else has ever made out so encyclopedic a case for this
ubiquitous and central modern notion. He quotes with approval a
description of "the print-made split between head and heart" as
"the trauma which affects Europe from Machiavelli to the present"
and thinks the Unconscious is a sort of slag heap where we dump
the débris left by the wasteful processes of a distorted sensory
equipment. Our materialist technologies have destroyed "Imagination, the Divine Body." What used to be the "ordinary transactions
between the self and the world" have now to be simulated in Symbolist poetry and called illogical. McLuhan shows signs of resistance to enslavement by the dissociation myth; he says much
modern primitivism is fraudulent or ignorant, and is anxious to
preserve whatever is good in the Gutenberg technology so that it
may be of benefit in the different future. But I don't think this is
sufficient to disarm one's critique of satisfaction. Why give this
splendid new dress to our old friend dissociation? The whole doctrine is itself a nostalgic reaction against typographic culture.

There is, naturally, a case for understanding better the success
of the doctrine. What matters is not whether the dissociation happened, but that we feel happier to suppose it did, and work on the
historical contours like the Ice Age hunters, or the millennialists;
it is one of those schemes described by Mircea Eliade as ways of
evading the terrors of actual history. We ought to ask ourselves
why at a moment like the present (after the relevant historiographi-
cal debate has been on for years) we find such obvious comfort in
historical or pseudo-historical explanations.

Mr. McLuhan's book is a work of historical explanation, and its merits as well as its defects are related to this. He tries to say everything relevant about a changing culture by free borrowing from many authorities, whose material is organized around a central myth. This is the method of the *specula,* or of the old hexameral commentaries, which origanized an encyclopedia into a commentary on the Six Days of Creation. All knowledge was therefore related and manageable; and the Fall explained why things had so evidently gone awry. This was the Genesis Galaxy. Mr. McLuhan substitutes the printing press for Genesis, and the dissociation of sensibility for the Fall. In so doing he offers a fresh and coherent account of the state of the modern mind in terms of a congenial myth. In a truly literate society his book would start a long debate.

Editor's Note: See Part 6, pp. 296–297 for McLuhan's comments.

20 the effect is of a lively, ingenious, but infinitely perverse <u>summa</u> by some medieval logician, who has given up theology in favor of sociology and knows all about the techniques of modern advertising.

—A. ALVAREZ

The Gutenberg Galaxy is a great overstuffed holdall of a book of a kind which occasionally emerges, like *The Meaning of Meaning,* from the philosophical demi-monde. It is crammed with unsorted bright ideas, killing references to unknown scholars, the answers to all our problems, prophecies for the future, and a single theory. Inevitably, it is slightly dotty.

Marshall McLuhan once wrote a brilliant book, *The Mechanical*

Bride, on the evils of advertising. Now he has developed a thing against print. Once upon a time, he thinks, man lived, warm and safe and organic, within the circle of the tribe, Popper's "closed society." But he was expelled from this paradise when he invented the phonetic alphabet. In the magical oral world before that, thought and action moved responsibly together. But

> ... literacy, in translating man out of the closed world of tribal depth and resonance, gave man an eye for an ear and ushered him into a visual open world of specialized and divided consciousness.

Meaning became the abstract property of words and words alone, wholly apart from the rest of physical awareness. Thus the occupational disease of literacy is schizophrenia, the separation of thought from feeling, the individual from the state, art from commerce, science from humanism and

> ... the visual faculty from the interplay with the other senses [which] leads to the rejection from consciousness of most of our experience and the consequent hypertrophy of the unconscious.

For someone who is so bitter about the abstracting power of words, Professor McLuhan wields a pretty formal vocabulary.

But this schizophrenia was, the author thinks, progressive. Since he himself appears to be something of a Thomist, he is willing to throw out Greek and Roman culture but not the Middle Ages. So he defends the Scholastic philosophers despite all their highly verbal, perverted chop-logic, on the grounds that at least their debates were oral, their learning a feat of memory, and their manuscripts were designed to illuminate God's world. The real fall from grace occurred when Gutenberg invented the printing press. It was this that, once and for all, made knowledge not only visual but also a marketable commodity: "The assembly line of movable types made possible a product that was as uniform and repeatable as a scientific experiment." McLuhan thinks that it was this mechanization of the products of the intellect, rather than the industrial revolution,

which began the process of homogenizing men into indistinguishable mass products of the social factories. And before you can
remonstrate that the Catholic Middle Ages may appear to many a
good deal more homogenized and conformist than the great period
of Renaissance and Protestant individualism, the professor pops in
with the counter-theory that print was also the means by which an
author was able to market his individuality on a wide scale. And
this, somehow or other, neutralized the personal achievement. So
poor Gutenberg is made responsible both for Newton's children—
the Mechanical Bride and her Mechanical Groom—and for Tamer-
lane's megalomania. It is all very puzzling.

Not that we need worry. For, according to McLuhan, the typographical, linear, and visual world of Gutenberg has come to its
last full stop. What Einstein did to physics and the Symbolists did
to the arts, Marconi has done to the means of communication. The
modern sensibility, like space, is rounded and apparently unified.
We are now safely in the Marconi Galaxy, in which electronics has
reduced the whole world once again to a small tribal community.

What will the new electronic man be like? Organic and tribal,
like Dr. Leavis' idealized aborigines? Or at one with his senses and
his God, like a kind of psychoanalyzed believer? McLuhan is
vague: Man will use "the techniqpe of suspended judgment," he
will not "insist upon visual sequence as a rational norm" since "the
electric puts the mythic or collective dimension of human experience fully into the conscious wake-a-day world" (though how the
author does not explain). Yet it never occurs to him that the new
style is as likely to be the end of feeling as the beginning of it.
After all, the triumph of electronics so far is the computer—that
is, the ability to repeat mechanically and market commercially the
abstract processes of thought itself.

It doesn't occurs to him because, for all its claims, his book is
essentially backward in its vision and method. His technique is
that of a mosaicist. The argument proceeds fitfully, through a
series of slogan-like glosses: "Heidegger surf-boards along on the
electronic wave as triumphantly as Descartes rode the mechanical
wave." In between are crammed not always relevant quotations
from various authorities, with comments by the author which often
twist them unjustifiably to his own ends. The effect is of a lively,

ingenious but infinitely perverse *summa* by some medieval logi-
cian, who has given up theology in favor of sociology and knows
all about the techniques of modern advertising. The impetus behind it all is, in short, a poignant nostalgia for the Schoolmen
themselves. Perhaps this is why the new Marconi priest turns out to
be only old Finnegan writ large. I had always suspected that *Finnegans Wake* was less a work for the future than the last manic
rattling of the bones of scholasticism. The way McLuhan draws it
continually from his magician's that makes me certain. Gutenberg's
invention may have led to the specialization of knowledge, but the
result of that has at least been to destroy the medieval belief that
there is a single answer to the whole world.

the style...prefers to rape our attention rather then seduce our understanding. —DAN M. DAVIN

21

Marshall McLuhan... supposes an ideal condition of man where all
the senses are in an ideal harmony. But he agrees that we have long
been exiled from our ideal condition; the galaxy or constellation
of technologies which the invention of the phonetic alphabet and
the printing machine made possible have upset the balance and
caused the visual element in our perception to become an exclusive
tyrant.

Our troubles began with the phonetic alphabet. This translated
man from the magical world of the ear to the neutral visual world.
All alphabets enable men to look at words privately and remove
the oral stimulus of sound, making a man separate from the world
of his fellows, detribalizing him and cutting him off from the community of action, condemning him to a world of linear time and
Euclidean space. But the phonetic alphabet is even worse.

At least the pictographic or ideographic alphabets are still related to a visual world of things and the components of things. The

phonetic alphabet puts a screen between men and things. It abstracts and makes men think and read from right to left; though that some of us reason in circles is not explicitly denied.

In Greek and Roman times the consequences were not too severe; there was an attenuation of the nonvisual senses but the practice of eloquence and rhetoric and the fact that writings could not be readily and uniformly multiplied was some protection. Even in the Middle Ages all was not yet lost; manuscripts were still difficult to reproduce, teaching was done by dictation and disputation and men read aloud. They were still not cut off from the oral world.

With the Gutenberg Galaxy—printing, paper, and the associated technologies—the phonetic alphabet was free to take its full effect. The process was vastly accelerated. Universal literacy became fatally possible. Books could be multiplied indefinitely, could be read in silence and become portable and private possessions. Protestantism, nationalism, private heterodoxies, and public schisms, a homogeneity of externals and an anarchy of privacies, all began to make their appearance, and with them our neuroses, and all our discontents.

But deliverance is at hand. "We are today as far into the electric age as the Elizabethan age had advanced into the typographical and mechanical age," says Mr. McLuhan. "Whereas the Elizabethans were poised between medieval corporate experience and modern individualism, we reverse that pattern by confronting an electric technology which would seem to render individualism obsolete and the corporate interdependence mandatory." We have come full circle, in fact, and through radio and television we are back in a world of sound. The example of the physicists and *Finnegans Wake* is there to assure us that we can escape from Newtonian space and from the Typographic time sense which is "cinematic and sequential and pictorial" to a new and more flexible space and a time sense where everything is simultaneous within a single field.

Meanwhile, we have our misgivings. True, Mr. McLuhan tells us his theme is "not that there is anything good or bad about print but that unconsciousness of the effect of any force is a disaster, especially a force that we have made ourselves." But might it not be that this assurance springs from an uneasy awareness on his part that in his assault on the phonetic alphabet and printing he is himself making use of both? His soldiers, too, are of lead. And is not a real hostility to the visual explicit in the clamor of his book's typography (unless he thinks our inward ear is now too degenerate to notice anything quieter than a shout)? The style, also, prefers to rape our attention rather than seduce our understanding. Otherwise, we might have been spared "analogate" and "audile-tactile" and the tedious repetition of "outering (uttering)."

Another explanation may be possible. Mr. McLuhan is a man with a formidable command of the secondary sources but gives the impression of having no deep acquaintance with the primary sources in anthropology, Greek and Latin literature, and medieval philosophy and theology. He confronts the characteristic impasse of the modern scholar who, in order to survey a broad field of thought within a single lifetime, has to become a specialist of specialisms without being an expert in all.

In dealing with the Greeks and Romans, especially, and the medieval schoolmen, his reliance on secondary authorities seems almost absolute and his bibliography relies suspiciously on translations. He does not always remember that the Greeks for whom Homer was first written down were not necessarily the same as the Greeks who read Homer in the time of Plato. His interpretations of Lucretius and Cicero are not those that every classical scholar would accept and his failure to discuss Virgil suggests that he has chosen only examples that can be wrenched to fit his case.

Again, when he talks of the Russians as people of an oral culture he does not make it clear whether he is talking of the people themselves or of their government.

But the whole argument depends too much on an exaggerated opposition between "audile-tactile" and "visual," neither term clearly defined. Primitive man in many ways had a more visual culture than we, as anyone knows who has seen the stars in the desert night or the London blackout.

One cannot escape the feeling that the book is a deeply felt attempt to intellectualize the obvious. We are left perhaps rather more fully aware than before we read it that the alphabet and the invention of printing played a great part in making us what we are —industrial even in our agriculture, urban even when we are rural (never rustic again). So far we can go with him. If we do not go further, we can nonetheless commend his book as an ingenious tract whose best elements are the occasional critical *aperçus*, the acute eye for a quotation and the fresh view of many interesting matters too long ignored or taken for granted.

22 paradoxically, if the book works it to some extent annihilates itself.
—RAYMOND WILLIAMS

It is now more than a year since I first read *The Gutenberg Galaxy*. In the intervening months the book has stayed in my mind, and I have often gone back to it. When I come to examine my curious reluctance to write about it, I find myself in unusual difficulty. I have no real doubt of the book's importance. No commonplace volume (and in commonplace here I include many works of sound and orthodox scholarship) could stay and move in the mind in this way. With this point taken, the simplest reaction—the simplest reviewing strategy—would be an enthusiastic acknowledgment of the originality and an illustrated rehearsal of the book's argument. It is just this, however, that I have been most reluctant to commit myself to, and not only because it has been done so often already, in the first flush of reviews. What seems to me to be necessary is to let the book's substance sink into the mind, to take on the importance of an experience. This, if we are serious about McLuhan's argument, if we have in any substantial way received it, is in any case inevitable. But, ironically, when this has happened, it is very difficult to return to the simple look at the book itself. It isn't easy, that is to say, to get back to judging the book as a "machine for thinking"; still less as a commodity which it is the reviewer's business to evaluate.

The experience that matters in the book is the structuring of a configuration—a "galaxy"—around the properties of print. This structuring is necessarily critical, since it is an essential part of

McLuhan's thesis that the inherited procedures of an educated mind are conditioned by the properties of print, so that only by an effort of critical imagination can these properties be seen. In turn, this critical imagination is now possible only because we are moving out of a print-culture, with its fundamental linear and uniform properties, into an electronic culture, with its new or restored properties of simultaneous configuration. The point of difficulty is then almost too simply seen: not only that the substance of the book is embedded in print, but that the normal reaction to it—given our present fields and procedures of advanced learning—will be in print also. Paradoxically, if the book works it to some extent annihilates itself.

McLuhan, of course, is aware of this situation. Few people are even comparably aware of the effect of the medium and structure of communication on the experience communicated. His offered solution is what he describes as a mosaic construction. The book is written as a series of *aperçus*, or, better (since the linear image of series is in part false), as a structure of insights. But there are two limitations on this. First, the inevitable serial element of the printed book, however discounted. Secondly, and perhaps not so inevitable, but certainly likely in an enterprise of such magnitude, the reliance on printed authorities. In one sense, evidently, McLuhan has assembled his book, from a very wide variety of sources, in a way at least comparable with that of the medieval scholars he describes. But of course he is sufficiently limited by his culture (and by its emphases of law and copyright) to have to stabilize this procedure, in part, at assembly: The acknowledgments to authorities have to be put in, and, more crucially, they have to be put in *as authorities*. My point is not mainly that some of these sources are, as I judge, more authoritative than others (by which I mean that what some say is more certainly true than what others say), though this has its own kind of importance. What I am really saying is that this kind of reliance on authorities (since the whole field is too vast to be crossed without them) ties the book in, to an important extent, to the limitations of the scholarship of print. When he cites an experience, it can escape this limitation; when he cites an historical interpretation, in my experience it usually does not.

These are not merely observations on method. Indeed, how could anyone intelligently review this book making the kind of separation of method and substance which would show it had not really been read? I make the points in this way as a preliminary to my most important point, which is that I think McLuhan, who has got further than anyone I know in seeing the characteristics of a print culture, remains limited by them in one decisive respect. The total effect of his book is, I think (I take as supporting evidence the ordinary accounts of it), the isolation of print as a causal factor in social development. I would be the last person to question an emphasis on the means of communication, and its necessary effects on perception, as a major social factor. But, though McLuhan puts in some qualifications about other causes, the effect and certainly the excitement of his argument is this kind of causal isolation. I believe it is entirely necessary, in the twentieth century, to bring history and the social sciences back to the whole man, after the mainly nineteenth-century isolation of what were seen as decisive political and economic factors. The bourgeois view of the world as a market reduced history and social investigation to quantitative and external material, and it is ironic that Marxism, potentially the greatest challenge to this view because it was aware of the sources of such a configuration, is itself now mainly limited to material of the same kind and its consequent methods. But then one does not remedy a distortion of this magnitude by seeking (perhaps unconsciously) a new single causal factor. I repeat that McLuhan acknowledges other causes, but he hardly names them and certainly gives them little attention. Print, like the price mechanism or the accumulation of capital, becomes the dramatic hero, whatever subsidiary characters are hopefully standing around and even at times taking part in the action. This is the penalty, I think, of McLuhan's real originality, in having to work his basic perception so deeply. But it has to be said, not only that a rewriting of historical development around the causal factor of print would require markedly more evidence than we have or is offered, but also that the pursuit of such evidence, in a linear way, might itself contradict the more significant perception, that the study of the relations of culture and communications leads us by sheer weight of evidence to thinking in terms of fields of forces rather than in terms of linear cause and effect. That is to say, the perception of the great importance of print and its institutions commands us not to isolate them, but to return them to the whole field. The solar system may then be called Gutenberg, but not, on any account, the galaxy.

And here, I think, especially as literary scholars (though the one leap we particularly can make is of great significance) we encounter great difficulty. I mean that to think in terms of active configurations, when we have left the poem and entered the rest of the world, is almost mind-breaking. The pre-Renaissance, or pre-Gutenberg, habits of mind have a good deal of attraction to the literary mind, and there has been a succession of subsequent defenders. But I think those habits are really useless to us, because they are not really field-thinking at all, or, rather, they are field-thinking only at a secondary level, a prime cause (structurally very similar to the price-mechanism or capital or print) being there confidently known and even, as God, capitalized. The principal intellectual effect of any habit of mind depending on an assumed prime cause is that all else is eclecticism. With all my respect for McLuhan, I cannot see that even he has escaped this disintegrating effect, an effect following from too early an integration around a single factor.

To argue this matter adequately would take me beyond the space of a review. I have abstained, quite deliberately, from adjectival treatment of the book, just because I respect it and what it is trying to do. I must say, in case my brief remarks should be misunderstood, that I regard McLuhan as one of the very few men capable of significant contribution to the problems of advanced communication theory, and *The Gutenberg Galaxy* as a wholly indispensable book. It must also be said that it is a considerable effect of his own work that it enables us to criticize him. In any case, from other sources and on other bearings, this radically important revaluation of our world will continue. McLuhan's discussion of the ending of print-culture, and his insights into the quite new configurations now being lived through, entitle us to look forward with exceptional interest to the analysis of these changes which he has promised for a forthcoming book.

Editor's Note: For McLuhan's response to Williams, see Part 6, pp. 283–284.

understanding

5 m.

the medium is the message.
—MC LUHAN

Although published in 1964, *Understanding Media* did not receive serious critical treatment in America until 1965. Then two essays appeared, distinct in manner and point of approach, which brought McLuhan to the attention of separate but complementary audiences. The first, published in the *New Yorker* in February of that year, was written by Harold Rosenberg, a shrewd and articulate student of popular culture and, in particular, of modernist trends in art. Dwight Macdonald's essay in *Book Week* was to follow. (It is interesting to note that various writers who have become aware of the McLuhan phenomenon more recently owe a great deal to the tone of Macdonald's piece.)

In the September, 1965, issue of *Books*, Jerome Agel, a very energetic and clever reporter, with an excellent feeling for literary scoops, devoted most of his publication to an illustrated, extensive report on McLuhan, the uproar in Canada that his ideas had caused, and the reception of *Understanding Media* in the United States and abroad. *Books* reaches a small but influential readership, and Agel's article provided an indispensable stimulus to a growing audience.

The selections in Part 5, illustrating representative views of *Understanding Media*, have been made on an interdisciplinary basis, with emphasis on education and theories of popular culture.

*　　*　　*

Harold Rosenberg (23) is the author of *The Tradition of the New*.

Dwight Macdonald (24) recently had a collection of his latest essays published as *Against the American Grain*.

Christopher Ricks (25) is the author of *Milton's Dream* and is a fellow of Cambridge University. An interesting comparison can be made between his essay and the piece by A. Alvarez in Part 4.

192

Jack Behar and **Ben Lieberman** (26) focus their debate on the application of McLuhan's ideas to secondary school education. Behar is a member of the faculty of the University of California, in San Diego; Lieberman is a New York critic.

John M. Johansen (27) is a practicing New York architect who, like many other architects, is unusually sympathetic to McLuhan's ideas.

George Steiner, Jonathan Miller, and **Andrew Forge** (28) in their 1966 BBC symposium presented one of the best public discussions of McLuhan's concepts. Steiner, a fellow of Churchill College, Cambridge, has written critical studies of Tolstoy and Dostoevski. Both a neurosurgeon and a man of the theater, Miller wrote and directed *Beyond the Fringe*. Forge teaches art history at Goldsmith College, London.

Benjamin DeMott (29), professor of English at Amherst, has written several novels. His manifesto first appeared in *Esquire*.

Susan Sontag (30) anticipated some of George Steiner's observations on McLuhan's role in the formation of the "new sensibility." This essay appeared in 1965 as the last chapter of her book *Against Interpretation*.

23 he is a belated whitman singing the body electric with thomas edison as accompanist. —HAROLD ROSENBERG

Understanding Media has a dry, professional-sounding title, suggesting a handbook on magazines and television for advertising men, in particular those charged with buying space and time. It was written, however, by Professor Marshall McLuhan . . . whose conception of pop culture is no more conventional than an electronic opera. McLuhan is more likely to write a manual for the angels that for Madison Avenue. *Understanding Media* carries the subtitle "The Extensions of Man," which alerts readers at the start that more is at issue in this book than the relative merits of news and entertainment packages. We all know that radio, the movies, the press do things to us. For McLuhan they also *are* us: "They that make them," he quotes the Psalms, "shall be like unto them." So *Understanding Media* is nothing less than a book about humanity as it has been shaped by the means used in this and earlier ages to deliver information.

McLuhan's account of the effects of the media upon the human psyche lies between fact and metaphor. The instrumentalities through which words, images, and other human signals reach us transform our bodies as well as our minds. Our eyes are bulged out by vacuum tubes, our ears elongated by transistors, our skin ballooned by polyesters. ("Clothing and housing, as extensions of skin and heat-control mechanisms, are media of communication.") In his first book, *The Mechanical Bride*, published a dozen years ago and unmistakably inspired by Duchamp's erotic apparatuses, McLuhan dealt with the pop creations of advertising and other word-and-picture promotions as ingredients of a magic potion, "composed of sex and technology," that was populating America with creatures half woman, half machine. "Noticed any very spare parts lately?" he inquired in a subhead of his title chapter. The

194

legs, bust, hips of the modern girl have been dissociated from the human person as "power points," McLuhan claimed, reminding the reader that "the Hiroshima bomb was named 'Gilda' in honor of Rita Hayworth." Man, to McLuhan, often appears to be a device employed by the communications mechanisms in *their* self-development. "Any invention or technology," he writes in *Understanding Media*, "is an extension or self-amputation of our physical bodies, and such extension also demands new ratios or new equilibriums among the other organs and extensions of the body. There is, for example, no way of refusing to comply with the new ratios or sense 'closure' evoked by the TV image."

In McLuhan's *The Gutenberg Galaxy*, the analysis of how the human organism has been remodeled by a single communications medium is turned into a full-scale interpretation of Western history. The outstanding characteristics of life in Europe and America from the Renaissance to the turn of the twentieth century are traced to the invention of movable type and the diffusion of the printed word. The streaming of letters across a page brought into being an "eye culture" that found symbolic representation in *King Lear*, with its blindings and its wanderers stripped naked by the storm. (McLuhan got his Ph.D. in English at Cambridge.) With Gutenberg began the technological acceleration of history that has made constant change the norm of social life. The portability of books, McLuhan says, allowed "alphabetic man" to feed his intellect in isolation from others, thus introducing individualism and the Hamlet-like division between knowing and doing, as well as split personality ("Schizophrenia may be a necessary consequence of literacy") and the conflict between the ego and its environment. The separation of seeing from the other senses and the reduction of consciousness to sight-based concepts were compensated for by the emergence of the world of the unconscious. The fixed position of the reader vis-à-vis the page, says McLuhan, inspired perspective in painting, the visualization of three-dimensional objects in deep space, and the chronological narrative. The uniformity and repeatability of the phonetic bits that make up a line of type strengthened mechanistic philosophies, serial thinking in mathematics and the sciences, and ideals of social leveling, and they were the model for the assembly line. In replacing vernacular with mass media, print generated the centralizing forces of modern nationalism: "The citizen armies of Cromwell and Napoleon were the ideal manifestations of the new technology."

Understanding Media is McLuhan's good-bye to Gutenberg and to Renaissance, "typographic" man; that is, to the self-centered individual. As such, it takes its place in that wide channel of cultural criticism of the twentieth century that includes writers like T. S. Eliot, Oswald Spengler, D. H. Lawrence, F. R. Leavis, David Riesman, Hannah Arendt. *Understanding Media,* McLuhan's most neatly ordered and most comprehensive book, is an examination of how the eye-extended, print-reading individualist of the past five centuries is in our time undergoing metamorphosis under the bombardment of all his senses by new electronic media, the first of which was the telegraph. With the loss of the monopoly of the column of type has come the breakup of its peruser, and with this a landslide of all print-based social and art forms; e.g., the mechanical assembly line gives way to automation, and perspective in painting to two-dimensional, overall composition. Thus the change-over of media is synchronized with revolutionary phenomena in production and in cultural life and with an extreme crisis of values.

Of all crisis philosophers, McLuhan is by far the coolest. Though his notion of the "externalization" or "numbness" induced in the consumer of today's popular culture accords with Eliot's "hollow men," Riesman's "other-directedness," and Arendt's "banality," he is utterly unsympathetic to any concept of "decline." The collective trance of his contemporaries is to his mind a transitional phenomenon—one that recurs in all great historic shifts from one dominant medium to another. Current unfeeling and anxiety parallel states prevalent in the early Renaissance, when the printed document was replacing the handwritten script. Regarding us all in this light, McLuhan is immune to despair; in his terms, the theory that the modern world is a cultural wasteland is meaningless. What, he might ask, makes the inwardness of yesterday preferable to the shallowness of tomorrow, if both are by-products of more or less effective devices for conveying information? As the phonetic alphabet carried man from tribalism to individuality and freedom, the new electric media are taking him beyond "fragmented, literate, and visual individualism." If man today is part machine, this is not an effect of the Industrial Revolution. Technologies have been a component of human living for three thousand years, and our loftiest feelings have derived from that segment of us that is least ourselves: "By continuously embracing technologies, we relate ourselves to them as servo-mechanisms. That is why we must, to use them at all, serve these objects, these extensions of ourselves, as gods or minor religions. An Indian is the servo-mechanism of his canoe, as the cowboy of his horse or the executive of his clock." In line with Toynbee (the idea of the Eskimo as a merman, the cowboy as a centaur, is his), McLuhan has superseded Marx's "fetishism of commodities" with a fetishism of the medium to explain the forms of belief by which men have been governed in various epochs. Societies in which the sacred played a greater role than it does in ours were simply those ruled by media of communication more primitive than the visual. "To call the oral man 'religious,' " McLuhan observed in *The Gutenberg Galaxy*, "is, of course, as fanciful and arbitrary as calling blondes bestial."

McLuhan, then, is a modernist to the hilt; his own "sacred" touchstones are Cézanne and abstract art, the new physics, *Finnegans Wake*. His is the kind of mind that fills with horror the would-be conservator of values (a Leavis, a Yeats, a Lukács). He is not tempted in the slighest to dig in at some bygone historical moment. Accepting novelty as inevitable, he is not only a modernist but a futurist. In his latest mood, he regards most of what is going on today as highly desirable, all of it as meaningful. His position is to be inside change; he is given over to metamorphosis on principle. The present worldwide clash between the new and the old arouses him to enthusiasm, since "the meeting of two media is a moment of truth and revelation from which new form is born." It is this appreciation of innovating forms that distinguishes McLuhan from other writers on popular culture. Instead of discovering menace in the chatter of the disc jockey and the inanities of the commercial, or relief in New Wave films or in Shakespeare and ballet on TV, McLuhan probes beyond the content of the media to the impact of each medium itself as an art form. What takes place at any moment in the rectangle of the comic strip or on the screen of the TV set may not be worth serious reflection. But as you look, or look and listen, in the particular way demanded by the comic strip or the television image, something is slowly happening to one or more of your senses, and through that to your whole pattern of perception—never mind what gets into your mind. Hence the first axiom of *Understanding Media* is "The medium is the message." Radio tells us about bargains in secondhand cars, the great books, the weather, but the ultimate effect of radio is that, day after day, it is displacing reading and reintroducing on a new, technological level the oral communication of pre-literate societies—or, as Mc-Luhan calls it, "the tribal drum." The effect of a tale differs depending on whether we read it, hear it, or see it on the stage. McLuhan therefore ridicules the reformist idea that changes in programming could alter the cultural mix now produced by the popular arts. "Our conventional response to all media, namely that it is how they are used that counts, is the numb stance of the technological idiot. For the 'content' of a medium is like the juicy piece of meat carried by the burglar to distract the watchdog of the mind. . . . The effect of the movie form is not related to its program content." In fact, McLuhan suggests that one medium always uses another medium as its subject matter: "The content of the press is literary statement, as the content of the book is speech, and the content of the movie is the novel." Whether or not this is so in every case, it provides a suggestive description of much contemporary art—for example, that of Rauschenberg, who through photographs and silk-screen reproductions makes news the content of painting.

A remarkable wealth of observation issues from the play of McLuhan's sensibility upon each of today's vehicles of human intercourse, from roads and money to games and the computer. After *Understanding Media*, it should no longer be acceptable to speak of "mass culture" as a single lump. Each pop form, this work demonstrates, has its peculiar aesthetic features: the comics, a crude woodcut style; TV, a blurred "iconic" image shaped by the eye of the viewer out of millions of dots (in contrast to the shiny completed image of movie film). A further aesthetic complexity of the popular media pointed out by McLuhan lies in their division into "hot" and "cool." The hot medium, like radio and news-papers, is aggressive and communicates much information, while the cool, like TV and the Twist (also open-mesh stockings and dark glasses), is reticent and tends to draw its audience into participa-tion. The varieties of aesthetic influences by which modern man is showered ought to dissolve the belief, prevalent among intellec-tuals, that today's man in the street, in contrast to the peasant or the bushman, has been cut down to a bundle of simple reflexes.

Responding to the man-made forms that flow continually through our senses, McLuhan arrives at happy conclusions for the future. No, man is not being impoverished by packaged cultural commodi-ties. On the contrary, it was the split personality created by the book who was deprived of sensual self-realization: "Literacy is it-self an abstract asceticism that prepares the way for endless pat-terns of privation in the human community." Though the shock of the sudden passage from mechanical to electrical technology has momentarily narcotized our nerves, integral man is in the process of formation. For the first time in history, the media are providing us with extensions not of one or more sense organs but of our sense structure as a whole, "since our new electric technology is not an extension of our bodies but of our central nervous systems." The mechanical age is departing, and with it the division of man within himself and his separation from his fellows. "Synaesthesia, or uni-fied sense and imaginative life, had long seemed an unattainable dream to Western poets, painters, and artists in general. They had looked with sorrow and dismay on the fragmented and impover-ished imaginative life of Western literate man in the eighteenth century and later. . . . They were not prepared to have their dreams realized in everyday life by the aesthetic action of radio and tele-vision. Yet these massive extensions of our central nervous systems have enveloped Western man in a daily session of synaesthesia." In-stant communication through the electric media, McLuhan goes on to argue, is ending the age-old conflict between city and country; by "dunking entire populations in new imagery" and bringing them together in the "global village," it is eliminating, too, the conditions that make for war.

In sum, McLuhan has built a philosophy of history on art criticism, which he has directed not at styles in literature, painting, or architecture but at the lowly stuff of everyday life. In doing this, he has also sought to recast the meaning of art and literature since the Renaissance by finding in Shakespeare, Pope, or Blake "galaxies" of meaning related to the aesthetics and metaphysics of print. He has experimented with form in his own writings; that is, he has tried to function as an artist. *The Mechanical Bride* was a kind of early pop art, with a layout like a museum catalogue and with headlines, clips of advertising art, comic-strip boxes. *The Gutenberg Galaxy* and *Understanding Media* regard the human habitation as an enormous art pile, a throbbing assemblage of things that communicate, and they try to make it comprehensible by means of a mosaic of exhibits and comments that the author's "circulating point of view" has assembled from widely separated fields; McLuhan is attempting to imitate in his writing the form of the TV image, which he describes as "mosaic." The effort to develop an open, expressive social-science investigation in place of the customary learned research report may in time produce important results; McLuhan's version of this new form has the virtue of allowing the author to pick up bits of observation (e.g., that girls in dark glasses are engaged in "cool" communication) that are usually excluded, and it also enables him to bring into focus a remarkable spread of information (e.g., the measurement of time by smell among the ancient Chinese and among modern brain-surgery patients). McLuhan's concern for style tempts him into discharges of epigrams, wisecracks, and puns. These have abated in *Understanding Media*, but the chapter titles are still haunted by gags ("Money: The Poor Man's Credit Card," "The Photograph: The Brothel-Without-Walls"). Some of this wit is low-grade ("Movies: The Reel World") even if we consider bad puns to be in keeping with the pop spirit. However, formulas like "If it works it's obsolete," to suggest the rate of change in media, and "Today, even natural resources have an informational aspect" more than balance the account.

McLuhan, then, is a kind of artist, and his quick leaps from datum to axiom ("Take off the dateline, and one day's paper is the same as the next") are often aesthetically pleasurable. In his communications-constructed world, the artist is the master figure—in fact, the only personage whom he differentiates from the media-absorbing mass. The artist, McLuhan believes, anticipates the changes in man that will be wrought by a new medium and through his work adjusts the collective psyche to it. Thus the artist provides an antidote to the numbness induced by change-over. Painting has long since gone beyond being a merely visual medium; praising someone for having a "good eye," as if a modern painting were an object to be taken in by a single sense, is tantamount to praising him for being out of date. A Kandinsky or a Mondrian is actually apprehended through a "resonating interplay" of the whole keyboard of sense and consciousness; no wonder that eye-trained people continue to ask, "What does it mean?" One of McLuhan's most valuable contributions is to help dissolve the craft-oriented concept that modern art works still belong in the realm of things contemplated instead of being forces active in "the unified field of electric all-at-onceness" of tomorrow's world community.

Unfortunately, despite his insights into form, McLuhan's organization of his own ideas is far from first-rate. As a composition, *Understanding Media* is often out of control; "circular" perspective becomes synonymous with going round in circles. Endlessly repetitious, the book, for all its rain of bright intuitions, creates a total effect of monotony. This repetitiousness probably reflects McLuhan's uneasiness about his ability to make himself clear. For there are in his thesis inherent ambiguities. Given the advanced nature of the electric media, the implication is that older forms, like the book and the stage, are obsolete and that film and comic strip are the art forms of the future. In clinging to a sense extension (the eye) that has been surpassed, the novelist is a reactionary—except for the beatnik who gives readings in coffeehouses. Even being an individual is retrogressive, so turn the dial and slip into the new global kraal. Much as McLuhan lauds the artist, he has pitted the pop media against him, in disregard of the fact that the masterpieces of this century have been paintings, poems, plays, not movies or TV shows. The point is that while McLuhan is an aesthete, he is also an ideologue—one ready to spin out his metaphor of the "extensions" until its web covers the universe; if clothes are media, and trees and policemen are, too—if, in short, all of creation "speaks" to us—McLuhan is discussing as media what used to be called "Nature," and his notion of the "sensuously orchestrated" man of the future is a version of the pantheistic hero. He is a belated Whitman singing the body electric with Thomas Edison as accompanist. Yet to expect Adam to step out of the TV screen is utopianism of the wildest sort. For McLuhan, beliefs, moral qualities, social action, even material progress play a secondary role (if that) in determining the human condition. The drama of history is a crude pageant whose inner meaning is man's metamorphosis through the media. As a philosophy of cultural development, *Understanding Media* is on a par with theories that trace the invention of the submarine to conflicts in the libido or the decline of the handicrafts to the legalization of interest on loans.

"Usury," Ezra Pound wrote in the *Cantos,*

> **. . . rusts the man and his chisel**
> **It destroys the craftsman, destroying craft;**
> **Azure is caught with cancer.**

McLuhan has taken with deadly literalness his metaphors of the media as extensions of the body and of a nervous system outside ourselves. "Man becomes, as it were, the sex organs of the machine world, as the bee of the plant world, enabling it to fecundate and to evolve ever new forms." His susceptibility to figures of speech leads him to describe possibilities of technological innovation as if they were already achieved facts. In his world, money and work are things of the past; we live on credit cards and "learn a living" as managers of computers, and the struggle, backwash, surprise of real events are somnambulistically brushed away. The chilly silence of science fiction reigns over a broad band of McLuhan's temperament.

These deficiencies might be decisive were there to arise a McLuhan "school" of cultural interpretation through media analysis.

If one judges McLuhan as an individual writer, however, what remain paramount are his global standpoint and his zest for the new. As an artist working in a mixed medium of direct experience and historical analogy, he has given a needed twist to the great debate on what is happening to man in this age of technological speed-up. Other observers have been content to repeat criticisms of industrial society that were formulated a century ago, as if civilization had been steadily emptied out since the advent of the power loom. As against the image of our time as a faded photograph of a richly pigmented past, McLuhan, for all his abstractness, has found positive, humanistic meaning and the color of life in supermarkets, stratospheric flight, the lights blinking on broadcasting towers. In respect to the maladies of de-individuation, he has dared to seek the cure in the disease, and his vision of going forward into primitive wholeness is a good enough reply to those who would go back to it. *Understanding Media* is a concrete testimonial (illuminating, as modern art illuminates, through dissociation and regrouping) to the belief that man is certain to find his footing in the new world he is in the process of creating.

he has looted all culture, from cave painting to <u>mad</u> magazine, for fragments to shore up against the ruin of his system. —DWIGHT MACDONALD

24

This is one of those ambitious, far-ranging idea-books that is almost certain to be a *succès d'estime* and may well edge its way onto the best-seller lists. It has all the essentials: a big, new theory about an important aspect of modern life—in this case what is called Mass Media, or Communications—that is massively buttressed by

data and adorned with a special terminology. An early example
was James Burnham's *The Managerial Revolution,* which wasted
a great deal of print, talk, and time two decades ago. Later, and
more respectable, examples are *The Lonely Crowd* ("other-
directed"), Norman O. Brown's *Life Against Death* ("polymorphous perverse"), and C. Wright Mills' *The Power Elite.*

Mr. McLuhan's book outdoes its predecessors in the scope and
novelty of its theory, the variety of its data (he has looted all culture, from cave paintings to *Mad* magazine, for fragments to shore
up against the ruin of his System) and the *panache* of its terminology. My only fear is he may have overestimated the absorptive
capacities of our intelligentsia and have given them a richer feast
of Big, New ideas than even their ostrich stomachs can digest. I
have a sneaking sympathy for "the consternation of one of the editors of this book" who, we are told on page 4, "noted in dismay
that 'seventy-five per cent of your material is new. A successful
book cannot venture to be more than ten per cent new.' " Not that
this fazes our author. "Such a risk seems quite worth taking at the
present time when the stakes are very high and the need to understand the effects of the extensions of man becomes more urgent by
the hour." If the worse comes to the worst, as the hours tick by,
no one can say that Marshall McLuhan . . . didn't do his best to wise
us up.

Compared to Mr. McLuhan, Spengler is cautious and Toynbee
positively pedantic. His thesis is that mankind has gone through
three cultural stages: a Golden Age of illiterate tribalism that was
oral, homogeneous, collective, nonrational, and undifferentiated; a
Silver Age (the terms are Ovid's, not his) that set in after the invention of the alphabet during which the spoken word began to be
superseded by the written word, a decay into literacy that was
facilitated by the fact that alphabetic writing is easier to learn and
use than Egyptian hieroglyphs or Chinese ideograms, whose desue-
tude he deplores; and the present Iron Age that was inaugurated
by movable-type printing, an even more unfortunate invention, and
that is visual, fragmented, individualistic, rational, and specialized. McLuhan's *The Gutenberg Galaxy* is really Volume 1 of the
present work, describing the sociocultural changes, mostly bad,

brought about by the post-Gutenberg multiplication of printed matter, with its attendant stimulation of literacy. A gloomy work.

Understanding Media is more cheerful. It is about a fourth Age
into which for over a century we have been moving more and more
rapidly, with nobody realizing it except Mr. McLuhan: the Electronic Age of telegraph, telephone, photograph, phonograph, radio,
movie, television, and automation. This is a return to the Golden
Age but on a higher level, as in the Hegelian synthesis of thesis and
antithesis; or a spiral staircase. These new media are, in his view,
making written language obsolete, or, in his (written) language,
the Electronic Age "now brings oral and tribal ear-culture to the
literate West [whose] electric technology now begins to translate
the visual or eye-man back into the tribal and oral pattern with its
seamless web of kinship and interdependence."

This preference for speech over writing, for the primitive over
the civilized—to be fair, McLuhan's Noble Savage is a more advanced model than Rousseau's, one equipped with computers and
other electronic devices that make writing, indeed even speech,
unnecessary for communication—this is grounded on a reversal of
the traditional hierarchy of the senses. Sight, hearing, touch was
Plato's ranking, and I imagine even in the Electronic Age few
would choose blindness over deafness or touch over either of the
other two. But McLuhan's 75 per cent of new material includes a
rearrangement to touch, hearing, sight, which fits his tropism toward the primitive. He seems to have overlooked the even more
primitive taste and smell, which is a pity, since a historical-
cultural view based on them would have yielded at least 90 per
cent new material.

If I have inadvertently suggested that *Understanding Media* is
pure nonsense, let me correct that impression. It is impure nonsense, nonsense adulterated by sense. Mr. McLuhan is an ingenious, imaginative, and (above all) fertile thinker. He has accumu-
lated a great deal of fresh and interesting information (and a great
deal of dull or dubious information). There is even much to be
said for his basic thesis, if one doesn't push it too far (he does).
I sympathize with McLuhan's poetic wisecrack about "the typographical trance of the West"—he is good at such phrases, maybe

he should have written his book in verse, some brief and elliptical form like the Japanese *haiku*. It is when he develops his ideas, or rather when he fails to, that I become antipathetic.

One defect of *Understanding Media* is that the parts are greater than the whole. A single page is impressive, two are "stimulating," five raise serious doubts, ten confirm them, and long before the hardy reader has staggered to page 359 the accumulation of contradictions, nonsequiturs, facts that are distorted and facts that are not facts, exaggerations, and chronic rhetorical vagueness has numbed him to the insights (as the chapter on Clocks, especially the pages on Donne and Marvell which almost make one forget the preceding page, which tries to conscript three Shakespeare quotations which simply won't be bullied) and the many bits of new and fascinating information: the non-English-speaking African who tunes in to the BBC news broadcast every evening, listening to it as pure music, with an overtone of magic; the literate African villager who, when he reads aloud the letters his illiterate friends bring him, feels he should stop up his ears so as not to violate their privacy.

If he had written, instead of a long book, a long article for some scholarly journal, setting forth his ideas clearly—and once—Mr. McLuhan might have produced an important little work, as Frederick Jackson Turner did in 1893 with his famous essay on the frontier in American history. At the worst, it would have been provocative, stimulating, maybe even seminal. And readable. But of course he wrote the book because he couldn't write the article. Like those tribesmen of the Golden Age, his mind-set doesn't make for either precision or brevity.

"Mr. McLuhan has an insoluble problem of method," Frank Kermode observed in his admirable review of *The Gutenberg Galaxy* in the February 1963 *Encounter*. "Typography has made us incapable of knowing and discoursing otherwise than by 'a metamorphosis of situations into a fixed point of view'; that is, we reduce everything to the linear and the successive, as computers reduce everything to a series of either-ors. And since he himself is unable to proceed by any other method, he cannot avoid falsifying the facts his book sets out to establish." He goes on to paraphrase a letter he received from McLuhan: "He says the ideal form of his book would be an ideogram. Or perhaps it could be a film; but otherwise he can find no way 'of creating an inconclusive image that is lineal and sequential.'" Alas. A writer who believes that truth can be expressed only by a mosaic, a montage, a *Gestalt* in which the parts are apprehended simultaneously rather than successively, is forced by the logic of the typographical medium into "a fixed point of view" and into much too definite conclusions. And if he rejects that logic, as McLuhan tries to, the alternative is even worse: a book that lacks the virtues of its medium, being vague, repetitious, formless, and, after a while, boring.

*   *   *

One way of judging a polymath work like this, or an omniscient magazine like *Time*, is to see what it says about a subject you know about. On movies, *Understanding Media* is not very understanding, or accurate. McLuhan is a fast man with a fact. Not that he is careless or untruthful, simply that he's a system-builder and so interested in data only as building stones; if a corner has to be lopped off, a roughness smoothed to fit, he won't hesitate to do it. This is one of the reasons his book is dull reading—it's just those quirky corners, those roughnesses that make actuality interesting.

Page 18: "The content of a movie is a novel or a play or an opera." This suits a McLuhan thesis: "The medium is the message," the content of a medium is always another medium, so the only *real* content is the technology peculiar to each medium, and its effects. Many movies, especially Hollywood ones, are made from novels and plays. But many are not, and those usually the best. "Even the film industry regards all of its greatest achievements as derived from novels, nor is this unreasonable." (By "not unreasonable" McLuhan means It Fits.) "All" is the kind of needlessly large claim McLuhan often makes: Common sense would suggest there might be a few films not derived from novels that are well-regarded by the industry. In fact, there are many; I imagine that even Hollywood—which has given Oscars to Bergman and Fellini,

after all—would include among the cinema's "greatest achievements" *Potemkin, Caligari, Ten Days That Shook the World, Citizen Kane, Intolerance, 8½, La Dolce Vita, L'Avventura, Grande
Illusion, Wild Strawberries*, and the comedies of Keaton and
Chaplin.

Page 287: Pudovkin and Eisenstein did not "denounce" the
sound film. Quite the contrary: Their famous 1928 Manifesto begins, "The dream of a sound film has come true" and concludes
that, if sound is treated nonrealistically as a montage element, "it
will introduce new means of enormous power . . . for the circulation . . . of a filmic idea." Again McLuhan knew this, for he refers
to the Manifesto, but he suppressed this knowledge for systematic
reasons.

Page 293: "This kind of casual, cool realism has given the new
British films easy ascendancy." On the contrary, British films of
the last decade—as the chief British film journal, *Sight & Sound*,
constantly laments—now stand low on the international scale. Mc-
Luhan makes this misjudgment because one of his theories is that
"cool" media suit the Electronic Age better than "hot" ones—I'll
explain shortly—so since British films are indeed on the casual-
cool side, either they must be ascendant or the theory must be
wrong.

                    *   *   *

An occupational disease of system-building that is perhaps even
worse than the distortion of reality is a compulsion to push the
logic of the system to extremes. The climactic, and much the long-
est, chapter in *Understanding Media* is the one on television. A
happy ending: TV is reforming culture by bringing us the real
stuff, tribal, communal, and analphabetic—none of that divisive
book larnin'—and restoring the brotherhood of man. It is the finest
flower of mankind's finest Age, the present or Electronic one.

In *The Gutenberg Galaxy*, McLuhan with his usual originality
denounces the "open" society of individual freedom we have kept
alive, with varying success, since the Greeks invented it. He prefers
a "closed" society on the primitive model ("the product of speech,
drum, and ear technologies") and he looks forward, as the Elec-

tronic Age progresses, to "the sealing of the entire human family
into a single global tribe." TV is the demiurge that is creating this
transformation. Already it has changed things in many ways, most
of them beneficial—I predict a brisk sale for the book on Madison
Avenue. Among them are: the end of bloc-voting in politics; the
rise of the quality paperback (had thought Jason Epstein was the
demiurge there, but maybe he got the idea from Jack Paar); the
recent improvement in our criticism ("Depth probing of words and
language is a normal feature of oral and manuscript cultures,
rather than of print. Europeans have always felt that the English
and Americans lacked depth in their culture. Since radio, and especially since TV, English and American literary critics have ex-
ceeded the performances of any European in depth and subtlety."
Well, an *original* judgment anyway); "the abrupt decline of baseball" and the removal of the Dodgers to Los Angeles; "the beatnik
reaching out for Zen" and also their public poetry readings ("TV,
with its deep participation mode, caused young poets suddenly to
present their poems in cafés, in public parks, anywhere. After TV,
they suddenly felt the need for personal contact with their public."
Agreed, but in opposite sense: The tripe manufactured all day and
night by TV may well have made poets feel the need for personal
contacts in their work); the picture window; the vogue for the
small car; the vogue for skiing ("So avid is the TV viewer for rich
tactile effects that he could be counted on to revert to skis. The
wheel, so far as he is concerned, lacks the requisite abrasiveness."
Skis seem to me *less* abrasive than wheels, but let it pass, let it
pass); the Twist; and the "demand for crash-programming in
education."

TV has been able to accomplish all this because it is not only
electronic but also very cool. Hot media (radio, cinema, photography) are characterized by "high definition" or "the state of
being well filled with data." Thus comic strips are cool because
"very little visual information is provided." He rates speech cool
("because so little is given and so much has to be filled in by the
listener"). McLuhan's own style, incidentally, is one of the hottest
since Carlyle: cf., the chapter headings: "The Gadget Lover: Nar-
cissus as Narcosis"; "The Photograph: the Brothel-without-Walls";

"The Telephone: Sounding Brass or Tinkling Symbol?"; "Movies: the Reel World" (now reelly).

TV is the coolest of media because the engineers havn't yet been able to give us a clear picture. Or, in McLuhanese: "The TV image is of low intensity or definition and therefore, unlike film, it does not afford detailed information about objects." (He can say that again.) So the viewer is forced to participate, to eke out imaginatively the poverty of what he sees, like the readers of those cool comic books—all very stimulating and educational. In the Mc-Luhanorama, Picasso is inferior to Milton Caniff because he goes in for "high definition." Another virtue of TV is that it "is, above all, an extension of the sense of touch, which involves maximal interplay of all the senses." Touch would seem to me to involve *less* interplay than, say, sight, and I have always thought of TV as oral and visual. But touch is No. 1 in the McLuhan hierarchy of the senses and TV is No. 1 in the McLuhan hierarchy of media and so . . .

Watching TV is also gregarious—"the TV mosaic image demands social completion and dialogue"—with the spectators chatting while *Gunsmoke* flickers by, and this is also good. (It doesn't seem to have occurred to McLuhan that TV may demand social completion simply because there isn't much of interest on the screen.) How different are the passive, isolated, mute movie-goers, who must put up with clear, complete, and sometimes even beautiful images that give them nothing to fill in (cinema is hot) and no chance for creative or social activity. They might as well be looking at a Mantegna or a Cézanne or some other high-definition, nonparticipatory image. "Since TV nobody is happy with a mere book knowledge of French or English poetry," McLuhan writes or rather proclaims. "The unanimous cry now is 'Let's *talk* French' and 'Let the bard be heard.' " Unanimous cries I doubt ever got unanimously cried. But I do like that "mere."

I found two statements I could agree with: TV is "an endless adventure amidst blurred images and mysterious contours"; and "TV makes for myopia." For the rest, the chapter reveals with special clarity two severe personal limitations on his usefulness as a thinker about media: his total lack of interest in cultural stan-

dards (he praises Jack Paar because his low-keyed, personal manner is well suited to a cool medium like TV—as it is—but has
nothing to say about the quality of the material Paar puts across so
coolly); and his habit—it seems almost a compulsion as if he
wanted to be found out, like a sick kleptomaniac—of pushing his
ideas to extremes of absurdity.

The most extreme extreme I noticed was the millennial vision
that concludes the chapter on "The Spoken Word: Flower of
Evil?":

> Our new electric technology that extends our senses and nerves
> in a global embrace has large implications for the future of
> language. Electric technology does not need words any more
> than the digital computer needs numbers. Electricity points the
> way to an extension of the process of consciousness itself, on a
> world scale, and without any verbalization whatever. Such a
> state of collective awareness may have been the preverbal
> condition of men. . . . The computer promises by technology a
> Pentecostal condition of universal understanding and unity. The
> next logical step would seem to be . . . to bypass languages
> in favor of a general cosmic consciousness which might be very
> like the collective unconscious dreamt of by Bergson.*
> The condition of weightlessness that biologists say promises a
> physical immortality may be paralleled by the condition of a
> speechlessness that could confer a perpetuity of
> collective harmony and peace.

I think Madame Blavatsky would have envied the writer capable
of the paragraph.

---

* Only McLuhan would see the conscious as "very like" the unconscious; in his
case, the resemblance may be close.—D. M.

Editor's Note: See Part 6, pp. 281–285 for McLuhan's comments.

25 the style is a viscous fog, through which loom stumbling metaphors.
—CHRISTOPHER RICKS

The importance of *Understanding Media* has nothing to do with worth. Marshall McLuhan is now a power in more than one land, and not only as Director of the Centre for Culture and Technology at Toronto. Since a great many people are concerned about the effects of TV, films, advertisements, and the press, they will turn more and more to a praised expert. And there is, too, a market for heady prophecies, especially those which skilfully and at the last moment substitute a sermon for a forecast. Like Jacques Barzun, Mr. McLuhan has the suspenseful air of being about to lift the veil. Does Telstar bode? Yes, indeed, and we may expect (excitement mounts), we may expect that

> **the time factor in every decision of business and finance will acquire new patterns. Among the peoples of the world strange new vortices of power will appear unexpectedly.**

"Unexpectedly" is about right, for all the help we actually get from Mr. McLuhan's clutch of crystal balls. The car has altered everything, "and it will continue to do so for a decade more, by which time the electronic successors to the car will be manifest." Nostradamus redivivus? A reader who crosses Mr. McLuhan's palm with two guineas may feel gulled.

Three themes cohabit, not very fruitfully. First: Electronics and "electric speed" are different in kind from the mechanical (which is linear, typographic, uniform, and repeatable). Our present culture partakes of both. The mechanical or typographic culture necessitated sequence, fragmentation, and specialization; but the new electronic culture "retribalizes," makes the world a village, and is organically instantaneous.

212

> Man can now look back at two or three thousand years of varying degrees of mechanization with full awareness of the mechanical as an interlude between two great organic periods of culture.

The second theme is "The Extensions of Man":

> Whereas all previous technology (save speech, itself) had, in effect, extended some part of our bodies, electricity may be said to have outered the central nervous system itself, including the brain.

Third:

> Political scientists have been quite unaware of the effects of media anywhere at any time, simply because nobody has been willing to study the personal and social effects of media apart from their "content."

These are important themes, but they are altogether drowned by the style, the manner of arguing, the attitude to evidence and to authorities, and the shouting.

Any medium has an effect *qua* medium, over and above its content. To have said so would have been to have written a sadder and a wiser book (and a shorter one). But Mr. McLuhan's contempt for people who attend to the "content" leads him to deny that content plays any part at all. "The medium is the message," he intones again and again. "The effects of technology"—and by technology he means all "extensions of man"—"do not occur at the level of opinions or concepts, but alter sense ratios or patterns of perception steadily and without any resistance." If he had said "do not occur *only* at the level of opinions"—but no, for him the sole effect is that of the medium itself. Literacy creates individualism, and "this fact has nothing to do with the *content* of the alphabetized words." "The effects of radio are quite independent of its programming." TV creates "total involvement in all-inclusive *nowness*," and "this change of attitude has nothing to do with programming in any way."

All of which means that *Understanding Media* cuts off its extension of man to spite its face. How can Mr. McLuhan possibly use the medium of the *book* (typographic, linear, fragmented) in order to speak in this way about the electronically instantaneous? On his own terms, a book cannot but enforce the typographic attitudes which he insists are cramping Western man. If his arguments are true, how silly to annul them by using a medium which has no option but to annul them.   ˙

He wriggles in this unmentioned predicament, and does his best to escape by abandoning all the sequential virtues of a book. He says the same thing on every page, and repeats whole chunks when he feels like it—which is perhaps one kind of instantaneity. He praises the Eastern ("oral") mode of thought: "The entire message is then traced and retraced, again and again, on the rounds of a concentric spiral with seeming redundancy." But if this "oral" tradition could be incorporated in a book, his arguments would all collapse. The attempt may be pluckily preposterous, but the outcome is not just "seeming" redundancy. The moral position, too, is shaky, and not even the quotation from Pope Pius XII about media quite manages to shore it up. Mr. McLuhan may insist that he is "withholding all value judgments when studying these media matters," but in fact his terms are about as neutral as a bigot. Who will be found to speak for literacy (which has "fragmented" and "mutilated") when the electronic culture is described in these terms—humble involvement and deep commitment, participation, heightened human awareness, and unifying the life of the senses? "Contemporary awareness had to become integral and inclusive again, after centuries of dissociated sensibilities"—does that withhold value judgments? And is it an act of neutrality to give a chapter to each of twenty-six media, but no chapter to the theater?

Very well—people were wrong to ignore the nature of a medium. But that doesn't beautify the airy hauteur to which the arguments rise whenever they confront facts, earthy political facts. Possibly radio does inevitably inflame, and TV does cool, but the authorial tone is too epigrammatically Olympian. "Had TV occurred on a large scale during Hitler's reign he would have vanished quickly. Had TV come first there would have been no Hitler

at all." Vanished? Like a Walt Disney ogre? So confident a magic
wand does not like the fact that there are facts. Can we be quite
so sure that Nazi TV would have had no choice but to intervene so
coolingly and so effectively? Is "content" (even anti-Semitic content) really a matter of total indifference in comparison with "the
medium proper"? Mr. McLuhan may perhaps be right, but Hitler
seems to me a subject where too serene a confidence in one's own
theories can easily look unfeeling. After all, there are those of us
who would have traded all of Pope Pius' words about mass media
for just a word or two about the massacre of the Jews.

Mr. McLuhan's confidence, quite without irony, sees the computer
as a type of the Holy Ghost: "The computer, in short, promises by
technology a Pentecostal condition of universal understanding and
unity." So much for greed, crowding, hunger, and all the hard
facts which make universal understanding and unity a matter of
intractable things as well as of language and media. When Mr.
McLuhan invokes his Pentecost, there is no doubt about the mighty
rushing wind, but where are the tongues of fire?

It seems that we have been fools, but now at last we will be put
right about it all, though our patient teacher can't quite prevent his
eyelid from drooping disdainfully. "It is not the increase of numbers in the world that creates our concern with population," rather
it is "our electric involvement in one another's lives." Our "concern" may well have been pricked by the media, but it is not entirely evolved from them, since there remains the glumly objective
fact of the increasing population, a fact which to any man who
wants to live as something more than "a student of media" is in
itself a cause of concern. Could it be that Mr. McLuhan averts his
eyes from the fact because the Catholic Church wishes it weren't a
fact? When the facts would be embarrassing, Mr. McLuhan passes
by on the other side. It seems that "literate man" is a warped creature, "quite inclined to see others who cannot conform as somewhat
pathetic." And then, without a pause: "Especially the child, the
cripple, the woman, and the colored person appear in a world of
visual and typographic technology as victims of injustice." But in
this world, the world of facts as well as of media, colored people
do not merely *appear* (thanks to tricksy typography) to be victims

of injustice, they *are* such. Not every single individual, of course, but quite enough for Mr. McLuhan's enlightened detachment to get tarnished. He long-sufferingly tut-tuts—how naive of people to be upset by circumstances, instead of realizing that it is all just the built-in preconceptions of media.

Media, apparently, and not moral convictions, get things done: "The real integrator or leveler of white and Negro in the South was the private car and the truck, not the expression of moral points of view." Notice "was," as if it were all a thing of the past, so that now the historian can bask in equanimity. Notice, too, that it isn't said that the truck was in the end the most effective or most important integrator or leveler—no, it was "the real" one, which leaves "moral points of view" (a prettily placid piece of phrasing) as merely unreal. As if there weren't enough people willing to be told that justice in the South (a) has been achieved, and (b) is no moral concern of theirs, without our author handing them warrant (don't worry, the truck'll change all that). This may all be unwitting, in which case it is the consequence of Mr. McLuhan's furious rebound. Since everybody else will talk about nothing but "content," he will talk about nothing but media—nice, neutral, omnipotent media.

There is a similar stoniness when he discusses "labor-saving" devices, toasters or washing-machines or vacuum cleaners: "Instead of saving work, these devices permit everybody to do his own work. What the nineteenth century had delegated to servants and housemaids we now do for ourselves." Oh no we don't. When we switch on the automatic washing machine, Mr. McLuhan and I are not in any meaningful sense doing the same *work* as servants used to do. There is something unimaginative about a deftness that is so very interested in "devices" and so little interested in how nineteenth-century servants really did work. "Today, in the electronic age, the richest man is reduced to having much the same entertainment, and even the same food and vehicles as the ordinary man." Try telling that to the many ordinary men who live in "the other America," let alone three-quarters of the globe. Mr. McLuhan may claim the license of a prophet, but even a prophet will be the more humane if he does not state as today's fact what may perhaps one day come to pass.

Such indifference to fact is not always politically disagreeable, but it is always absurd. Literate societies don't like B.O.? That must be because the odor "is far too involving for our habits of detachment and specialist attention." But why shouldn't it just be that we don't like the smell? Ah, but what about "the strange obsession of the bookman with the press-lords as essentially corrupt"? That must, it seems, be due to the antagonism of the book to the newspaper as a medium. Yet what if it weren't a strange obsession, but a fact, that press-lords are corrupt?

The style is a viscous fog, through which loom stumbling metaphors. And Mr. McLuhan's subject, after all, is the imagination and the emotions. Nothing could be less imaginative than all this talk of "a complex and depth-structured person," especially as the depth resembles a sump: "People begin to sense a draining-away of life values." What we need is "the mosaic of the press" which "manages to effect a complex many-leveled function of group-awareness." Fortunately "the tactile mesh of the TV mosaic has begun to permeate the American sensorium"—hence the "complex togetherness of the corporate posture." What makes it all so grisly is that this unfelt, unfeeling, and nerveless style is forever insisting on how media grip, how they touch, how they create.

The tastes are of a piece with the style. He asserts that ours is "one of the greatest ages of music, poetry, painting, and architecture alike." Later he comes to think that this was a bit half-hearted, so he steps it up: "The arts of this century" have an "ascendancy over those of other ages comparable to that which we have long recognized as true of modern science." And the justification for such a claim? Well, there is the "extraordinary intensity" of Agatha Christie's *Labours of Hercules*. And there are advertisements.

The ads are by far the best part of any magazine or newspaper. More pains and thought, more wit and art go into the making of an ad than into any prose feature of press or magazine.

Anybody who thought that advertisements have as much ugly lying as witty art would simply be exposing himself as one of the "media victims, unwittingly mutilated by their studies." "Ads are ignored or deplored, but seldom studied and enjoyed"—as if enjoyment could not but follow study, as if it weren't even a possibility that one might study and then deplore. Since he so admires advertisements, it is not surprising that he uses them as evidence. Is Mrs. Khrushchev's plain cotton dress an icon of thrift? Yes—a "very ingenious ad" has said so. Are the Greeks more sensuously involved? Yes—a travel guide has said so. *Vogue* proves one fact (and I don't mean about *Vogue*), and *Life* another, as if they were irreproachable works of history.

Mr. McLuhan uses his authorities about as convincingly as his evidence. No doubt there is still a lot to be said for Bergson and Toynbee, but it is not now possible to plonk down their names as if they settled a matter. Mr. McLuhan invokes Lynn White's *Medieval Technology and Social Change* for its argument that at a particular time the stirrup profoundly affected ways of life—but he does not mention that there are unridiculous historians who believe that the arguments are important but the evidence (especially as to dating) far from complete. Similarly, great play is made with that dread "dissociation of sensibility" which at some unspecified date overtook Western man—as if any scrupulous cultural historian now thought the phrase anything but a faded bright idea. It is not only those who have been twisted by literacy who will find all these arguments short on evidence. Perhaps Mr. McLuhan's history is more accurate than are his literary quotations. The audacity is impressive, as when he takes E. E. Cummings as a type of the poet whose work is for the ear and not for the eye: Cummings must be "read aloud with widely varying stresses and paces," since "people who feel that poetry is for the eye and is to be read silently can scarcely get anywhere with Hopkins or Cummings." I would like to hear Mr. McLuhan rendering Cummings' "gRrEaPsPhOs." But even so great a vocal skill would not be a substitute for cogency or clarity of argument. Or for an accurate text of Cummings—Mr. McLuhan does not give us Cummings' spelling, capitalization, hyphenation, lineation, or spacing. The masters of the subtle schools are controversial, polymath. Mr. McLuhan shifts from ham to ham, stirring the water in his bath.

Editor's Note: See Part 6, p. 298 for McLuhan's comments.

he doesn't want ideas but action.
—JACK BEHAR 26

the greatest defect of mc luhan's theory is the complete rejection of any role for the content of communication.
—BEN LIEBERMAN

Behar:

   The Gutenberg Galaxy gave us McLuhan's major thesis about the new world of sensibility being created under the aegis of the electronic media, and at the center of this new book are the formulae that figured prominently in it. Briefly, the picture that emerges is something like the following: Pre-literate or tribal man lived in a rich oral-aural world, one structured by myth and ritual, its modes of awareness being "tactile" and "auditory," its values communal and sacred. (Here, of course, McLuhan finds the perfect myth, one centering in collective participation, that so attracts him and us; and from it grows a rather familiar mystique of the organic in the repeated use of the notion of "unified sensibility.") The Gutenberg revolution exploded the world of tribal man, creating via print the open society, modern individualism, privacy, specialization, mechanical-repeatable techniques, etc., all at the cost—a very heavy one, for McLuhan—of cutting us off from a rich auditory experience. Hence, fragmented, specialized, impoverished modern man is Gutenberg Man, a necessary victim of the visual emphasis given by printing technology. The electronic revolution, however, once more makes oral-aural experience central, promising liberation from the impoverishing effect of print, demanding participation rather than print-fostered passivity, and

219

restoring us to wholeness and harmony in the reconstituted tribal society. McLuhan apparently believes, then, that the problem of contemporary "fragmentation" is being solved whether we know it or not, that Utopia is unnecessary when we have begun to be projected, via our electronic technology, into an incredibly rich world of auditory experience that begins to wipe out our disabling legacy from the mechanical age of Gutenberg. We may yet find salvation in a happy, active, outgoing sensorium in Paradise Regained.

Certainly there is an obvious craving in our society for a more richly orchestrated life of the senses, for oral-aural modes of experience and communion with others, and in a somewhat over-popularized way, for a kind of revolt against passive, consumer-oriented roles. We are becoming devoted to the idea of full-time creativity for everyone, to process rather than to product, to "getting with" things rather than imposing oneself on them, to "acting out" rather than "reading up on." But to find, as McLuhan does, the TV image the trigger of all this is going rather far—too far, I would suppose. Some of us may find what McLuhan calls the "tactile mesh" of the TV image a quite maddeningly abstract idea. On the other hand, McLuhan's analysis of newspaper form as "mosaic" is perfectly valid, and here the formula of "simultaneity" and "total field" awareness seems to work, as does the notion that the mosaic of newspaper form tends to neutralize the "hot" point of view reserved for the editorial pages. Perhaps McLuhan presses so hard on the idea of the mosaic-like TV image because he is desperate to come by at least a token reality of "community" and the new "ritual" forms on which it can be based. What he needs to do is to define "involvement" and "participation" so that these large terms are not simply produced on the analysis of perceptual schema. We tend to regard "involvement" as (in part) distinct from the way a person looks at the TV image.

In the drama the book makes of opposing worlds of sensibility, where does McLuhan stand? What is he after in foisting so heavy a load of subliminal work on the backs of the media? On the whole, quite like the literary men whose culture-bound responses to the media he makes light of, he wants collective involvement in a "ritual process," and he sees TV, the newspaper, and radio as providing this at a "magical" communal level. He doesn't want ideas ("point of view") but action, a magical process working itself out, communal awareness restored, participation "in depth" made possible, the "Africa within" released to the sound of the tribal media. And indeed, it is easy to conclude that, for all the many sharp observations McLuhan gives us on the workings of the media, what he finally desires is a kind of religion. He is, like Blake and Lawrence, whose names occur in these pages, a foe of "single vision and Newton's sleep," and logically, then, an advocate of "ritual." But it is odd that McLuhan's proto-religious longings should fasten on the TV image and the electronic revolution.

The large question McLuhan's book raises seems to be this: How can we see to it that the necessary specialist sensibility, fostered by whatever happens to be the form of our media indoctrination, doesn't come to dominate the whole field of our awareness? McLuhan doesn't want us to resemble the teen-ager caught up in the self-mesmerization of the Twist, happily submerged in the trance. He refers to "autonomy," and he says about education that it must be regarded as "civil defense against media fallout." Yet he is so bound to the idea of the subliminal power of the media to impose their assumptions about the structuring of primary social processes on those who use and are used by them that he can't descend to what is inevitable—some fairly grubby educational programming. We don't want simply a subliminally enjoyable interplay of the sense—a kind of electronic *symboliste* madness, however liberating—or the total triumph of habits print technology has fostered. If we live indeed at a moment of crucial cultural change, when the assumptions imposed by print technology begin to strike us as making for some inevitable distortions and a harmful imbalance, then we must assess what resources we have that allow for righting the balance. Righting the balance, however, will not give us anything so comprehensive as "unified sensibility," so it is a rather foolish messianism to talk as McLuhan does about this.

The world which the media have helped to build is inescapably the one in which we live. Keeping watch over the media is one of the ordinary daily chores. It follows, I think, that we cannot help but act as analysts of content, not merely of the apparently unconditioned power of media *forms* to create or to transform the conditions of our lives.

$$* \qquad * \qquad *$$

Lieberman:

The Cult of McLuhanacy now has its full gospel. Everything is explained by seeing electric (= instant) information and communication become the whole of matter and energy; the central Mystery that every good cult needs is provided in the phenomenon that the very *form* of the communication media not only creates all change without the slightest regard for *content*, but has this causal effect despite the fact that there is no such thing as causality.

If you do not understand this, at least do not dismiss it as caricature. It is doctrine very seriously laid forth, with a very profuse profusion of printed language (a form the Master seems to deplore). For the details, you will have to read the book if you can. It will be hard enough, here, in limited space, even to cover the main points.

McLuhan's message is that the media aren't what people think they are (especially not what scholars and media people think they are), and we can't understand the vast technological and cultural changes now upon us if we don't understand media. Unfortunately, McLuhan is so full of jerry-built theory, dogmatic overgeneralizations, nonsequiturs, disorganized successions of parenthetical observations, and bewilderingly swift and large leaps among high peaks of misconception, that he makes little contribution himself to that understanding. On the contrary. It will take years to unravel a defenseless student who takes McLuhan's "facts" literally.

Nevertheless, and lest this review begin to sound critical, it must be said strongly that the book does perform a useful negative service for the mature reader, and even more for any encrusted communicator who can somehow be brought to plunge into McLuhan's super-souped-up style.

McLuhan is right to thrust out at the pipsqueak communication theories of the academicians and at the smug assumptions of most of the media leaders. We certainly have no communication theory today that is anywhere close to encompassing the realities and ramifications of communication. It is literally appalling to see how little effort is made to study and understand (much less teach) communication *per se* in major colleges and universities. No one can even get his feet wet in *Understanding Media* without at least feeling viscerally that the usual views of communication are utterly superficial and wrong, and that something drastic ought to be done about the matter.

But McLuhan unfortunately does not seem able to organize himself into a coherence that can fit the internal facts of the communication complex itself, much less the relationship of the communication complex to the industrial complex, the educational complex, the political complex, and all the other polarized but interdependent facets of our total society. It is not enough to say, as he does, that the advent of the electric media has made everything one nonlinear whole that needs no delineating. And in any event, as fuzzy a little tail as even McLuhan's ABC (All-Being Communication) trying to wag a dog as big as all mankind Past, Present, and Future really is preposterous.

Nor does it help too much that McLuhan thrusts at the excesses of specialism in our society, including specialist teaching. When he lays the blame at the print media and proclaims that the new electr[on]ic media have already completely change the situation, he reveals the frail substance of his insight. The specialist phenomenon is a necessary, inevitable development, arising out of and creating our whole technology—not just communication—and it was growing long before the "explosion" of phonetic literacy. It *does* need to be counterbalanced as our society becomes too complex for the innate generalist sense in each of us to keep our total effort a workable whole. And despite McLuhan's dangerous complacency which arises from his mystic generalist role for the "implosion" of electronic media and automation, we *are* in real danger of either splintering into paralysis and doom or else accepting a conformist pattern that will make us into an ant society. A lot of us are going to have to work hard to restore the generalist balance, but McLuhan's faith in radio, TV, and the computer—as media which have already changed the reality and thus eliminated the danger—is not the clarion call to duty.

Unfortunately, as has been perhaps hinted, McLuhan has no real positive contribution to make in this book. He produces a great confusion of aphorisms, striking sentences, arresting allusions, hindsightful insights, and breathtaking inferences. It may well be that some of them are great and will be quoted millennia hence as imperishable truths. But it is possible to suspect also that if so, this will be true simply by the laws of probability invoked in the spewing out of a torrent of statements of one kind or another—just as a pack of monkeys can theoretically, in due time, type out a Shakespearean play. But is it worth the prodigious waste of paper, and even more the staggering work of wading through all those near-miss typings to find the gems?

Not that McLuhan's creative process is sheer probability, like the monkeys. He has what can only be called an eclectic mind, an eclecticism sent skittering over all sorts of facts and artifacts by the electric charge of a neglected truth. Using *Understanding Media* as a fascinating casebook, the process in McLuhan goes something like this:

> —Any straw in a field is a straw in the wind if it happens to have at least one characteristic that is also characteristic of the point being made.
> —Any straw in the wind is the complete clue of a great new condition of the human mind or society.
> —Any clue to a great new condition of the human mind or society that is going to develop from some new communication medium is the evidence that this change has already been effected.
> —(Corollary) Any such change was caused entirely by a new communication medium.
> —(Corollary) Any such change is also revolutionary, permanent, and tied to some great past.

To test all the implications, ramifications, and conclusions which this kind of creativity puts onto even one typical McLuhan page would take years. But, to repeat, would it be worth it?

One reason for fearing not is the way McLuhan can base whole chunks of his theory (if that's what it is) on the most simple and yet staggering distinctions based on sheer error. One example must suffice, but it is central: his analysis of TV.

He finds TV different from film, to say nothing of print media, because (page 164) "From the three million dots per second on TV, the viewer is able to accept, in an iconic grasp, only a few dozen, seventy or so, from which to shape an image. The image thus made is as crude as that of the comics." And from that stems the dichotomy which leads to the whole social change and the complacency mentioned earlier. What an incredible misconception of what the eye sees! Yet one must accept this starting point, and the inferences which follow, or the "understanding" of media throughout the whole book is made meaningless.

The greatest defect of McLuhan's theory, however, is the complete rejection of any role for the content of communication. One can only assume that the irony that his own work creates "content" exclusively is lost upon McLuhan. At any rate, he ignores the power of ideas, of values, of emotions, of cumulative wisdom—to say nothing of the hard facts of geography, economics, politics, and the human glory and tragedy of life and death. "The medium is the message," and there is no other. Just like that. The truth is overwhelming in its pristine simplicity, as great a stroke of genius as Einstein's $E = mc^2$. And the result, unleashed, is a comparable radioactivity that creates horrible mutations. McLuhan bombs a landscape already in critical condition, and then strews his special seed for the growth of the new truths he sees.

Well, let us end ungrudgingly and say that his bombing is useful. Even that his seeding is a prodigious and noble gesture. But let us hope that very few readers believe he has reseeded our land with a viable, useful crop of truth. There will have to be new seed, certainly, and a tremendous amount of patient work to cultivate the new truths that our new technological society needs to replace the old—but glibly Marshalled McLuhanacies are only going to grow weeds that will need pullling if they take root at all.

27 the experience we derive from our buildings will be drawn from a fusion of the senses: the impact swift, instant, condensed, total; the message immediate, direct, possibly crude, unedited, unrehearsed, but real.

—JOHN M. JOHANSEN

Most of us for some time have been aware of the field of cybernetics and the vast effects of the current electronic revolution. Norbert Wiener, in his book *The Human Use of Human Beings* (1954), presented these matters most vividly. Since that time electronics has made possible accelerated development of computers for data processing, worldwide communication systems by Telstar, and guidance of weapons and spacecraft. Already several newspapers have installed computer typesetting; soon we will have three-dimensional TV, and at the Massachusetts Institute of Technology a team is developing a nationwide computer network that will make all knowledge, whether stored or presently recorded, instantly available anywhere. Publishing will almost surely undergo a radical transformation; the book will be replaced by research packages assembled to suit specific needs. The take-over by datamation of traditional methods is borne out by the recent news that the Radio Corporation of America has bought out Random House: a very significant event. In addition, cybernetics has already had its influence on teaching, psychology, language, and mathematics.

In each period of well-established cultural achievement, there is apt to be a consistency in the thinking and experience of the arts, science, and philosophy. In his book, *Music, History and Ideas*, Hugo Leichtentritt points out that in the seventeenth century, for

226

example, as the concept of infinity became widely accepted for the first time in scientific thinking, it was also expressed in the endless vistas of the Baroque painters and sculptors, and in music by the elaborate and boundless developments by composers of the fugue and concerto. Although it may be disputed whether such consistencies in any time were conscious or unconscious, the fact remains that consistencies are indeed found and that for us today there are likely to be similar consistencies. It is with this background in mind that I am prompted, after reading Marshall McLuhan's *Understanding Media*, to examine the new aspects of experience predicated by the electronic revolution, and find their effects, established or predictable, upon our architecture. While certain of our architects who seem not to be aware of the present need reorientation, other architects, who sense the current change, deserve encouragement, reassurance, and a cause around which to rally their valuable talents.

The effects of the electronic age upon architecture may be felt in the following ways:

First, the overwhelming presence of electronic devices will lead to a degree of imitation in the design of our buildings. We witnessed this happening in the 1920's and 1930's when Le Corbusier romanticized and imitated the machine and industrial products. Mies van der Rohe expresses the industrial processes of rolled steel in the application of standard sections to the facades of his buildings; and Walter Gropius made his great contribution by bringing design talent to manufacturing and building methods. But with the passing of the industrial age, we may now expect an architecture conceived more as a computer, of components rigged on armatures or chassis connected by circulation harnesses. The use itself of electronic terms conjures up new mental pictures of architecture. There should be a new kinetic quality in this manner of assemblage that will be more convincing than buildings that imitated moving mechanical parts yet did not themselves move. Interchangeability of parts with different circuit patterns for various performances may suggest that very different building types, the house, the high-rise office building, and the theater, will be assembled of different combinations of the same components or sub-assemblies.

Habitable chambers may be arranged not for closest physical connection, but according to most practical circuiting. Circuit patterns, whether for public use or mechanical equipment, will be shown vividly coursing through, overlaid or circumventing one another as one now sees them in the rear view of a TV cabinet. Intercommunication systems themselves, although less conspicuous, will be given expression. *Plug-in City,* the science-fiction proposal by Peter Cook in 1964 in England, is certainly a bold effort to state our environment in new terms. In this design, buildings old and new were to be plugged into, or removed, at will from a vast raceway of service conduits providing power, water, sewage, and transportation. Here, however, the value of this liberating idea derives from a sense of city organization rather than from imitation. So although this influence through direct imitation may be the most readily apparent visually, it is probably the least significant or valuable.

The second influence will be felt through the use of the computer. Already scaled drawings are made from architectural data. Even perspectives are constructed when a computer is given plan and elevation. However, more influential in the design process will be the instantaneous assembly, organization analysis, and conclusion of controlling conditions or determining design factors which can relieve us of endless calculation, research, and comparative study. The effect will be to make the building in process of design as malleable as clay, which can be manipulated and recomposed or reorganized before our eyes. The aid then is more in planning; the architect will see alternate solutions of building types, configurations, and functional organizations simultaneously and instantaneously, by programming different design data into the computer. This will also free the architect's mind, we hope, for greater aesthetic evaluation and judgment, or intuitive flow of creative ability.

Third, architecture must constantly be thought of in new terms that have force and meaning for us today. Such a term is "Cyborg," which may be defined as the entity resulting from the application of attachments to the human body of any mechanical or electronic device, to extend and enlarge the performance of its physical or mental faculties. The computer as an extension of the brain is of course the most revolutionary. But why cannot the buildings we live in be considered "extensions of man"—of their inhabitants? The control of natural or artificial light relieves diaphragm adjustment for the eye. The floor platforms and the elevator assist the legs in setting our position in space. The protective walls and roof supplement the limited and inadequate protection provided by our epidermis. Air conditioning is an addition in extension of the nasal functions of constant air temperature control and of the cilia hairs which filter out dust. The concept of "building and man as Cyborg" may well free our thinking architecturally; the extension of man as grafted or as portable equipment and the more fully equipped building may soon be indistinguishable. Then again, as we can already see in terms of self-opening doors and fully programmed temperature control, the building itself will eventually develop into a sensory organism with feedback and consciousness of its own performance.

A fourth influence will be electronic communication itself used within or between buildings. The telephone obviously has already decentralized cities, administrative and government agencies, and much of light industry. In a similar way, the parts of buildings will be decentralized. As McLuhan says, the implosion due to electronic communication will cause an explosion of population and physical plant. Within the building, rooms and departments will be more loosely assembled, as is already true of one college in the West. It is fully equipped for communications, and can provide 136 lectures simultaneously at any time at any student study on the campus. This arrangement replaces the lecture halls with dormitory rooms or individual student study cubicles possessing total reception. The library will be metamorphosed into a single computer room with limited staff space, which will receive data from its own tape library or from any other library or fact-storage center; it will select, edit, xerox, and transmit written and pictorial material.

Generally then, with proximity of building elements no longer necessary for reasons of communication, the building design will be more loosely conceived. The long conduit will replace the short corridor. The new functional configuration will be found to be consistent to or sympathetic with the aesthetic configuration, which for satisfaction of our reconditioned psyche will follow its own process.

However, aside from the planning and organizational aspects of our buildings, the architectural expression is of particular interest and concern. The fifth influence will be the most subtle but the most inevitable of all: that of our reconditioned minds and senses. The architect will undergo—has already partially undergone—a retraining of his perceptive habits, his psyche, his methods of thinking, his language, the relative acuteness of his senses and his aesthetic values. The influence upon him will be partially subliminal, the change in his design partially unconscious. He will produce sooner or later, inevitably, a new architecture.

The sixth and last influence, as I see it, will also be upon aesthetic content, but will be governed by conscious awareness of our changing technology and environment. From what has already been said, it is rather unlikely that a number of the fanciful tacks of current architectural expression will find a place. Historic revival —neoclassic and neobaroque opera houses and museums, neomedieval castles to house factories, neo-Gothic dormitories, and the "mono-pitch school"—is out-of-date. The air terminal that looks like a bird: the "architecture of imagery" is out-of-date. And since the mechanical age has been replaced by the electronic age, buildings styled after machines are out-of-date. Those who do not derive their forms from the experience of our present environment upon our changing habits of perception are out-of-date. Those who approach architecture from an academic or fine arts or "masterwork" point of view, the "beauty seekers" and the formalists, have no place. As Wiener observed, a rigid deterministic world has given over to one of contingency and organic incompleteness and probability. We can therefore assume that perfectionism and rationalism are irrelevant. For architects oriented in these directions offer society no interpretation or reconciliation with our technological environment—instead, merely an escape. For, as Mr. McLuhan says, we must first understand our environment if we are to control it.

In the mechanical age, action and reaction were not closely connected in time, response was slow, involvement limited, consequences of our actions unreal. In the electronic age, action and reaction are almost simultaneous. "We have extended the central nervous system itself in a global embrace, abolishing time and space," writes McLuhan. This separation of action and reaction or consequence formerly meant noninvolvement. Now, with the technological extension of the self including all mankind, we necessarily participate, and in depth, in the consequences of every action. The theater of the absurd dramatizes the dilemma of Western man who appears not to be involved with the consequences of his actions. The electric speed of bringing all social and political functions together in sudden implosion has heightened human awareness to an intense degree; and the partial, specialized, or detached point of view will not serve in the electronic age. The "all-inclusive image" prevails. Wholeness, empathy, and depth of awareness is of our time.

The images of the electronic world are continuous, simultaneous, nonclassified, or noncodified. They run counter to the traditional Platonic compartmentation of ideas and things, and counter to the analytic and rational processes of thought. Images are abstracted and require the viewer's involvement and participation for their complete transference. They represent a continual flow of data, not measured or measurable. This process has been described as a "mosaic" effect of composite impressions producing a total comprehension. Many effects and impressions are absorbed by the viewer instantaneously, involving a fusion of all the senses. The spectator becomes part of the system or process and must supply the connections. He is the screen upon which images are projected. Images as on TV are low definition, therefore require high participation. In this sense, the new experience is anti-"square," since "squares" don't get involved. It is "cool," in that the message is implicit. The new media deal in slang rather than in eloquence, since slang is the outgrowth of firsthand experience and the immediate scene; not restated, refined, edited, but real. No detached point of view, whether of physical position or state of mind, is longer possible.

Now we may attempt to restate these experiences and attitudes in architectural terms. If we have been reconditioned to an intensely heightened awareness of places and events, the viewer will expect all parts and aspects of buildings to be made known, to be immediately comprehensible, not as a composite impression but as an all-inclusive image. Buildings will reveal themselves totally. They will clearly express their elements, functions, and processes. The viewer will identify with them, feel an empathy with them. "Package design" is out-of-date, and there will be a conscious attempt to force an expression of elements and processes to the exterior, or by pulling apart the elements to allow the viewer to see in depth within, possibly to inner buildings. We are not interested in the epidermis or skin, only, but insist on knowing the mesoderm and the endoderm; that is, the bones and internal organs.

Intercommunication systems within the building will further allow the pulling apart of elements, relieving the current prosaic and boring compactness and density in favor of a vastly more interesting form—space composition effected by the multiple impact of many parts.

The "facade" in the traditional sense, no matter how richly sculpted or how irregular or bold, will disappear in favor of separate habitable enclosures posed freely in space. If it can be said at all that there will still be a facade, it will be a composite of all facets of all enclosures, their four walls, roof, and soffit. To use Mr. McLuhan's words, it will become a "mosaic" of facades, a bombardment of the eye by many images. Already I find among the drawings of my current designs, not only the four exterior elevations, but many more sheets devoted to the interior elevations; the inward and side-facing facets.

In this heightened human awareness which the viewer will be trained to feel, occupants will not be lost from view when in the building, but their infusion through space will be seen from outside as well as in. Or, if occupants themselves are not in view, the loci of their coursing will be felt by the shaping of the habitable spaces and passages; we will feel in the enclosed forms the loci of their movements.

The rational, analytic aspects of architecture will give over to a nonclassified accretion of elements in continuous uninterrupted flow without any particular sequence. As modern physics no longer sees a universe in which everything happens precisely according to law, which is compact, tightly organized, and in which everything is governed by strict causality, so too, our impressions will not be ordered, controlled, or in sequence. Impact will derive from group effects, and on every view, the mosaic of staccato images will present themselves. Views will not be selected or limited, but will include unplanned peripheral sensations; adjacent, oblique, marginal experiences; adjunct images of other functions, structures, or mechanics. Perhaps the view of a stairway, for example, will be inseparable in a composite view of other elements, or may itself be purposely broken into multiple images.

As buildings become looser assemblages, less finite and static, they will become volatile, will reach out and fuse with adjoining buildings and lose their identity in a continual froth of space-form. It would appear that the current concept of the city as one continuous building is borne out. The individual building appears to be many; the campus, neighborhood, or city may in fact be one. The total architectural environment, as McLuhan has said, will be a mythological world in which all things are connected in the human mind and experience, as opposed to the Aristotelian classified world of knowledge and exact definition. We are now closer to the flux, continuous currents, coalescence, and change of the earlier philosopher Heraclitus. If architectural elements are not defined or codified, recognizable symbols will not be used, and there will be no fixed architectural language.

The experience we derive from our buildings will be drawn from a fusion of the senses: the impact swift, instant, condensed, total; the message immediate, direct, possibly crude, unedited, unrehearsed, but real. Textures of exposed finishes, for example, allow us to feel with our eyes from a distance; or we see with our sense of touch.

Our designs will use architectural slang. Eloquence in architecture, now so much in vogue, will be out. Slang will be used because as in speech, it is direct, vivid, brash, effective, sometimes ingeniously poetic, and has always to do with immediacy in time and situation; with firsthand experience. This is indeed typical of modern communications. Architects will make known through their design the fact that they have had immediate participation in "pre-living" their buildings, while occupants will in actual "re-living" read back the firsthand experience. Like the computer, the building has "memory," by which previous conditions can be recalled. The architect will reveal his processes of design, and the contractor's processes of construction—may in fact show the building in stages, even incomplete or unresolved in order to allow the viewer to participate in the processes. This is "cool architecture," that is, low definition, high participation, as in electronic communications today. The viewer is required or encouraged to extend his powers to "make the connection," as McLuhan says; to fill in that additional content which is only implied. Low definition will mean that the architectural expression is implicit, not explicit, understated, not overstated, suggested, not hammered home.

Akin to this characteristic is the coming insistence that the architect and occupants will not be detached from the realities of architecture, in the sense that they will not take a detached or contrived point of view, be it academic, preciously professional, or one of personal isolation. Since we cannot detach ourselves from conditions and events as they really are anywhere on the world—or off —we are in fact there. We no longer will have patience with the hypothetical, the make-believe, the isolated event out of natural context, with sophistries, stunts, or mannered poses. Architecturally this would condemn historic revival, literary reference, moralizing, academic or fine arts attitudes.

As electronic communications have made it possible to assume a station point anywhere in time and space, our way of viewing our buildings will change for all time. Not only is the fixed axial reference point of the Renaissance out-of-date, but so also is the "Space Time," or moving, station point conceived by Siegfried Giedion, which might be said to represent the mechanical age of the wheel. Now I would make the observation that we will have a new station point of the electronic age: one that is multiple and simultaneous, a "simul-station." Obviously we don't change our physical position within a building as instantaneously as we follow an intercontinental discussion by Telstar. However, we may now be trained to project ourselves into positions, to identify ourselves with many other stations and circumstances. Buildings then will be designed by architects who can project themselves in this way, and for occupants who will easily respond with this same developed faculty of identification in space. Applied literally, any or all station points, fixed positions, or loci of moving occupants will be identified and expressed. Rooms or other spaces can be designed to suggest by scale and form, their use; passages, tunnels, bridges, tubes, troughs, arches, platforms can be so vividly expressed as to make us extend ourselves in space, as it were.

Finally, Mr. McLuhan's observation that "the medium is the message" has its parallel in architecture. This simply means that the influence of the vehicle by which the message is sent is greater than that of the message itself. Correspondingly, the building as an instrument of service has greater effect upon our lives than the functional service itself. To any serious architect this is hardly new. We should expect today, however, that this will be recognized more than ever. Further, we can fulfill our social purpose by designing buildings not as "consumer commodities," or as "diet for the privileged," as McLuhan says, but as instruments for explaining and helping all to understand and adjust to our often bewildering environment of rapid technical change. Great and responsible artists and thinkers in all times both have been affected by their technology, and have helped to find a meaning in it for their society. It should certainly be expected of the architect today that he be aware of the vast growth and influence of the electronic revolution, that his perceptive habits be retrained, and that his architecture in turn be a consistent and valid expression of his times.

28 as for blake, mc luhan is his successor over and over again. —GEORGE STEINER

he often opens doors to chaos. —JONATHAN MILLER

in his work there is an icy undertone which strikes terror. —ANDREW FORGE

STEINER: We're talking to you, we're in a studio, we're around a table. You don't see us as you might in television; you aren't reading what we're going to say as you might, let's say, in a book or in a record of this broadcast. Now McLuhan has taught us to feel that this makes an enormous difference; that what we're saying, the way we're saying it, the way you're hearing it—its entire meaning —is wrapped up in the medium, in the particular medium we're using. Now if he's right, and I think a lot of us feel that he is, and that he's opening many, many new doors—the way we're going to think about books, about language, about communication, about the different arts—is going to be radically affected by the thought of this enormously exciting iconoclast in Toronto.

MILLER: Well I certainly agree that everything that McLuhan says opens new doors. I think he often opens doors to chaos, but enough of the doors that he opens are exciting and productive to make him worth studying. It seems to me that his real interest lies in the fact

that he has done something which very few people have done publicly before. That is: to focus attention on the devices through
which we obtain knowledge. These aspects have largely been
ignored in the past, or at least have been a province of philosophers or else of neuro-physiologists, and I think for the first time
what McLuhan has done is to bring the nervous system right into
the center of the discussion of ordinary communications and of
human knowledge in general.

FORGE: My interest in Marshall McLuhan comes from the following point, that my major concern is to do with visual arts and here
is somebody who is arguing a complete view of the world as a
whole, taking in all the media of ordinary human communication.
He extends this to include things like motorcars, clothes, etc., and
yet he is discussing these things from what appears to me to be a
position related, very, very closely related, to that which a painter
or a sculptor has to adopt when he's trying to interpret his work to
a layman. If you put a landscape painting beside a figure sculpture, the really meaningful difference between the two is that one
is a painting and the other is a sculpture—not that one is a landscape and the other a figure. Perhaps I'm over-simplifying this
unjustifiably, but it seems to me that essentially this is the kind of
argument, the kind of way of looking at things, that McLuhan is
inviting us to extend throughout our physical and intellectual life.

STEINER: I think he has combined two very central perceptions
which you mention. The first, the total picture. Now it's almost a
cliché. We live in a complex system of information, physically,
physiologically, nervously, humanly, and he's saying that never
has there been as much information—that striking phrase of his,
"information fallout"—masses of information which can barely be
absorbed. At the same time, I think it's fair and important to mention here his Catholicism, in background, in scholastic thought.
He's saying either we get some sense of unity back out of this, or
we have something worse than chaos; we are in a kind of flat, unimaginative set of responses which are falling further and further
behind the available opportunities of using information and of

living it. And if we think why in so many academic places he can't get a hearing, this is because traditional ways of thinking about specialized fields are lagging further and further behind the obvious, anxious need to nonspecialize. And to think of a total space, of a total relationship, in our living.

MILLER: There's a strange division in this country [England] between those people who are concerned with the visual arts and those who are concerned with the written or spoken word. There's a belief that these belong to two completely separate departments of human activity and that it's unprofitable to bring the two together in any way at all. The result is that you find, for example, in schools of architecture and in art schools a huge underground of people who are fascinated by the idea of communications and a strange scholasticism amongst people concerned with languages. People in the language departments seem to have absolutely no idea of the ferment of ideas going on at the moment in the visual arts. I mean, quite apart from their complete failure to acknowledge what's going on in scientific study or communications, which is why I mentioned the nervous system.

FORGE: About this matter of neglect or rejection of McLuhan in academic circles—don't you think that this has something to do with certain ambiguities in McLuhan's own attitude which for some reason or other he has refused to expose fully?

MILLER: I think that one of the reasons why he's neglected, particularly by people who study English, is that his English is deplorable. He writes in a way which outrages elementary laws of literary aesthetics. He leaps from object to object of jargon. He has appalling puns and slang associations in his prose. It's full of often very poorly assimilated ideas taken from cybernetics, and from modern science, and he misuses the terms a great deal. He often contradicts his own definitions a great deal. The result is that anyone exposed to this for the first time is confronted simply by a sort of seasickness. Simply because there seems to be no set, stable ground at all.

STEINER: Let me for a moment interrupt and be devil's advocate. I agree with you absolutely. I think he doesn't have an ear. He's a lousy writer. Fine. I think I would hear him saying now, "Look here, this is more important than you think because possibly the code, the medium, of linear, logical, argumentative discourse, which you're all asking for isn't on any more." In other words, McLuhan's bad writing is almost an illuminative instrument of obsolescence.

MILLER: This is absolutely true. The strange irony, of course, is that he happens to be writing about that very subject in such a way that his own prose is going to be destroyed because he's questioning the basis of prose. Only a little while ago he wrote to me, as a result of something I'd written in the newspapers, about this bad prose. And then the first thing he said in the letter was, "We must understand that prose is no longer a useful technique for getting ideas across. It's too linear, it's too extended. You have to get things across by means of puns because puns condense ideas into single images."

FORGE: And incidentally, I think it's worth saying that the first book that I read by McLuhan I didn't read in any order; and the second time I read I conscientiously started at the beginning and read it right through, and I found that there was nothing to choose.

STEINER: But there we belong to an awfully important radical group. As Nietzsche says, "I hope nobody will call himself a philosopher any more after this." Certain op sculpture and op art has a built-in time bomb which says, "You've seen me, it's a happening." McLuhan is related to our present sense of those important thinkers who are deliberately subverting their own case.

MILLER: Wittgenstein says, "Of what one cannot speak one must remain silent." What's interesting about McLuhan is that he refuses to remain silent on this very point. He believes that there is a point where apparently language is broken down in the lines of getting ideas across, and he is trying to open up the possibility of

not remaining silent, of being communicative by using new techniques which language has perhaps not provided.

STEINER: Like Norman Brown, with whom there are many links,
McLuhan's tremendously concerned with leisure. And what's going
to happen in an increasingly leisure-programmed society. He's
thinking of art almost under a more general theory of play—a
game theory of some kind—acceptable to far more people than
"art" is in any traditional, cultural sense. He hasn't got this right
at all. But again, as so often in McLuhan, I think he's on a very
important track. The game is going to become a much more important category of which art may be only one phase.

MILLER: I think this is one of the critical points where McLuhan
finds himself neglected and rejected by the traditional academics.
You see, the strange thing about McLuhan is that having, as it
were, put out this idea that the medium is the message and pre-
cedes the message, he actually has come to a point where the
medium for him is even more interesting than the message. The
actual amount of value judgment and interesting content is mini-
mal in all his work. It's amazing how little account of the stories
in a film or a television series or a novel ever occurs in his work.
It's amazing how little subject matter is dealt with when he talks
about painting. He seems to have less and less interest in content.
It's very strange and rather touching to hear him talk about things
like jazz and things of this sort and to hear how inaccurate he is
about it all, and how little he really knows about the details of the
thing.

STEINER: Oh he stopped doing his homework, I think, years ago—
like many people who brilliantly explode ideas and then harvest
them. There's a lot of homework that needs doing but there are
nevertheless very powerful political social implications in his
work. One of them is that this information fallout, this admass
culture, is good; there is a positive romantic, post-romantic, almost
pastoral implication that there are terrific energies loose and that
they are creative, that it's incredibly snobbish not to live with them,

in them, and use them. And this is a very powerful humanistic position, after all.

MILLER: And this surely brings up the other point which really has, I think, engendered most of the hostility. It's the fact that he is so willing to accept and treat seriously aspects of popular culture. Now I'm absolutely sure that this really is the origin of most of the hostility. The fact is that he will talk about television and there is still an apparently ineradicable hostility to television and to popular media, to films, as being things which can be talked about seriously. There is this aristocracy of print still, and I think what he's coming up against is the ancient snobbery against new media, and against the new forms that are coming out.

FORGE: I am very conscious of the warmth in which he accepts this enormous range of information and so on, this tremendous warmth. At the same time there is a kind of undertone, an icy undertone, which strikes terror, I believe. When, for instance, he talks about men as the servo-mechanisms of their machines or as the sexual organs of machines, it's not the phrase which is so frightening but a suspicion at the back of one's mind that one's not altogether sure whether he welcomes this or whether he abhors it.

MILLER: If you ever question him on this, he will say, "I have no value judgments to make on this. I am just simply reporting on what is the case."

FORGE: At the same time, it's very charged—the way in which he talks about it. I don't know if this is completely out of line, but it reminds me very much of Burroughs, who seems to me in a way the artist who most closely relates to this kind of absolute ambiguity with regard to machines and to extensions of the nervous system.

STEINER: I'd want to worry about that one, because if it's Burroughs it's not going to be Rabelais. And I would suggest that Rabelais is at almost every point crucial to McLuhan's argument, and to the way McLuhan thinks about words and language. Rabelais and Joyce, who are immensely different from Burroughs. You may be right; we may be again here at something he hasn't resolved. Can I just take up one point on what Jonathan was saying, which seems to me central. Jonathan was saying snobbery; people won't accept. But we have a very new problem here. The television show, the pop song, the film, are not easily repeatable except in very special and limited conditions. Are we now moving into a completely different orientation where the work of art is important and great and energetic, whatever you wish to say, but for the first time in human history it is not preservable. It's a one-time event. And this is going to need a real re-orientation of our way of thinking about a work of art, and we get roughly something like this: a long oral period, then a very short, (his Gutenberg Galaxy) period of recordable, memorable art, and perhaps again the beginning of a number of multiple oral things. And the very fact that we can talk this way and know that the problem of death enters here—the problem of the death of the work of art and the death of the person who remembers having seen it, but cannot transmit the experience—we partially owe to McLuhan. And there is a really big door about stability in the experience which the literary theorists haven't opened, and nobody since Blake I think has really quite seen. As for Blake, McLuhan is his successor over and over again.

Editor's Note: See Part 6, pp. 279–280, 291–294 for McLuhan's comments on Steiner and Miller.

a literary self that amounts to an amalgam of bogie and dr. huer might not seem everybody's dish: but the thing obviously meets a felt need.

29

—BENJAMIN DE MOTT

A marvy year for Marshall McLuhan, take it all in all. Tom Wolfe compared him with Darwin, Freud, and Einstein; Susan Sontag said in public she thought he was swell. London saw him as an epoch maker and intellectual frontiersman (*Encounter* and the *Times Lit Supp*), and *The New Yorker* reviewed him rapt. What is more, academe—after a period of sitting tall but silent on his bandwagon —began talking out loud about his work. (One example: A recent international convocation of savants at Southern Illinois University spent days discussing the "communications revolution" in open session—mainly in McLuhanian terms.) Success being what it is, wasps and carpers were doubtless waiting for the man a piece or two up the road. But no amount of carping could obscure the facts of his rise. Overnight the author of *Understanding Media* had emerged as Midcult's Mr. Big. And ahead of him lay a shot at mass adulation and the title of Everyman's Favorite Brain.

The secret of this ascent isn't instantly visible to casual reportorial eyes. Marshall McLuhan is no literary old pro blessed with a power base and a rich experience at name-making. An English professor for most of his working life (Wisconsin, Assumption, St. Louis), he moved on from teaching only quite recently to his present post as director of Toronto University's Centre for Culture and Technology. And despite long years in the classroom, he has no credit reserves in the trade—no stretch of unheralded, scholarly labor of the kind fellow professionals pant to puff. McLuhan avoided book-writing until he was forty. His first work, *The Mechanical Bride* (1951), was an analysis of the sex-power-horsepower ploy by which two generations of ad men have sold us our annual car. (Not much there for the Modern Language Association.) And after the *Bride* appeared, the author resumed his silence as a bookman and maintained it for another full decade and more.

Nor can it be said—still on the mystery of the McLuhanian boom—that here is a case of a late-blooming stylist, somebody who had to turn fifty to turn a slick phrase. In terms of style, this flower has yet to bud. Marshall McLuhan's present reputation rests on two books—*The 'Gutenberg Galaxy* (1962) and *Understanding Media* (1964); both are sometimes stimulating, but neither is pretty prose. One problem is that of opacity (McLuhan's pages are dense with stoppers like "sense ratios," "interiorizations of alphabetic technology," and the like). Another is that the favored method of organization has a bit too much in common with that of an impresario squirrel. *The Gutenberg Galaxy* looks gathered, not written: a paste-up from a hundred histories of math, political theology, nationalism, and fur-trading, and from a thousand "other authorities." (Walt Whitman and Walt Whitman Rostow, Cicero and Father Ong, de Chardin and de Beauvoir, Rabelais, Riesman, and Shakespeare, the Opies, Powys, and Poe—name your hero, he surely is here.) The man's work reads for pages at a stretch like a Marboro clearance ad:

"Clagett [author of *The Science of Mechanics in the Middle Ages*] presents the treatise of Nicholas of Oresme *On the Configurations of Qualities* in which Oresme says: 'Every measurable thing except numbers is conceived in the manner of continuous quantity.' This recalls us to the Greek world in which as Tobias D. Dantzig points out in his *Number: The Language of Science* (pages 141–142): 'The attempt to apply rational arithmetic to a problem in geometry resulted in the first crisis in the history of mathematics. . . .' Number is the dimension of tactility, as Ivins explained in *Art and Geometry* (page 7)," etc.

Furthermore, the two leading articles of this thinker's gospel can't be called easy to grasp. The first is a theory of culture which contends that communications media impose a wide range of assumptions "subliminally." (The form of the media, not the content, structures men's values, according to McLuhan; the form also determines the content of the senses and the very look of the world.) The second is an interpretation of history which claims that revolutionary transformations of media occur periodically through the ages, and that one such transformation is in progress right now. (A five-hundred-year-old "typographic and mechanical" era is ending and an "electric galaxy of events" has begun; the new "galaxy" offers experiences of simultaneity and heightened interdependence in which traditional values—privacy, independence and so on—are engulfed.) Neither of these items is wholly lacking in interest, and McLuhan's historical chapters are often enlivened by canny, comprehensible remarks. But the key idea, to repeat—that of the centrality of *form* in the media as the determinant of social structure and individual minds—is to most men unfamiliar and abstract. An author who makes it into his dogma would ordinarily be ill-advised to brood overmuch about fame.

That Marshall McLuhan is now in position (if he chooses) to brood about nothing else owes a little to his skill with the magic of the modern. "Baby, it's what's happening" is a regularly sounded ground theme in his work. The basic language is video-mesh, circuits, and data processing. Injunctions to *Think Modern!* appear on page after page. ("We still have our eyes fixed on the rearview mirror looking firmly and squarely at the job that is receding into the nineteenth-century past.") The right names—Cage, Camp, Bond, Van Der Beek, the whole of the switched-on mob—are fingered throughout like sacred medals. The farthest-out art—electric landscapes, pop happenings, or whatever—is treated either as classic or already passé, and idols of the hour are probed intensely, like important neglected codes:

"The Beatles stare at us with eloquent messages of changed sensory modes for our whole population, and yet people merely think how whimsical, how bizarre, how grotesque. The Beatles are trying to tell us by the antienvironment they present just how we have changed and in what ways."

Old times and old-timers do turn up, as indicated—especially in *The Gutenberg Galaxy*. But even they swim into the reader's ken to a definite R-and-R beat. (Who was Christopher Marlowe? The man, says McLuhan, turning dead Kit hummingly on, who "set up a national P.A. system of blank verse." Who was Heidegger? A cat who "surfboards along on the electronic wave." What were the Middle Ages? *"The Late Show* for the Renaissance.")

Among other crowd-pleasing elements in the McLuhanian equation, the author's literary persona rates a word. At some moments this writer plays Inside Dopester (I called the Kennedy-Nixon election, he announces, I knew exactly why Jack would win). At others he's simply a Scrappy Little Professorial Guy. Enemies as various as George Bernard Shaw ("he lost his nerve") and General Sarnoff ("the voice of the current somnambulism") are worked over in his books; Lewis Mumford, Arnold Toynbee, and dozens more are patronized, and English profs ("literary brahmins") come off naturally as jerks. The author also does a turn as Kitsch Cynic, mocker of goodie-good types—and it is here that he shows his best stuff, speaking again and again with the clarity of last night's knowing cabby or this week's issue of *Time*. People who are easily shocked give him the laughing fits. ("The historian Daniel Boorstin was scandalized by the fact that celebrity in our information age was not due to a person's having done anything but simply to his being known for being well-known. Professor Parkinson is scandalized that the structure of human work now seems to be quite independent of any job to be done.") And he likes interrupting the argument to defend the innocent guilty and to lean on moralizing twerps:

"So great was the audience participation in the quiz shows that the directors of the show were prosecuted as con men. Moreover, press and radio ad interests, bitter about the success of the new TV medium, were delighted to lacerate the flesh of their rivals. Of course, the riggers had been blithely unaware of the nature of their medium, and had given it the movie treatment of intense realism, instead of the softer mythic focus proper to TV. Charles Van Doren merely got clobbered as an innocent bystander, and the whole investigation elicited no insight into the nature or effects of the TV medium. Regrettably, it simply provided a field day for the earnest moralizers. A moral point of view too often serves as a substitute for understanding in technological matters."

A literary self that amounts to an amalgam of Bogie and Dr.

Huer might not seem everybody's dish; but the thing obviously meets a felt need.*

And the same can be said about McLuhan's gamesmanly ploys as a historian. A specialist in unnoticed causes, this scholar never delves into a historical situation without emerging with "major factors" nobody quite hit on before. The handling in *Understanding Media* of the advent of philanthrophy a century ago is typical of his cunning moves. Why did "even the hardiest of the rich dwindle into modest ways of timid service to mankind"? Because of the invention of the telegraph, McLuhan explains—and does not stop for questions. What is the key factor in the Southern civil-rights struggle? The internal-combustion engine. ("The real integrator or leveler of white and Negro in the South was the private car and the truck, not the expression of moral points of view.") Why were the Jews murdered by the million? Because radio came before TV. ("Had TV come first there would have been no Hitler at all.") The talent in question isn't the kind treasured by trad historians, but it is what is called provocative and universally pleasing to wits.

In the end it won't do, though, to pretend that Marshall Mc-Luhan's secret is a matter either of mere wit or mere newsiness or mere literary self-creation. The truth is more complicated—and more painful—than that. Grasping it means facing up to the dozen different kinds of stratagem by which this author empties facts and agonies from the world he thinks of as "Now." Some of these stratagems depend on tricks of futuristic projection, displacements of present-day reality which treat desperate hopes as facts. (Write that "the real integrator of the white and Negro *was*," and you imply that the struggle has already been won.) Other tricks include sudden weird tonal abstractions—see the flip comment about TV and Hitler—deadenings of feeling and sympathy that distance

---

* There are occasional bad break-downs or inconsistencies in this public literary mask. McLuhan stands forth usually as a man quite unafflicted by any sense of inferiority. "I am in the position of Louis Pasteur," he tells his reader repeatedly. Yet the word *humility* comes not infrequently to his lips. For example: His address at Southern Illinois, which began with a summary of likenesses between Marshall McLuhan and Plato, ended with the assertion that "I really feel shatteringly humble." It was a sequel that left some alert listeners confused.

holocaust and shame. Still others con the reader into a frankly theatrical view of experience, a vision that insulates him from immediacies and shows forth all life as a production or stunt. Taken singly, needless to say, none of the stratagems would rank as original, amazing, or troubling; taken in concert they have powerful and obnoxious effect. The complaint isn't that Professor McLuhan puts together a thoroughly fantastic account of the situation of contemporary man; it is that he sets himself up, speaking bluntly, as the constituted pardoner of this age—a purveyor of perfect absolution for every genuine kind of modern guilt.

Do I chide myself for trivial failings—my laxness as a parent, my sins of permissiveness, my failure to exact respect from the kids? Do I worry about rearing lay-abouts incapable of work or thought?—Oh but come *on*, says Marshall McLuhan, a benign forgiving face, the truth is your children are grand:

"Some people have estimated that the young person, the infant and the small child, growing up in our world today works harder than any child ever did in any previous human environment—only the work he has to perform is that of data processing. The small child in twentieth-century America does more data processing—more work—than any child in any previous culture in the history of the world. . . . We haven't really cottoned on to the fact that our children work furiously, processing data in an electrically structured world. . . ."

Do I feel bad about my *own* laziness, say—my own unending belt of mindlessness in front of TV? Situation comedy, secret agents, mean mockeries of domestic life. . . . Has my intellectual appetite gone dead? My mind turned slush?—Forget it, says this Constant Comforter. The medium is the message, and whatever you think you are doing in front of the box, the fact is you're being expanded-extended-improved. "TV has opened the doors of audile-tactile perception to the nonvisual world of spoken languages and food and the plastic arts. . . ." TV has transformed "American innocence into depth sophistication, independently of 'content'. . . ." TV has "changed our sense-lives and our mental processes. It has created a taste for all experience in *depth*. . . . And oddly enough, with the demand for the depth, goes the demand for crash-programming [in education]. Not only deeper, but further, into all knowledge has become the normal popular demand since TV."

Or am I bugged by my pointless affluence, my guilt about having fat on my hide at a time when sores of starvation are the rule for hundreds of millions elsewhere?—But don't be *silly*, says my adviser, you're being ridiculous again. You're mired in outmoded thinking, you're the victim of moldy figs. Oh, yes, we've all heard about the underdeveloped nations, the "ascent into history," the necessity of hard labor, the problems of locating resources, building factories, educating work forces, creating credit systems, and the like. But *we* know, don't we now, *we* know that we have it within us practically at this instant to do the miracle of our choice whenever we choose:

"The computer will be in a position to carry out orchestrated programming for the sensory life of entire populations. It can be programmed in terms of their total needs, not just in terms of the messages they should be hearing, but in terms of the total experience as picked up and patterned by all the senses at once. For example, if you were to write an ideal sensory program for Indonesia or some area of the world that you wanted to leapfrog across a lot of old technology, this would be possible if you knew in the first place its present sensory thresholds, and, second, if you had established what kind of sensory effect a given technology like radio or literacy had upon sensory life as a whole."

Or suppose I am simply worried about my *natural* self, my condition as part of the creation, my indecencies to the life around me that is coextensive with mine. I deface the garden, Earth, with cigarette butts, billboards, beer cans. I pollute the streams with uncycled wastes from my factory. Should I not then despise myself as a rapist?

Well, do what you like, answers Marshall McLuhan sniffishly, but you are a bit of a wag. Men may have been a bit hard on the planet in the past—but full amends are about to be made. If you'll just be patient a minute or two, you'll see us doing a kind of honor to this Little Old Earth that will more than make up for the past:

"If the planet itself has thus become the content of a new space created by its satellites, and its electronic extensions, if the planet has become the content and not the environment, then we can confidently expect to see the next few decades devoted to turning the planet into an art form. We will caress and shape and pattern every facet, every contour of this planet as if it were a work of art, just as surely as we put a new environment around it."

In sum: give it all over, is the message. Give over self-doubt, self-torment, self-hatred. Give over politics. Give over conscience. Relax, go soft and complacent, accept your subliminal perfectability. Before us, almost at hand, is a moment of revelation when it shall be shown that "we are living in a period richer" than that of Shakespeare, that our time is properly thought of as "the greatest of all human ages, whether in the arts or in the sciences." And while we are waiting, there are worthy acts to be done. We can cut ourselves off from our depressions. We can look beyond the trivia of daily life—beyond entanglements with wives and children and employers, beyond neighbors, bond issues, tax bills, and the rest. We can overcome the tired sense that there are urgent local and international issues, and learn to see the dropout, the teach-in, even the casualty himself, as part of The Greater Showbiz:

". . . we now experience simultaneously the dropout and the teach-in. The two forms are correlative. They belong together. The teach-in represents an attempt to shift education from instruction to discovery, from brainwashing students to brainwashing instructors. It is a big dramatic reversal. Vietnam, as the content of the teach-in, is a very small, misleading Red Herring. It really has nothing to do with the teach-in as such any more than with the dropout. The dropout represents a rejection of nineteenth-century technology as manifested in our educational establishments. The teach-in represents a creative effort to switch the educational process to discovery, from package to prove."

Thus will we rise to the certainty that style and method are all, that the visible—Vietnam or wherever—is not in any real sense *there*. And having done this we can take off absolutely, fly up from the nonworld of consciousness into the broad sanctuaries of ecstacy and hope. ("The computer, in short, promises by technology a

Pentecostal condition of universal understanding and unity . . . a perpetuity of collective harmony and peace.")

It is here, of course, precisely here—in the gift of oblivion—that the heart of the McLuhanian munificence is found. This writer does bestow on his reader a welcome grant of hip modernity. He stimulates in addition a voluptuous sense of mastery (to say "The Middle Ages were *The Late Show* for the Renaissance" is rather like cornering a Corvette). And whether or not the basis of his sunniness is sheer terror, his work does rank as the strongest incitement to optimism yet produced in this age. But the great gift offered is, ultimately, the release from consciousness itself. Those who accept it have clearly won a deliverance, a free way up and out.

Are they so reprehensible, it is asked? Poor men, the ignorant, the hopeless, have to buy *their* release from pushers. The Professor's enthusiasts spend less and get more. They buy a guarantee that the disorder, chaos, and misery around them are but veils and shadows, lies told by the stupid conscious mind—yet they make no sacrifice whatever of their ability to function in the workaday world. In the act of discounting their own senses and anxieties, they rise up to form an elite—men dignified by their access to the knowledge that nobody knows what's what. If they are at bottom blind devotees of the subliminal dogma, they have at least kept their self-respect.

—And in any case what *is* the compulsion to Gloomsville that makes it shameful to smile with a Happy Prof? By what laws are we obliged to speak and act always as though tragedy, endless tragedy, were the perpetual human lot? Is it really a badge of reason to hold at every hour of day and night that—as Santayana claimed—"the only true dignity of man is his capacity to despise himself"?

The frustration that breathes in these questions, the boredom with canting pessimism, the thirst for a freshening of life, the longing for an inward sense of courage—these are doubtless the deepest secrets known by our new King of Popthink, the deepest needs his elixir is designed to meet. And making light of the needs is no less inhuman than exploiting them. The best that can be done is to repeat the questions that consciousness—were there any of it left around—would probably feel bound to raise, *viz.:*

How much can be said for an intellectual vision whose effect is to encourage abdication from all responsibility of mind?

Or: What good is this famous McLuhanacy if it makes men drunk as it makes them bold?

30 the basic unit of contemporary art is not the idea, but the analysis of and extension of sensations. —SUSAN SONTAG

In the last few years there has been a good deal of discussion of a purported chasm which opened up some two centuries ago, with the advent of the Industrial Revolution, between "two cultures," the literary-artistic and the scientific. According to this diagnosis, any intelligent and articulate modern person is likely to inhabit one culture to the exclusion of the other. He will be concerned with different documents, different techniques, different problems; he will speak a different language. Most important, the type of effort required for the mastery of these two cultures will differ vastly. For the literary-artistic culture is understood as a general culture. It is addressed to man insofar as he is man; it is culture or, rather, it promotes culture, in the sense of culture defined by Ortega y Gasset: that which a man has in his possession when he has forgotten everything that he has read. The scientific culture, in contrast, is a culture for specialists; it is founded on remembering and is set down in ways that require complete dedication of the effort to comprehend. While the literary-artistic culture aims at internalization, ingestion—in other words, cultivation—the scientific culture aims at accumulation and externalization in complex instruments for problem-solving and specific techniques for mastery.

Though T. S. Eliot derived the chasm between the two cultures from a period more remote in modern history, speaking in a famous essay of a "dissociation of sensibility" which opened up in the seventeenth century, the connection of the problem with the Industrial Revolution seems well taken. There is a historic antipathy on the part of many literary intellectuals and artists to those changes which characterize modern society—above all, industrialization and those of its effects which everyone has experienced, such as the proliferation of huge impersonal cities and the predominance of the anonymous style of urban life. It has mattered little whether industrialization, the creature of modern "science," is seen on the nineteenth- and early twentieth-century model, as noisy smoky artificial processes which defile nature and standardize culture, or on the newer model, the clean automated technology that is coming into being in the second half of the twentieth century. The judgment has been mostly the same. Literary men, feeling that the status of humanity itself was being challenged by the new science and the new technology, abhorred and deplored the change. But the literary men, whether one thinks of Emerson and Thoreau and Ruskin in the nineteenth century, or of twentieth-century intellectuals who talk of modern society as being in some new way incomprehensible, "alienated," are inevitably on the defensive. They know that the scientific culture, the coming of the machine, cannot be stopped.

The standard response to the problem of "the two cultures"—and the issue long antedates by many decades the crude and philistine statement of the problem by C. P. Snow in a famous lecture some years ago—has been a facile defense of the function of the arts (in terms of an ever vaguer ideology of "humanism") or a premature surrender of the function of the arts to science. By the second response, I am not referring to the philistinism of scientists (and those of their party among artists and philosophers) who dismiss the arts as imprecise, untrue, at best mere toys. I am speaking of serious doubts which have arisen among those who are passionately engaged in the arts. The role of the individual artist, in the business of making unique objects for the purpose of giving pleasure and educating conscience and sensibility, has repeatedly been called into question. Some literary intellectuals and artists have gone so far as to prophesy the ultimate demise of the art-making activity of man. Art, in an automated scientific society, would be unfunctional, useless.

But this conclusion, I should argue, is plainly unwarranted. Indeed, the whole issue seems to me crudely put. For the question of "the two cultures" assumes that science and technology are changing, in motion, while the arts are static, fulfilling some perennial generic human function (consolation? edification? diversion?). Only on the basis of this false assumption would anyone reason that the arts might be in danger of becoming obsolete.

Art does not progress, in the sense that science and technology do. But the arts do develop and change. For instance, in our own time, art is becoming increasingly the terrain of specialists. The most interesting and creative art of our time is *not* open to the generally educated; it demands special effort; it speaks a specialized language. The music of Milton Babbitt and Morton Feldman, the painting of Mark Rothko and Frank Stella, the dance of Merce Cunningham and James Waring demand an education of sensibility whose difficulties and length of apprenticeship are at least comparable to the difficulties of mastering physics or engineering. (Only the novel, among the arts, at least in America, fails to provide similar examples.) The parallel between the abstruseness of contemporary art and that of modern science is too obvious to be missed. Another likeness to the scientific culture is the history-mindedness of contemporary art. The most interesting works of contemporary art are full of references to the history of the medium; so far as they comment on past art, they demand a knowledge of at least the recent past. As Harold Rosenberg has pointed out, contemporary paintings are themselves acts of criticism as much as of creation. The point could be made as well of much recent work in the films, music, the dance, poetry, and (in Europe) literature. Again, a similarity with the style of science—this time, with the accumulative aspect of science—can be discerned.

The conflict between "the two cultures" is in fact an illusion, a temporary phenomenon born of a period of profound and bewildering historical change. What we are witnessing is not so much a conflict of cultures as the creation of a new (potentially unitary) kind of sensibility. This new sensibility is rooted, as it must be, in *our* experience, experiences which are new in the history of humanity—in extreme social and physical mobility; in the crowdedness of the human scene (both people and material commodities multiplying at a dizzying rate); in the availability of new sensations such as speed (physical speed, as in airplane travel; speed of images, as in the cinema); and in the pan-cultural perspective on the arts that is possible through the mass reproduction of art objects.

What we are getting is not the demise of art, but a transformation of the function of art. Art, which arose in human society as a magical-religious operation, and passed over into a technique for depicting and commenting on secular reality, has in our own time arrogated to itself a new function—neither religious, nor serving a secularized religious function, nor merely secular or profane (a notion which breaks down when its opposite, the "religious" or "sacred," becomes obsolescent). Art today is a new kind of instrument, an instrument for modifying consciousness and organizing new modes of sensibility. And the means for practicing art have been radically extended. Indeed, in response to this new function (more felt than clearly articulated), artists have had to become self-conscious aestheticians: continually challenging their means, their materials, and methods. Often, the conquest and exploitation of new materials, and methods drawn from the world of "nonart" —for example, from industrial technology, from commercial processes and imagery, from purely private and subjective fantasies and dreams—seems to be the principal effort of many artists. Painters no longer feel themselves confined to canvas and paint, but employ hair, photographs, wax, sand, bicycle tires, their own toothbrushes, and socks. Musicians have reached beyond the sounds of the traditional instruments to use tampered instruments and (usually on tape) synthetic sounds and industrial noises.

All kinds of conventionally accepted boundaries have thereby been challenged: not just the one between the "scientific" and the "literary-artistic" cultures, or the one between "art" and "nonart"; but also many established distinctions within the world of culture itself—that between form and content, the frivolous and the serious, and (a favorite of literary intellectuals) "high" and "low" culture.

The distinction between "high" and "low" (or "mass" or "popular") culture is based partly on an evaluation of the difference between unique and mass-produced objects. In an era of mass technological reproduction, the work of the serious artist had a special value simply because it was unique, because it bore his personal, individual signature. The works of popular culture (and even films were for a long time included in this category) were seen as having little value because they were manufactured objects, bearing no individual stamp—group concoctions made for an undifferentiated audience. But in the light of contemporary practice in the arts, this distinction appears extremely shallow. Many of the serious works of art of recent decades have a decidedly impersonal character. The work of art is reasserting its existence as "object" (even as manufactured or mass-produced object, drawing on the popular arts) rather than as "individual personal expression."

The exploration of the impersonal (and trans-personal) in contemporary art is the new classicism; at least, a reaction against what is understood as the romantic spirit dominates most of the interesting art of today. Today's art, with its insistence on coolness, its refusal of what it considers to be sentimentality, its spirit of exactness, its sense of "research" and "problems," is closer to the spirit of science than of art in the old-fashioned sense. Often, the artist's work is only his idea, his concept. This is a familiar practice in architecture, of course. And one remembers that painters in the Renaissance often left parts of their canvases to be worked out by students, and that in the flourishing period of the concerto the cadenza at the end of the first movement was left to the inventiveness and discretion of the performing soloist. But similar practices have a different, more polemical meaning today, in the present post-Romantic era of the arts. When painters such as Joseph Albers, Ellsworth Kelly, and Andy Warhol assign portions of the work, say, the painting in of the colors themselves, to a friend or the local gardener; when musicians such as Stockhausen, John Cage, and Luigi Nono invite collaboration from performers by leaving opportunities for random effects, switching around the order of the score, and improvisations—they are changing the ground rules which most of us employ to recognize a work of art. They are saying what art need not be. At least, not necessarily.

The primary feature of the new sensibility is that its model product is not the literary work, above all, the novel. A new nonliterary culture exists today, of whose very existence, not to mention significance, most literary intellectuals are entirely unaware. This new establishment includes certain painters, sculptors, architects, social planners, film-makers, TV technicians, neurologists, musicians, electronics engineers, dancers, philosophers, and sociologists. (A few poets and prose writers can be included.) Some of the basic texts for this new cultural alignment are to be found in the writings of Nietzsche, Wittgenstein, Antonin Artaud, C. S. Sherrington, Buckminster Fuller, Marshall McLuhan, John Cage, André Breton, Roland Barthes, Claude Lévi-Strauss, Sigfried Giedion, Norman O. Brown, and Gyorgy Kepes.

Those who worry about the gap between "the two cultures," and this means virtually all literary intellectuals in England and America, take for granted a notion of culture which decidedly needs reexamining. It is the notion perhaps best expressed by Matthew Arnold (in which the central cultural act is the making of literature, which is itself understood as the criticism of culture). Simply ignorant of the vital and enthralling (so called "avant-garde") developments in the other arts, and blinded by their personal investment in the perpetuation of the older notion of culture, they continue to cling to literature as the model for creative statement.

What gives literature its preeminence is its heavy burden of "content," both reportage and moral judgment. (This makes it possible for most English and American literary critics to use literary works mainly as texts, or even pretexts, for social and cultural diagnosis—rather than concentrating on the properties of, say, a given novel or a play as an art work.) But the model arts of our time are actually those with much less content, and a much cooler mode of moral judgment—like music, films, dance, architecture, painting, sculpture. The practice of these arts—all of which draw profusely, naturally, and without embarrassment, upon science and technology—is the locus of the new sensibility.

The problem of "the two cultures," in short, rests upon an un-educated, uncontemporary grasp of our present cultural situation. It arises from the ignorance of literary intellectuals (and of scientists with a shallow knowledge of the arts, like the scientist-novelist C. P. Snow himself) of a new culture, and its emerging sensibility. In fact, there can be no divorce between science and technology, on the one hand, and art, on the other, any more than there can be a divorce between art and the forms of social life. Works of art, psychological forms, and social forms all reflect each other, and change with each other. But, of course, most people are slow to come to terms with such changes—especially today, when the changes are occurring with an unprecedented rapidity. Marshall McLuhan has described human history as a succession of acts of technological extension of human capacity, each of which works a radical change upon our environment and our ways of thinking, feeling, and valuing. The tendency, he remarks, is to upgrade the old environment into art form (thus Nature became a vessel of aes-thetic and spiritual values in the new industrial environment) "while the new conditions are regarded as corrupt and degrading." Typically, it is only certain artists in any given era who "have the resources and temerity to live in immediate contact with the en-vironment of their age. . . . That is why they may seem to be 'ahead of their time.'. . . More timid people prefer to accept the . . . previ-ous environment's values as the continuing reality of their time. Our natural bias is to accept the new gimmick (automation, say) as a thing that can be accommodated in the old ethical order." Only in the terms of what McLuhan calls the old ethical order does the problem of "the two cultures" appear to be a genuine problem. It is not a problem for most of the creative artists of our time (among whom one could include very few novelists) be-cause most of these artists have broken, whether they know it or not, with the Matthew Arnold notion of culture, finding it histori-cally and humanly obsolescent.

The Matthew Arnold notion of culture defines art as the criticism of life—this being understood as the propounding of moral, social, and political ideas. The new sensibility understands art as the extension of life—this being understood as the representation of (new) modes of vivacity. There is no necessary denial of the role of moral evaluation here. Only the scale has changed; it has become less gross, and what it sacrifices in discursive explicitness it gains in accuracy and subliminal power. For we are what we are able to see (hear, taste, smell, feel) even more powerfully and profoundly than we are what furniture of ideas we have stocked in our heads. Of course, the proponents of "the two cultures" crisis continue to observe a desperate contrast between unintelligible, morally neutral science and technology, on the one hand, and morally committed, human-scale art on the other. But matters are not that simple, and never were. A great work of art is never simply (or even mainly) a vehicle of ideas or of moral sentiments. It is, first of all, an object modifying our consciousness and sensibility, changing the composition, however slightly, of the humus that nourishes all specific ideas and sentiments. Outraged humanists, please note. There is no need for alarm. A work of art does not cease being a moment in the conscience of mankind when moral conscience is understood as only one of the functions of consciousness.

Sensations, feelings, the abstract forms and styles of sensibility count. It is to these that contemporary art addresses itself. The basic unit for contemporary art is not the idea, but the analysis of and extension of sensations. (Or if it is an "idea," it is about the form of sensibility.) Rilke described the artist as someone who works "toward an extension of the regions of the individual senses"; McLuhan calls artists "experts in sensory awareness." And the most interesting works of contemporary art (one can begin at least as far back as French symbolist poetry) are adventures in sensation, new "sensory mixes." Such art is, in principle, experimental —not out of an elitist disdain for what is accessible to the majority, but precisely in the sense that science is experimental. Such an art is also notably apolitical and undidactic, or, rather, infra-didactic.

When Ortega y Gasset wrote his famous essay *The Dehumanization of Art* in the early 1920's, he ascribed the qualities of modern art (such as impersonality, the ban on pathos, hostility to the past, playfulness, willful stylization, absence of ethical and political commitment) to the spirit of youth which he thought dominated our age.* In retrospect, it seems this "dehumanization" did not signify the recovery of childlike innocence, but was rather a very adult, knowing response. What other response than anguish, followed by anesthesia and then by wit and the elevating of intelligence over sentiment, is possible as a response to the social disorder and mass atrocities of our time, and—equally important for our sensibilities, but less often remarked on—to the unprecedented change in what rules our environment from the intelligible and visible to that which is only with difficulty intelligible, and is invisible? Art, which I have characterized as an instrument for modifying and educating sensibility and consciousness, now operates in an environment which cannot be grasped by the senses.

Buckminster Fuller has written:

> In World War I industry suddenly went from the visible to the invisible base, from the track to the trackless, from the wire to the wireless, from visible structuring to invisible structuring in alloys. The big thing about World War I is that man went off the sensorial spectrum forever as the prime criterion of accrediting innovations. . . . All major advances since World War I have been in the infra and the ultrasensorial frequencies of the electromagnetic spectrum. All the important technical affairs of men today are invisible. . . . The old masters, who were sensorialists, have unleashed a Pandora's box of nonsensorial controllable phenomena, which they had avoided accrediting up to that time. . . . Suddenly they lost their true mastery, because from then on they didn't personally understand what was going on. If you don't understand you cannot master. . . . Since World War I, the old masters have been extinct. . . .

But, of course, art remains permanently tied to the senses. Just

---

* Ortega remarks, in this essay: "Were art to redeem man, it could do so only by saving him from the seriousness of life and restoring him to an unexpected boyishness."

as one cannot float colors in space (a painter needs some sort of surface, like a canvas, however neutral and textureless), one cannot have a work of art that does not impinge upon the human sensorium. But it is important to realize that human sensory awareness has not merely a biology but a specific history, each culture placing a premium on certain senses and inhibiting others. (The same is true for the range of primary human emotions.) Here is where art (among others things) enters, and why the interesting art of our time has such a feeling of anguish and crisis about it, however playful and abstract and ostensibly neutral morally it may appear. Western man may be said to have been undergoing a massive sensory anesthesia (a concomitant of the process that Max Weber calls "bureaucratic rationalization") at least since the Industrial Revolution, with modern art functioning as a kind of shock therapy for both confounding and unclosing our senses.

One important consequence of the new sensibility (with its abandonment of the Matthew Arnold idea of culture) has already been alluded to—namely, that the distinction between "high" and "low" culture seems less and less meaningful. For such a distinction—inseparable from the Matthew Arnold apparatus—simply does not make sense for a creative community of artists and scientists engaged in programming sensations, uninterested in art as a species of moral journalism. Art has always been more than that, anyway.

Another way of characterizing the present cultural situation, in its most creative aspects, would be to speak of a new attitude toward pleasure. In one sense, the new art and the new sensibility take a rather dim view of pleasure. (The great contemporary French composer Pierre Boulez entitled an important essay of his twenty years ago, "Against Hedonism in Music.") The seriousness of modern art precludes pleasure in the familiar sense—the pleasure of a melody that one can hum after leaving the concert hall, of characters in a novel or play whom one can recognize, identify with, and dissect in terms of realistic psychological motives, of a beautiful landscape or a dramatic moment represented on a canvas. If hedonism means sustaining the old ways in which we have found pleasure in art (the old sensory and psychic modalities), then the new art is antihedonistic. Having one's sensorium challenged or stretched hurts. The new serious music hurts one's ears, the new painting does not graciously reward one's sight, the new films and the few interesting new prose works do not go down easily. The commonest complaint about the films of Antonioni or the narratives of Beckett or Burroughs is that they are hard to look at or to read, that they are "boring." But the charge of boredom is really hypocritical. There is, in a sense, no such thing as boredom. Boredom is only another name for a certain species of frustration. And the new languages which the interesting art of our time speaks are frustrating to the sensibilities of most educated people.

But the purpose of art is always, ultimately, to give pleasure— though our sensibilities may take time to catch up with the forms of pleasure that art in a given time may offer. And, one can also say that, balancing the ostensible antihedonism of serious contemporary art, the modern sensibility is more involved with pleasure in the familiar sense than ever. Because the new sensibility demands less "content" in art, and is more open to the pleasures of "form" and style, it is also less snobbish, less moralistic—in that it does not demand that pleasure in art necessarily be associated with edification. If art is understood as a form of discipline of the feelings and a programming of sensations, then the feeling (or sensation) given off by a Rauschenberg painting might be like that of a song by the Supremes. The brio and elegance of Budd Boetticher's *The Rise and Fall of Legs Diamond* or the singing style of Dionne Warwick can be appreciated as a complex and pleasurable event. They are experienced without condescension.

This last point seems to me worth underscoring. For it is important to understand that the affection which many younger artists and intellectuals feel for the popular arts is not a new philistinism (as has so often been charged) or a species of anti-intellectualism or some kind of abdication from culture. The fact that many of the most serious American painters, for example, are also fans of "the new sound" in popular music is *not* the result of the search for mere diversion or relaxation; it is not, say, like Schoenberg also playing tennis. It reflects a new, more open way of looking at the world and at things in the world, our world. It does not mean the renunciation of all standards: There is plenty of stupid popular music, as well as inferior and pretentious "avant-garde" paintings, films, and music. The point is that there *are* new standards, new standards of beauty and style and taste. The new sensibility is defiantly pluralistic; it is dedicated both to an excruciating seriousness and to fun and wit and nostalgia. It is also extremely history-conscious; and the voracity of its enthusiasms (and of the supercession of these enthusiasms) is very high-speed and hectic. From the vantage point of this new sensibility, the beauty of a machine or of the solution to a mathematical problem, of a painting by Jasper Johns, of a film by Jean-Luc Godard, and of the personalities and music of the Beatles is equally accessible.

a **d**ialogue: ——→

6

Q. & A.

— GERALD E. STEARN

31 even hercules had to clean the augean stables but once! —MC LUHAN

Marshall McLuhan and I met twice over a period of six weeks and tape-recorded twenty hours of random discussions. Later I transcribed his remarks and my questions and shaped them into a formal interview. In our two meetings, so far as possible, I limited myself to the role of cipher. I never argued a case, nor did I take it upon myself to disagree with what might be regarded as an evasive or incomplete reply.

The following dialogue is arranged in a pattern similar to that of the book's structure—the questions directed at McLuhan follow, roughly, the order of presentation of the material used to demonstrate the evolution of his system of analysis and the range of his critical adversaries. Obviously, McLuhan did not "answer" all of his critics; and his responses are in no way a formal defense of his views. He seemed quite charmed by this method of critical involvement and considered the dialogue not an opportunity to destroy opponents so much as a playful exercise in the development of his own thoughts.

* * *

q. will there ever be silence? —GERALD E. STEARN
a. objects are unobservable. only relationships among objects are observable. —MARSHALL MC LUHAN

STEARN: What originally led to your interest in media and the effect of media upon our culture?

McLUHAN: I was gradually made aware of these things by other people—artists, the new anthropological studies. As you become aware of the different modes of experience in other cultures—and watch them transformed by new, Western technologies—it is difficult to avoid observation. It becomes inevitable to assume that what happens to other people and cultures can happen to us. My present interest is an extension of, and derivative of, my literary work.

266

If I could get a team of media students going, I would happily retire back into literary studies. I find media analysis very much more exciting now simply because it affects so many more people. One measure of the importance of anything is: Who is affected by it? In our time, we have devised ways of making the most trivial event affect everybody. One of the consequences of electronic environments is the total involvement of people in people. The Orientals created caste systems as an area of classified immunity.

Here perhaps my own religious faith has some bearing. I think of human charity as a total responsibility of all, for all. Therefore, my energies are directed at far more than mere political or democratic intent. Democracy as a by-product of certain technologies, like literacy and mechanical industry, is not something that I would take very seriously. But democracy as it belongs very profoundly with Christianity is something I take very seriously indeed.

There have been many more religious men than I who have not made even the most faltering steps in this direction. Once I began to move in this direction, I began to see that it had profound religious meaning. I do not think it my job to point this out. For example, the Christian concept of the mystical body—all men as members of the body of Christ—this becomes technologically a fact under electronic conditions. However, I would not try to theologize on the basis of my understanding of technology. I don't have a background in scholastic thought, never having been raised in any Catholic institution. Indeed, I have been bitterly reproached by my Catholic confrères for my lack of scholastic terminology and concepts.

STEARN: When one looks back at your first book, *The Mechanical Bride*, it appears as a strident, moral tract. What is your present attitude toward the *Bride* and how is it related to your more recent interests?

McLUHAN: *Mechanical Bride* is a good example of a book that was completely negated by TV. All the mechanical assumptions of American life have been shifted since TV; it's become an organic culture. Femininity has moved off the photographic, glamor cake altogether into the all-involving tactile mode. Femininity used to be a mingling of visual things. Now it's almost entirely nonvisual. I happened to observe it when it was reaching the end of its term, just before TV.

In 1936, when I arrived at Wisconsin, I confronted classes of freshmen and I suddenly realized that I was incapable of understanding them. I felt an urgent need to study their popular culture: advertising, games, movies. It was pedagogy, part of my teaching program. To meet them on their grounds was my strategy in pedagogy: the world of pop culture. Advertising was a very convenient form of approach. I used advertising in the *Bride* because of legal considerations—no permissions were needed. Otherwise I would have used picture stories of any sort from movies, magazines, anywhere. I had thirty or forty slides and gave little talks to student groups. I invited them to study these ads. In England, at Cambridge, when I arrived there, it had become popular to look at films and the popular culture around us as something to be studied and understood as a "language." Wyndham Lewis did various studies on pop culture. Leavis has a book called *Culture and Environment.* There was a similar interest in popular speech idioms, language, the *Wake. The Waste Land* is full of these pop-cult forms. Pound's *Cantos* have similar forms. Pound has a very useful guide to the *Cantos* called *Kulchur.* In doing the *Bride* I was merely trailing behind some interesting predecessors. I discovered that when you take anything out of the daily newspapers and put it on the screen, people go into a fit of laughter. Like Mort Sahl. He would take random items from the press and read them out to an audience straightforwardly. People never notice the outrageous humor until something is removed from its form. Because it's environmental and invisible. The moment you translate it into another medium it becomes visible—and hilarious.

Movies on TV are, in a sense, a parody. Just using one form over another form creates that comic effect. When movies were new it was suggested that they were a parody of life. The transcript of ordinary visual life into a new medium created hilarious comedy. The word parody means a road that goes alongside another road. A movie is a visual track that goes alongside another visual track, creating complete terror. I did take time to read the language of the form and discovered that most people couldn't read that visual language. If I merely reprinted ads, without any appended dialogue, the book would have been hilarious in any case. That kind of book ought to be an annual. When you change its environment you flash perception onto it.

In the *Bride* there is far more following of lines of force than simply moral judgments.

Wyndham Lewis was a great influence on me because of his pop-cult analysis. I found Lewis far too moralistic for my tastes. I greatly admired his *method*. Lewis looked at everything as a painter first. His moral judgments never interested me. He was horrified by Bergson and the time philosophy because it seemed to him to destroy various aspects of our Western culture. He said the whole Western culture was based on sight. But he moralized all his life about "ear people" like Bergson who were undermining the visual facets of Western culture. He attacked Spengler in the same way.

Lewis Carroll looked through the looking glass and found a kind of space-time which is the normal mode of electronic man. Before Einstein, Carroll had already entered that very sophisticated universe of Einstein. Each moment, for Carroll, had its own space and its own time. Alice makes her own space and time. Einstein, not Lewis Carroll, thought this was astonishing.

STEARN: Did you learn anything from editing *Explorations* or from your contributors?

McLUHAN: Giedion influenced me profoundly. *Space, Time and Architecture* was one of the great events of my lifetime. Giedion gave us a language for tackling the structural world of architecture and artifacts of many kinds in the ordinary environment. He learned this language from his preceptor, Wölfflin, whose principles of art history revolutionized the entire language of art criticism at the end of the nineteenth and the beginning of the twentieth centuries.

Wölfflin, in turn, had studied with Burckhardt. But Wölfflin was a much abler man than Burckhardt. He moved the European world into a haptic orbit and discovered the structure of various art

schools. He approached them not descriptively—not by classification—but structurally. Giedion began to study the environment as
a structural, artistic work—he saw language in streets, buildings,
the very texture of form.

We started *Explorations* when we felt we had something to say.
We stopped it when we felt that we had said it. We decided to write
books and free ourselves from the kind of slavery involved in a
repetitive operation like publishing a journal. We did discover that
readers like a journal that appears on an irregular basis. Most
readers of most journals are very unhappy about their regular
appearance.

STEARN: Blissett's parody-critique, written in 1957, seems to have
anticipated some of the later criticism directed at the *Galaxy* and
Understanding.

McLUHAN: The complaints about irregular, disconnected, irrational elements in *Explorations* show a complete unawareness. Connected sequential discourse, which is thought of as rational, is
really visual. It has nothing to do with reason as such. Reasoning
does not occur on single planes or in a continuous, connected
fashion. The mind leapfrogs. It puts things together in all sorts of
proportions and ratios instantly. To put down thoughts in coded,
lineal ways was a discovery of the Greek world. It is not done this
way, for example, in the Chinese world. But to deny that the Chinese have access to reason would be ridiculous. They do not
have rational discourse at all by Western standards. They reason
by the act of interval, not by the act of connection. In the electric
age we are moving into a world where not the connection but the
interval becomes the crucial event in organization. For people to
waste their time lamenting the disappearance of logic and rational,
connected discourse when they are really under the illusion that
this is actually related to man's reasoning powers is simple non-
fact. It is rather sad for people to waste a great deal of energy and
moral indignation on things that don't exist, and never have.

On the other hand to say or even suggest that continuous connected discourse is valueless is something I would *never* say. All
that I will say is that it isn't rational, it's visual. Why not be accu-

rate? If you're going to order life visually, that is how it is done. Now if you're going to be rational you may have many other ideas about spacing. Once you move into an ear world (for example, the musician moves by interval, not by connection), once you move out of the visual order, you at once discover new modes of rationality. In the electric age we are discovering new modes of rationality. I am not saying this is a "good" thing. I'm simply trying to understand what is happening and how it's done.

All that Blissett is attempting to record here is the sense of lack of connection between events in *Explorations*. The moment you see that the problem is to invent tools—probes—rather than to make continuous (I never saw the parody before today) connected statements, you alarm writers like Blissett. They really think that connected statements are a means of organizing energy and perceptions. They are actually a way of reporting things already seen. You take a statement and turn it around, using it as probe into the environment instead of using it descriptively—as a means of packaging information, already picked up—the idea of using language and statement as probe in this sense just baffles them. On the other hand if they waited around long enough to find out what you were doing they might say, "Oh, why didn't you tell me." If just never dawns on these people, and they're so put off! Their perceptions are so irritated by what they immediately encounter that they never wait around to discover anything. The immediate effect of encountering new forms is, for many people, the cause for scampering back into old ones, where they feel more at home, more comfortable. They are using the language of the consumer, of the person who collects impressions and who is a passive receiver of impressions. This is the language of the dilettante, the amateur, of the fragile, ever so delicate, person. These people put all their energies into dull and conventional materials, second and third rate matters.

Explorations became an international magazine because it had something to say to the world, something new. It excited a lot of people. The idea that one could run something of real international interest and excitement in a backward area like Canada charmed them. Canadians are all a very humble bunch. They take it for granted that everything they do must be second rate. Carpenter and

I just blithely assumed that, since nearly everything in the world is second rate at best, there was no reason why we couldn't do something that was first rate right here. So it happened.

STEARN: The anthropologist, Dell Hymes, claims that some of your comparisons go to "ludicrous extremes" and he cites your remarks in the *Galaxy* that "print . . . made bad grammar possible" and: "Nobody ever made a grammatical error in a nonliterate society."

McLUHAN: Obviously he's not talking about native societies. He is talking about illiterate American speech. Natives are bewildered when they hear grammatical errors in their tongue committed by visiting anthropologists who don't know how to speak Urdu or Eskimo. Until anthropologists arrive, the native has never heard a grammatical error in his own tongue. Suppose you made a grammatical error in slang. No child ever made a grammatical error in slang. It would just be funny. Slang is an oral form in which we have infallibility. On the other hand, try to write down slang and everybody is going to make mistakes. Etienne Gilson is fond of using American slang and frequently gets it wrong—"Now we come to zee brass tacks."

One of the more unfortunate features of the entire anthropological enterprise in the twentieth century is that its practitioners are almost entirely and unconsciously literate. They approach structures of nonliterate and oral societies with many of the expectations and patterns which they have acquired from their own highly literate society. Margaret Mead and I have discussed this at some length. She told me of a strange event that occurred in the Admiralty Islands. When she returned there, she had copies of some of her books. Some of the natives noticed that the copies were the same. They got very excited. This was the first time they had seen two books that were alike. They were so excited they said, "They're the same! They're the same!" Now this is an oral, illiterate response to literacy. The idea that you can have the same thing repeated exactly was, to them, a miracle. Now that is a genuine and legitimate response to the printed word. Literary people have never had that response.

The anthropologists of our time have been extremely guilty of importing, uncritically, literate assumptions into nonliterate areas of study; of using models of perception that have no relevance to their materials. These models are constructed of literacy, visual points of view. Anthropologists, for example, assume that vision, as they perceive it in its Western mode, is normal to mankind, that other people see this way too. Anthropologists write about these societies without correcting the bias of their own visual habits. I have been much influenced by anthropology in the sense that I have uncovered material very useful in studying media. Hymes is a very good example of the uncritical, literate anthropologist importing literate assumptions into a nonliterate *world*.

Ted Carpenter has written me about the Hymes critique of the *Galaxy*:

> Hymes is bluffing. He pretends that much is known about the shifting of sense ratios by the new extensions of man. The authorities he cites make no contribution to this subject, nor do anthropologists or linguists generally. They cannot even be trusted to recognize the significance of such an approach when they encounter it. Hymes is merely defending his own unconscious, literate stake in a field he doesn't understand.

> Anthropologists see themselves as daring explorers, way out in front. Most are actually nineteenth century in outlook. They deal with data atomistically and feel free to abstract them and create regularities for them. Their visual models are highly ethnocentric, totally ill-suited to understanding nonliterate patterns. Models offered by Joyce, Klee, and Pound are ignored. The alienation theme of Man vs. Environment, so dear to the nineteenth century, survives among them like a watch ticking in the pocket of a dead man.

> Yet anthropologists hold a monopoly on a body of data of prime importance to the understanding of environments as natural extensions of man. Their models blind them to the significance of these data; professionalism prevents them from accepting ideas which threaten existing management. Hymes' review is a classic example of this combined blindness and fear.

In objecting to McLuhan's forceful style, Hymes misses the point that technology is explicitness. Rumors that Al Smith ate peas with a knife would not have hurt him prior to 1920. Americans didn't become self-conscious about eating habits until films made these explicit. Remember the film comedy with eyeglasses equipped with windshield-wipers for protection while eating grapefruit? Such films are now immensely popular in Russia.

Language etiquette was linked to print, just as table etiquette was linked to film. The sudden interest in linguistic decorum during the reign of James I arose when print made grammar clearly visible. Similarly, typewriters increased dictionary sales. Bad penmanship could no longer conceal bad spelling.

The press and typewriter speeded up information flow, creating the need for more explicit rules of language, just as the motorcar created the need for more explicit traffic regulations.

It was Western man, not McLuhan, who carried the individualizing capacity of print, and the lineal nature of the thinking it fosters, to "ludicrous extremes."

McLuhan suggests that lineal thinking alone is not capable of grasping and understanding our world in a global manner. He offers no single-minded, oversimplified exegesis, but opens the way for multiple models simultaneously applied. One obstacle to such an all-at-once analysis is the single-minded, oversimplified, obsolete approach which Hymes seems to be saying offers "an adequate view of human history."

STEARN: Perhaps the most repeated and passionate dissents emerge from what many critics call your historicism. John Simon's charge —that you play the history of ideas game none too well—has been repeated quite often. You have said that without radio, no Hitler; that the Russians have an "ear" culture and consequently found the U-2 a sensory intruder, not merely the belligerent act of a hostile power.

McLuhan: The Russians find it unbearable to have "eyes" around their environment. Just as we hate the idea of having "ears" in our own—*vide*: the microphone in the embassy eagle. The Russians live much more by ear than we do. Their new high-rise apartments are at once transformed into villages. All communication between fellow apartment dwellers is like that of a village square. They must live this way. In India, for example, when they tried to put in cold running water, it pulled the village women away from the well. This destroyed community life. They had to remove the pipes. You cannot put running water into an aural community without distressful circumstances.

When you make a structural analysis, you follow lines of force and follow not just one but many, at various levels of the culture, observing patterns. All semiliterate or "backward" cultures are aural cultures, whether it's Ghana or China. They organize space differently, at all times. The Eskimo world is an ear one. When asked to draw maps, they draw areas they've never seen. From their kyacks they've heard water lapping against shores. They map by ear and it later proves quite adequate when checked by aerial photo. Except that there is always an exaggerated area where they've camped. That part receives a stress or bulge in their map. The natural world of nonliterate man is structured by the total field of hearing. This is very difficult for literary people to grasp. The hand has no point of view. The ear has no point of view.

Years ago when I was working with Carpenter on anthropological matters, I used acoustic and auditory space frequently as a basic counterploy to visual Western man. I gave it up because I found that the literary people made desperate attempts to visualize auditory space. But you cannot visualize auditory space, that is: a total field of simultaneous relations, without center or margin. Carpenter has remarked that anthropological materials are now beginning to be made up and published by natives themselves— their own stories are being retold by natives themselves. And the results are totally different from what the anthropologists said earlier. We now realize that a nonvisual culture cannot be reported by a visual man.

A prose statement is a reduction to visual terms, like legal language—which is an extreme, unrealistic case of visual organization.

It isn't accidental that the primary arts of Russia are music and ballet. They are not a literary people at all. The world of Dostoevski is not literary. It's a newspaper world, like Edgar Allen Poe or Dickens (an Ann Landers type). This does not contradict the fact that they take literacy far more seriously (and literally) than the West does. Russians, for example, are quite agitated about the telephone.

Russia never had a Renaissance, in terms of space. Realism, perspective art, is avant-garde for them. When you have the means of realistic representation, you also have the means of mechanical production. Mechanical production comes out of visual realism in the Western world. What we think of as realism is to them (Russians) absolute fantasy.

Kafka isn't realism in our world. It's allegorical fantasy (like Bosch). Similarly, Western visual man would have great difficulty in "reading" a tactile piece of information.

To pre-literate man, space was sacred.

A lot of this aural culture is found now in the Negro world. The reason that they are so far ahead of us in the arts is, quite simply, that they haven't trained their visual sense to the point of suppressing the other senses. In music—dance and song—Negroes are ahead.

The generations gap between parents and children is quite simple —children are auditory, nonvisual in their orientation. Teen-agers are returning to a backward phase.

All literate cultures sentimentalize all primitive cultures, whether as anthropologists or new neighbors of Negroes. We sentimentalize their primitive state automatically as superior to our own. This confuses a lot of perception, of course.

STEARN: Is the Cold War then merely a sensory conflict?

MCLUHAN: We have a huge cold war going on inside our own borders concerning territorial conflicts, ambitions, jurisdictions, economic demands, etc. These are hugely exaggerated misunderstandings born of sensory divergencies. Our inability to understand them mutually exasperates our negotiations in dealing with them. This exasperation is quite independent of the actual sources of conflict. The same with Castro and dealing with Cuba, with its intensely backward, aural culture. The Cuban way of thinking and feeling about problems is quite alien to our modes of understanding. It's the same with the American Southerner, who has very backward, aural ways of thinking and feeling. It's very hard for the literate North to give him credit for being honest and sincere at all.

De Tocqueville was able to predict certain developments in American culture by contrasting the lack of auditory background in America with its ability to blueprint its development in visual, literate terms. He was making equations. He encountered a new land in which literacy had no opposition, except from Indians. Visual literacy marched unimpeded by any other sensory mode. For the first time in the history of the world, a great new technology encountered a great, new space.

De Tocqueville could not blueprint older, European cultures. But to an ear-oriented European, the American literate culture was quite visible. Mrs. Trollope spoke about auditory, nonvisual factors —which the English even in our time find impossible to deal with. They are unable to realize that they have a class struggle based upon ear culture. We acept literacy and they don't. Literacy wipes out tonality. Americans have never permitted a tone of voice to dictate a man's importance in this world. The English use that criterion entirely as a basis of judging human excellence. In highly literate, visual America it is correct spelling and grammar, not correct intonation. T. S. Eliot lacked an English voice and they did not accept him there. Pound just romped through England wearing a mask of outrageous Yankee dialect. They accepted that. The British are unaware of their auditory culture; we're quite unaware of our visual culture.

STEARN: Similarly, you claim that the war in Vietnam is, more or less, a creature of television.

McLUHAN: Without an informed public there would be no war. We live in an informational environment and war is conducted with information. TV news coverage of Vietnam has been a disaster as far as Washington is concerned because it has alienated people altogether from that war. Newspaper coverage would never alienate people from the war because it's "hot," it doesn't involve. TV does and creates absolute nausea. It's like public hangings—if there were public hangings there would be no hangings. Because public hangings would *involve* people. The distant statistical fact— "At 5:30 this morning so and so was executed"—that's hot. Washington is still fighting a "hot" war, as it were, by newspaper means and the old technologies. The effects of the new technologies on war coverage is not something Washington is prepared to cope with. In Washington people do not concede that the news on TV and news in the press are dissimilar.

TV has begun to dissolve the fabric of American life. All the assumptions—all the ground rules—based on visuality, superficiality, blueprinting, connectedness, equality, sameness—disappear with TV.

STEARN: If you shut off TV, then we would end the war in Vietnam and at the same time set back the civil rights movement?

McLUHAN: Oh yes. But there is an alternative: Put hundreds of extra lines on the TV image, step up its visual intensity to a new hot level. This might serve to reverse the whole effect of TV. It might make the TV image photographic, slick, like movies: hot and detached. Bell Telephone is now operating with eight-thousand-line TV images, not eight hundred, quite beyond the fidelity of any known photographic process.

STEARN: Why hasn't this been tried?

McLUHAN: You might well inquire. No one believes these factors have any effect whatever on our human reactions. It's like the old days when people played around with radium, painting watch dials and they licked the brushes. They didn't believe radium could affect people.

STEARN: George Steiner claims that you have much to tell us about Freud and Marx. Have they influenced you at all?

McLuhan: Marx's statement should have been: "If you want to change the world, you have to understand it." Freud's notion of ever-increasing repression is simply a remark on the ever-increasing visuality, blueprinting of society. Electronic conditions provided a release from that visuality. I've read Freud and Jung and used them to make discoveries of my own—just as any literary person has been influenced by them. For example, Freud's *Interpretation of Dreams* reveals the amazing power that all people have in their dream life of invention and poetic discovery, that the most ordinary person in his dream life is a tremendous poet. Most Freudians are concerned with the subject matter of this poetry. That never interested me. I was always fascinated by the amazing ingenuity, symmetry, and inventiveness of the dreamer. We all have these tremendous unused powers which we use surreptitiously. We are afraid to use them in our waking lives. Except the artist. The artist uses in his waking life the powers an ordinary person would use in his dream life. The creative man has his dream life while awake. This is the meaning of the title *Finnegans Wake*— mankind is approaching that state of dreaming wide awake. Come Marconi, as environment, dream life became art form. The old romantic dream becomes art form.

Marx was looking in the rear-view mirror of Adam Smith and Ricardo. I'm looking in the rear-view mirror of Joyce, Carroll, the Symbolists, Adolph Hildebrand. They related the sensory life of metomorphosis and transformation in contact with new technology.

Stearn: George Steiner has remarked adversely on your concept of the "global village."

McLuhan: This is amazing confusion of mind here on the part of Mr. Steiner. There is more diversity, less conformity under a single roof in any family than there is with the thousands of families in the same city. The more you create village conditions, the more discontinuity and division and diversity. The global village absolutely insures maximal disagreement on all points. It never occurred to me that uniformity and tranquillity were the properties of the global village. It has more spite and envy. The spaces and times are pulled out from between people. A world in which people encounter each other in depth all the time.

The tribal-global village is far more divisive—full of fighting—than any nationalism ever was. Village is fission, not fusion, in depth. People leave small towns to *avoid* involvement. The big city *lined* them with its uniformity and impersonal milieu. They sought propriety and in the city, money is made by uniformity and repeatability. Where you have craftsmanlike diversity, you make art, not money. The village is not the place to find ideal peace and harmony. Exact opposite. Nationalism came out of print and provided an extraordinary relief from global village conditions. I don't *approve* of the global village. I say we live in it.

It's like the universe. Margaret Fuller said, "I accept the universe," and Carlyle said, "Yes, you'd better."

I accept media as I accept cosmos. They assume I'm for or against Gutenberg. Bunk! I think of technologies as highly identifiable objects made by our own bodies. They feel that technologies are strange, alien intruders from outer space.

STEARN: When you say that technologies are extensions of man, are they as well extensions of man's will?

McLUHAN: In the ordinary sense of subliminal wish and drive—yes. Man, however, never intends the cultural consequences of any extension of himself.

STEARN: What are we to do with all this information? How does it affect our consciousness?

McLUHAN: When man is overwhelmed by information, he resorts to myth. Myth is inclusive, time-saving, and fast. Children are driven today into mythic thinking. When environmental effects shift beyond a certain point, everybody agrees on a new strategy.

To be conscious or unconscious is to make a certain order of experience. I possess no theory of consciousness. But that says nothing. Throughout my work, however, I am saying that awareness is being pushed more and more out into the environment. Technology pushes human awareness out into the environment. Art becomes environment. Our environments are made of the highest levels of human consciousness.

STEARN: Many readers have been shocked and confused by what they consider idiosyncratic methods in your work. For example: A number of critics suggest that your books are repetitious and, in Dwight Macdonald's words, "ultimately boring."

McLUHAN: Macdonald's is the kind of confusion that comes to the literary mind when confronted with a drilling operation. Repetition is really drilling. When I'm using a probe, I drill. You repeat naturally when you're drilling. But the levels are changing all the time. Macdonald thinks *that's* repetition. There is a complete unawareness of what is going on in the book. His remark that the book might have been an article reveals another fallacy of the literary mind—that the purpose of facts is for classification. The idea of using facts as probes—as means of getting into new territories—is utterly alien to them. They use facts as classified data, as categories, as packages.

Literally, *Understanding Media* is a kit of tools for analysis and perception. It is to *begin* an operation of discovery. It is not the completed work of discovery. It is intended for practical use. Most of my work in the media is like that of a safecracker. In the beginning I don't know what's inside. I just set myself down in front of the problem and begin to work. I grope, I probe, I listen, I test—until the tumblers fall and I'm in. That's the way I work with all these media.

Depth operations are natural to modern studies in all fields including psychiatry and metallurgy and structural analysis. In order to inspect any situation structurally you have to inspect it from all sides simultaneously, which is a sort of cubist gimmick. A structural approach to a medium means studying its total operation, the *milieu* that it creates—the environment that the telephone or radio or movies or the motorcar created. One would learn very little about the motorcar by looking at it simply as a vehicle that carried people hither and thither. Without understanding the city changes, suburban creations, service changes—the environment it created—one would learn very little about the motorcar. The car then has never really been studied structurally, as a form.

If you look at print not as a conveyer belt of data but as a structure somewhat different from the spoken word, somewhat different from manuscript culture, then you are at once in a world where you have to repeat yourself furiously in order to capture all facets simultaneously. The literary form is truly not adopted to simultaneity and structural awareness and this of course is inherent in the very first acts of writing in early times when a vast amount of human awareness was tossed out. Very little of the qualities of speech can be captured by written form, very little of nuance, very little of the drama and action of speech can be captured by written form whatever. But today, with the oscillograph, tape recorder, and various electronic devices, speech is being felt in depth and discovered in structural multi-facet-ness for the first time in human history. So naturally anybody who has become vividly aware of the many, many structural facets of speech, when confronted with the literary form, is aghast at its impoverished character. It's very abstract—it has eliminated most language and speech from its medium. The moment you begin to look at speech as a structure you quickly understand why writing as a structure really cannot deal with much speech. The great poets, starting with Baudelaire and Rimbaud, were quite aware of this and began to substitute all sorts of new literary techniques as a way of capturing the multi-facet-ness of speech. Symbolism discovered that in order to capture the live drama of speech you have to break up the sentence and break up language. That's what Symbolism means—it comes from the Greek *symbaline*—to break things into bits and reassemble them into patterns. This was a monetary or economic configuration in the Greek world—break things into single bits and give them out to various parties in a transaction. Symbolism attempted to capture a much larger portion of human speech and language. Anybody who has to have a very thorough initiation into Symbolist art—both painterly and poetic—would not really be in a very good position to look at Gutenberg technology or its rivals in electronic circuitry.

Macdonald (and other literary critics) have never thought for one minute about the book as a medium or a structure and how it related itself to other media as a structure, politically, verbally, and so on. It's not peculiar to Macdonald. It's true of the entire academic world, of the whole journalistic world. They have never studied any medium.

STEARN: Are you an "enemy of the book?" John K. Jessup (in the *Yale Review*) claims that you have "sold the pass of reason and joined the assault on it." Your observations have become infatuations. George P. Elliott says your relationship to the book as "form" appears somewhat ambivalent. Raymond Williams' comment that if one follows your argument—specifically that print culture conditions our mind—then paradoxically, if the book [*The Gutenberg Galaxy*] works, "it to some extent annihilates itself." Have you, after Blake, "become what you behold."

McLuhan: It is customary in conventional literary circles to feel uneasy about the status of the book and of literacy in our society. Macdonald and others, heaven knows, are nineteenth not twentieth-century minds. Therefore anybody who looks at it in a kind of clinical spirit is regarded as hostile, and an enemy of the book.

My own motivation in studying all media began with my commitment to literature as a profession and I quickly became aware that literature had a great many enemies. (They are all of our own making. We have created them.) I discovered that the enemies of literature needed very careful scrutiny and study if the literary man was to manage to extricate himself from this new jungle. So the literary people, I became aware, were so uneasy about the surround of enemies that any attention given to literature as such was considered unfortunate and, as Dwight Macdonald says, "gloomy." And it's a past subjunctive. Any attention to the book is regarded as unfriendly because it is felt that the book will not bear scrutiny any more. Now, in the same way, any attention to new media which are in the ascendant, whose gradient is climbing rapidly, is considered as an act of optimism. Anybody who would direct intellectual attention to a new medium must be an optimist because the rear-view look of the nineteenth-century mind in contemplating literature is essentially a pessimistic one. That's why I say "past subjunctive." There are only two cases, you see, in classifying one's relation to almost anything in merely literary terms—you are either "for" or "against." It's as simple as that. So if you write about the book you must be against it because the book is declining in terms of its overall cultural role. If you write about new media in the ascendant, you must be in favor of it. Such is the Western devotion to facts that the mere stating of any case is considered a hostile act. The idea of stating without approval or disapproval is alien to the literary man who finds classification indispensable for order.

STEARN: When Eric Goldman asked you on "The Open Mind" if media change—the electronic revolution of our time, for example —was a "good" or "bad" thing, you replied:

> Now, you see, you have slipped into the literary language of the classifier. The visual man is always trying to check things out by classification and matching.
>
> Goldman: I have set it in the language of the social commentator. You have said something is happening in our society. We now have a medium which is bombarding us, all of our senses.
>
> McLuhan: But when you say "good," is it good in relation to what? You know, the social scientist—
>
> Goldman: Is it good in relation to the established values of the West, let us say?
>
> McLuhan: You remember what the social scientist said to a friend of his: "How is your wife?" And the other social scientist replied, "Do you mean is she better? If so, in relation to what?"

McLuhan: Classification, for the literary man, is the be-all and end-all of observations. That's why Macdonald attempts to classify me. In the medical world, classification is a form of dismissal. If the doctor says it's measles, that's it, it's over with. The rest is just routine. But classification is not the beginning of the study of a problem—it's the end. For me any of these little gestures I make are all tentative probes. That's why I feel free to make them sound as outrageous or extreme as possible. Until you make it extreme, the probe is not very efficient. Probes, to be effective, must have this edge, strength, pressure. Of course they *sound* very dogmatic. That doesn't mean you are committed to them. You may toss them away.

There is an alternative to classification and that is exploration. This doesn't easily register with nineteenth-century minds. Most nineteenth-century minds are helpless in discussing contemporary forms. They have never acquired the verbal means of grappling with a pictorial world. Macdonald has no verbal strategies for even coping with the movies, let alone more subtle or more recent forms, like radio or television.

I'm perfectly prepared to scrap any statement I ever made about any subject once I find that it isn't getting me into the problem. I have no devotion to any of my probes as if they were sacred opinions. I have no proprietary interest in my ideas and no pride of authorship as such. You have to push any idea to an extreme, you have to probe. Exaggeration, in the sense of hyperbole, is a major artistic device in all modes of art. No painter, no musician ever did anything without extreme exaggeration of a form or a mode, until he had exaggerated those qualities that interested him. Wyndham Lewis said: "Art is the expression of a colossal preference" for certain forms of rhythm, color, pigmentation, and structure. The artist exaggerates fiercely in order to register this preference in some material. You can't build a building without huge exaggeration or preference for a certain kind of space.

This question of repetition bothers them most because they are looking for values or a "point of view." Now values, insofar as they register a preference for a particular kind of effect or quality, are a highly contentious and debatable area in every field of discourse. Nobody in the twentieth century has ever come up with any meaningful definition or discussion of "value." It doesn't work any longer in economics, let alone humanist affairs. It is rather fatuous to insist upon values if you are not prepared to understand how they got there and by what they are now being undermined. The mere moralistic expression of approval or disapproval, preference or detestation, is currently being used in our world as a substitute for observation and a substitute for study. People hope that if they scream loudly enough about "values" then others will mistake them for serious, sensitive souls who have higher and nobler perceptions than ordinary people. Otherwise, why would they be screaming.

Anybody who spends his time screaming about values in our modern world is not a serious character. You might as well start screaming about a house that's burning down, shouting, "This is not the act of a serious man!" When your old world is collapsing and everything is changing at a furious pitch, to start announcing your preferences for old values is not the act of a serious person. This is frivolous, fatuous. If you were to knock on the door of one of these critics and say "Sir, there are flames leaping out of your roof, your house is burning," under these conditions he would then say to you, "That's a very interesting point of view. I personally couldn't disagree with you more." That's all these critics are saying. Their house is burning and they're saying, "Don't you have any sense of values, simply telling people about fire when you should be thinking about the serious content, the noble works of the mind?" Value is irrelevant.

STEARN: But if "value is irrelevant" what about the *content* of media? In your discussions with Eric Goldman this same point was raised:

> Goldman: Mr. McLuhan, a number of commentators have said that as they understand your view, you really don't think that changing the contents of television would change much about this process. . . .
>
> McLuhan: No. You may have seen a New Yorker joke. A couple are watching TV, and one says, "When you think of the vast educational potential of TV, aren't you glad it doesn't?"
> This is based on the assumption, you see, that it is the content that does the educating, not the medium. Now, if it should be just the other way around—and very few people have asked themselves anything about that—then it would be understandable why these things happen involuntarily and unasked.

Goldman: Take "Peyton Place." If you put on "Peyton Place"
or if you put on a news documentary, the contents are radically
different in that case, but still from your point of view the
medium is transcending the contents in significance so far as
the person out there is concerned.

McLuhan: It's like changing the temperature in a room. It
doesn't matter what's in the room at all, or what pictures are on
the wall, or who is in the room. If the temperature drops forty
degrees suddenly, the effect on our outlook, our attitude,
is profound.
Media are like that. They just alter the total social temperature.
Since TV, the whole American political temperature has cooled
down, down, down, until the political process is almost
approaching rigor mortis. These facts of media are not the
areas in which they look—after all, the medical profession was
in the habit of looking in the wrong places for causes and
effects for many centuries, and nobody has come up with
any suggestions for how to control media or the social
impact of technologies until now.

McLuhan: Many people would rather be villains than nitwits. It
occurs to me just now that moral vehemence may provide ersatz
dignity for our normal moronic behavior. It would be possible to
extend my media analysis to include the idea that the normal
human condition, when faced with innovation, is that of the brain-
washed idiot who tries to introduce the painfully learned responses
from one situation into new situations where they apply not at all.
The reason that I refrain in the book from pointing out this obvious
moral is owing to the discovery, represented by the book itself, that
this helpless and witless condition of persistent irrelevance of response is unnecessary at the first moment that we recognize this
pattern of response and its causes. It is this discovery that fills
me with optimism. The moralist has instinctively translated my
forward-looking discovery into backward-looking misanthropy.
Moral bitterness is a basic technique for endowing the idiot with
dignity. Guilt and remorse are retrospective by definition and
exempt the guilty party from any redeeming act of expiation or

creative renewal. Guilt and remorse are forms of despair and sloth. Any charge of nonmoral fervor with regard to my work merely points to my own effort to protect reader and critic from the rage and indignation which they have richly earned. For many years I have observed that the moralist typically substitutes anger for perception. He hopes that many people will mistake his irritation for insight. Is this not one of the great attractions of Marxism? While lacking all insight into the processes with which it is concerned, it yet provides an intensely dramatic role for the corporate expression of dissatisfactions that elude the understanding.

Do I "approve of 'Peyton Place' or of Jack Paar?" No! But they're trying to classify Paar with a good or bad "thing," not attempting to find out *what* he's doing or what effect he's having or what's really going on. They are trying to fit him into some sort of encyclopedia of culture. They find *concept* a much more convenient form of human activity than *precept*. They ask me to judge what I observe. Cocteau said: "I don't want to be famous. I just want to be believed." Any artist would say that he doesn't want people to agree or disagree with him. He just wants them to notice. I expect my audience to participate with me in a common act of exploration. I want observations, not agreement. And my own observation of our almost overwhelming cultural gradient toward the primitive —or involvement of all the senses—is attended by complete personal distaste and dissatisfaction. I have no liking for it.

Since, however, this new cultural gradient is the world, the *milieu*, in which I must live and which prepares the students I must teach, I have every motive to understand its constituents, its components, and its operations. I move around through these elements as I hope any scientist would through a world of disease and stress and misery. If a doctor, surgeon or scientist were to become personally agitated about any phenomenon whatever, he would be finished as an explorer or observer. The need to retain an attitude of complete clinical detachment is necessary for survival in this kind of work. It is not an expression of approval or a point of view or outlook. It's only a strategy of survival. Anybody who enters this kind of work with strong feelings of approval or disapproval, nineteenth-century-style point of view, fixed positions, "From where I'm sitting I would say that this is an abomination and degradation of all human values," etc.—anybody who enters any situation in our time with any such commitments has completely polished himself off the scene as an observer. He's had it. So our literary fraternities—nineteenth-century liberals if you like—are completely helpless to even approach the material of their own culture. They are so terrified, so revolted, they don't even know how to get near it and they've never bothered to acquire the means of studying or of observing it.

This so-called primitivism—and it is so fatuous in our time, so uncritical—one of the more ridiculous aspects of Picasso, if you like—it's a form of surfboarding, just riding any old wave that happens to be around. On the other hand, primitivism, D. H. Lawrence style, has become in itself almost a form of *camp*. That is why we have suddenly abandoned it in favor of *camp*, which is a new artistic attitude toward our own junkyard. The sudden resolve to tackle our own junkyard as art work is a hopeful indication that we are prepared after all to look at the environment as that which is capable of formulation, patterning, shaping. It still lacks the awareness of what effects environments have upon us. They still seem to imagine that you can take it or leave it. You know the old literate attitude toward advertising in the thirties: "Personally, I can take it or leave it. I'm just not interested in it." These are the helpless victims of all advertising, these people who think that merely by subjecting themselves to it without taking an interest in it they can be immune. The idea of immunity from environments and environments created by media—so long as one concentrates upon noble content—is a cherished illusion in literary circles. I heard a Tom Swiftie the other day—" 'Don't talk to me of icebergs,' said the captain of the *Titanic* sanctimoniously." The literary professions are somewhat in that position. There are many who imagine that we can disregard these forms and their operations on human sensibilities.

Similarly, there are those who feel they can expose themselves to a hideous urban environment so long as they feel they are in a state of literary grace, as it were; that the forms of life are not in themselves communicative; that only classified data register in our apparatus. People would never dream of valuing their daily experiences in terms of what they happen to see or hear *that* day.

Media like print or radio or television—which are much more environmental and pervasive forms assailing their eyes and ears all day long—these are invisible. It was only in the nineteenth century that artists, painters, and poets began to notice that it was the environmental form itself, as humanly constituted, that really provided people with the models of perception that governed their thoughts. The literary people still cherish the idea that we can fight off the sensory models imposed on our sensorium by environment, by content, by the classifiable part of the environment. It's somewhat the predicament that Malraux sees in his museum without walls. As long as you can see art inside a museum you can, as it were, protect it from all sorts of vulgarity. What happens when photoengraving and various new technologies make it possible to have far more art *outside* walls of museums than *inside*? How do you maintain taste and artistic standards when you can vulgarize the greatest art with an environment? These are the problems assailing the literary world but which have never been looked into by literary people, journalists, and reviewers.

As a person committed to literature and the literary tradition, I have studied these new environments which threaten to dissolve the whole of literary modality, the whole traditions of literary achievement, and I don't think that these are merely threats to classifiable literary values that can be fended off by staunch moralism or lively indignation. We have to discover new patterns of action, new strategies of survival.

This is where William Burroughs comes in with his *Naked Lunch*. When we invent a new technology, we become cannibals. We eat ourselves alive since these technologies are merely extensions of ourselves. The new environment shaped by electric technology is a cannibalistic one that eats people. To survive one must study the habits of cannibals.

STEARN: Why are some critics so outraged by your work?

McLUHAN: Any new demand on human perception, any new pressure to restructure the habits of perception, is the occasion for outraged response. Literary people prefer to deal with their world without disturbance to their perceptual life. In the sixteenth century, when new forms of perception came into existence with things like printing, people underwent terrified responses as recorded by Hieronymous Bosch. The world of Bosch shows space—the old familiar, comfortable, sensible space of all right-thinking people—medieval, iconic, discontinuous. Against that space he juxtaposes the new world of perspective and three-dimensional space with its strange vanishing point and continuum. By putting these two spaces together he gets the "Temptation of St. Anthony." Quite similarly, Kafka takes the plausible, reasonable, literary modes of discourse and narrative and immediately juxtaposes them with something else—creating metamorphosis, change of structure, change of perception. By putting the three-dimensional world against the metamorphic world of changed structure he gets the same degree of nightmare and terror that Bosch got by putting his two spaces together. Now Bosch was merely recording a response of his age to the experience of pictorial space. To the world of the sixteenth century, rational, three-dimensional, pictorial space was a world of absolute horror. There is no literary horror in the presence of mass culture that could match the horror which the sixteenth century felt in the presence of three-dimensional, rational space. To them it was absolute disaster, absolute spiritual disruption. In our time the plunge through the looking glass of Lewis Carroll into the discontinuous, space-time world of electric technology has created the same sense of the plunge into the abyss, the plunge into the irrational on the part of our contemporaries that we associate with existentialism. Our contemporaries are mistaken, in many ways, as to the causes of their present discontent. On the other hand, they are not mistaken about the demands on their sensibilities and on their perceptions. To shift out of a nineteenth-century, rational space into a twentieth-century space-time, noncontinuum is an experience of great discomfort because it puts one's whole sensorium under terrible pressure.

STEARN: "The communications expert," one of your detractors has remarked, "cannot communicate," underlining Jonathan Miller's observation: "McLuhan opens many doors, including the doors of chaos."

McLUHAN: Communication, in the conventional sense, is difficult under any conditions. People prefer *rapport* through smoking or drinking together. There is more communication there than there ever is by verbal means. We can share environments, we can share weather, we can share all sorts of cultural factors together but communication takes place only inadequately and is very seldom understood. For anybody to complain about lack of communication seems a bit naïve. It's actually very rare in human affairs. This has been studied in our time by F. C. Bartlett in his book *Remembering* or I. A. Richards, and others. The most skilled students of poetry, when their reading and understanding of a poem are checked, are found to be monstrously mistaken. It isn't only country bumpkins who have difficulty reading good poems—it is the professors of literature. They too have a very inadequate relation to the world of poetry and prose. Practical criticism created a mortal terror in the academic world in 1929 because it revealed that the best students and professors were quite incapable of reading ordinary poems.

There is a kind of illusion in the world we live in that communications is something that happens all the time, that it's normal. And when it doesn't happen, this is horrendous. Actually, communication is an exceedingly difficult activity. In the sense of a mere point-to-point correspondence between what is said, done, and thought and felt between people—this is the rarest thing in the world. If there is the slightest tangential area of touch, agreement, and so on among people, *that* is communication in a big way. The idea of complete identity is unthinkable. Most people have the idea of communication as something matching between what is said and what is understood. In actual fact, communication is *making*. The person who sees or heeds or hears is engaged in making a response to a situation which is mostly of his own fictional invention. What these critics reveal is that the mystery of communication is the art of making. What they make in difficulties, confusions, vague responses is natural. It goes on all the time in all human affairs as between parents and children, for example. We are always improvising interpretations of everything we do, see, feel, and hear. With ingenuity, with great skill, we improvise responses in order to enable us to continue our relations with our fellows.

Platonic dialogues come out of an oral rather than a literary culture. In a highly literate culture, the dialogue form becomes repugnant. It came back with radio and panel shows. Highly literate people speak on one level, in a monotone. "Good" prose is spoken this way. A level of form, one plane. You cannot discuss multi-relationships on a single plane, in a single form. That's why the poets of our time have broken all the planes and sequences, forming a cubist prose. "I don't follow you"—as if that had anything to do with reasoning. It has to do with lineality and visuality. Logical or connected discourse is highly visual and has very little to do with human reasoning.

STEARN: If you consider your prose an art form, then your books might be considered as extensions of McLuhan, poetical or artistic outbursts having nothing to do with media?

McLUHAN: The "suggestion" is delightful and far too flattering, based, I think, on an almost ethereal whimsy. But it implies that I have used media analysis as a means of private self-expression. Of course when you talk back to the environment you begin to use it as a means of self-expression. However, I am antienvironment. I am not in awe of media or their contents. For example: When you talk back to ads as I did in *The Mechanical Bride*, they become your servants. Since you cannot survive the effects of media if you huddle or hide, you must rush out and kick them in the guts—give them what for—right in the midriff. And they respond very well to this treatment. Media, after all, are only extensions of ourselves. The road to understanding media effects begins with arrogant superiority. If one lacked this sense of superiority—this detachment—it would be quite impossible to write about them. It would be like an octopus attacking the great pyramids.

The propriety of Mandarin prose, the mask of the upper-middle-class Mandarin world, is simply ludicrous. In *Beyond the Fringe*, when the cast wanted to appear superbly ludicrous, they put on that mask. It is a comic mask, good only for laughs. I can speak "slight" Mandarin prose any time, without effort at all. What we call "acceptable prose" moves along on a single plane while puns do not. When you are dealing with a variety of facets simultaneously, you cannot use that kind of prose. I'm talking that kind of prose right now. The kind Miller thinks I cannot write. I talk it all day long in the classroom. I don't use slang, puns—I use Mandarin prose, the only form of discourse I employ. But when I sit down to write about complicated problems moving on several planes, I deliberately move into multi-level prose. This is an art form. The prose that he's complaining about I consider a serious art form. The prose he considers perfectly natural and conventionally acceptable is a kind of prose that comes in with a high visual cultivation and disappears with aural culture.

In the sense that these media are extensions of ourselves—of man—then my interest in them is utterly humanistic. All these technologies and the mechanisms they create are profoundly human. What does one say to people who cannot see extensions of their own bodies and faculties, who find their environments invisible? They call these same environments alien, nonhuman and search for a "point of view." This is simply the inability to observe ordinary data. Content analysis divorces them from reality.

They are talking about art as a blood bank, as stored precious moments of experience. The idea that art's job is to *explore* experience too never dawned on them. The job of art is not to store moments of experience but to explore environments that are otherwise invisible. Art is not a retrieval system of precious moments of past cultures. Art has a live, on-going function. Milton's phrase —"A great book is the precious life-blood of the master spirit." The humanist fault, since the Renaissance, has been to sell art totally short. Since Gutenberg, art has become a retrieval system. Before, art was a means of merging with the cosmos. My critics' notion of art is incredibly defective and feeble. Blake regarded art as exploratory. He thought of it as a means of uniting all the human faculties, aspiring to the unity of the imagination. Art-as-probe is survival. They are saying: "Without art, what impoverished lives we would lead."

Programmers of computers are still using the old print technology—storage. Computers are being asked to do things that belong to the old technology. The real job of the computer is *not* retrieval but discovery. Like the human memory, the process of recall is an act of discovery.

The dream is a way of processing waking experiences in a pattern which is nonlineal, but multi-leveled. Freud is very literary. His technique of analyzing and presenting his material is elegantly literary. And this is why he is the darling of literary men. Jung is much less literary, much less lineal, much more auditory.

STEARN: Do you *personally* enjoy Jack Paar?

McLUHAN: I've only looked at Paar to try to understand TV. I would never dream of looking at Paar for entertainment. I look at advertising in much the same way. I find it diverting.

I use Jack Paar or any successful practitioner of the art of a particular medium as an instrument of observation. I use them as probes. I'm concerned with Paar's content because that belongs to the old medium. Movies used the gramophone. Books used old manuscripts. This is inevitable. The fact that any new medium must use the old medium as content does not raise the factor of values at all. Questions of value should have been raised when that content was new. We do not measure the success or meaning of any particular day of our lives by the things we have said or seen. The actual use of our faculties day by day is never considered. But we do consider it a great advantage to be able to use our eyes, ears, etc. This is the way we use media—as extensions. Therefore it doesn't matter what's on, what matters is that we have use of our faculties. I'm quite prepared to live the life of Confucius or Plato, day in, day out, in my conversations.

Most media, though, are pure poison—TV, for example, has all the effects of LSD. I don't think we should allow this to happen.

I don't think these literary critics are serious. I don't think they're honest. They don't insist on high standards in the daily life use of their faculties. It is only when they see poor content in some old medium that the question arises. If anyone tried to value painting by the subject matter he would be in a very poor position. Years ago, before I wrote the *Bride*, I had a moralistic approach to all environmental facts. I abominated machinery, cities, everything except the most Rousseauistic. Gradually, I became aware of how useless this was and I discovered that artists of the twentieth-century had a different approach and I adopted it.

STEARN: Frank Kermode quoted a letter of yours to the effect that *The Gutenberg Galaxy* might have been expressed as an ideogram and that you are very much concerned with your own problems of communication.

MCLUHAN: I'm trying to get my audience involved in perceptions. So I use their language. The language of their environment.

The idea that the *Galaxy* might have been presented as an ideogram is true. That's the very form it is in. It could also be expressed as a Happening. The word "galaxy" really expresses the simultaneous interplay of factors that are not directly connected at all. It is this pattern of interplay that is both the essence of the electronic speed-up and also the antithesis of the old mechanical connectedness which passed for rationality for centuries.

The literary quotations I use in the *Galaxy* are not intended as footnotes or as part of my argument. They are there as heuristic probes. I could substitute for any one of those quotes twenty or thirty other citations.

The mosaic is a world of intervals in which maximal energy is transferred across the gaps. This is the "massage" effect. *The Gutenberg Galaxy* is a world in which energy is generated in the intervals, not by the connections. And the massage—the shaping, the twisting, the bending of the whole human environment by the technology—the reconditioning of the entire human environment by this technology—is a violent process, like all new technologies often revolting, as well as revolutionary. That is why Joyce calls them "thunders." All revolutionary events are nauseating.

I personally find very little joy in the effects of media. The only satisfaction I derive is learning how they operate. This is cool, in that it is at once involvement and detachment.

I expect my readers to do more work than I did. But I'm offering them opportunities, roles of initiative. When people approached T. S. Eliot and said, "Mr. Eliot when you were writing 'Sweeney Among the Nightingales' in that passage XYZ did you mean. . ." he would wait patiently and say, "Yes. I must have meant that, if that's what you got out of it." Now Eliot was saying that the reader was co-poet. The reader's job was to make poems. Not to get his essence but to make a poem with the ingredients handed to him. This shocked literary people. That a poet would say, as Eliot did, "I never thought of that but I must have meant it if you got that out of it." That's the way I feel about critical responses. Many of the meanings people get—in so far as they are related to media— are not the ones I had in mind but they might serve very well as exploratory devices. When critics say, "One gets a lot of misconceptions and misunderstandings from these pages," they're being naïve. Not to understand the media of discourse is naïve. What sort of people am I dealing with? Isn't this the kind of image that the Europeans have always had of Americans—naïve, superficial? They are betraying enormous naïveté here. After all when I mark themes of graduate students, I expect naïveté there. And I'm not surprised when I find it in the pages of various American journals. They're no better than the ordinary graduate student.

STEARN: Some critics have argued that "hot and cool" are artificial polarities which permit you to build a system of analysis that fits your whimsy, not your evidence.

MCLUHAN: Perhaps I should have set up polarities on media rigid and frigid. It's very difficult to have a structure of any sort without polarities, without tension. For example, the triangle is the most economical way of securing an upright object. Without polarities, without contraries—this is Blake's whole notion of hateful contraries—without polarities, there is no progression, no structure. For a literary person who likes things to move along in one direction on one plane, polarities are distressing. I must know how media are structured to discover what they are doing, to me and my environment. *Media, hot* and *cool* are not classifications. They are structural forms. These are slang terms from the musical world where they have high, structural meaning. "System" means something to look at. You must have a very high visual gradient to have systemization. In philosophy, before Descartes, there was no "system." Plato had no "system." Aristotle had no "system." My own interest in studying media is a "systems development" approach. "Systems development" is a structural analysis of pressures and strains, the exact opposite of everything that has been meant by "systems" in the past few centuries. "Systems development" is the opposite of "systems" in the philosophical sense. It is concerned with the inner dynamics of the form.

A system has almost entirely visual connotations—as with Newton. The great difficulty of approaching the space-time world, after the Newtonian intrusion, is that one is deprived of visual means of fitting things in. In Newton's world, you fit things into the world. The environment is thought of as a wraparound space into which things are placed like pictorial painting or perspective art. Prior to perspective paintings, each object made its own space (for example, the flat Byzantine world). With the coming of perspective, things began to press down. They had a thrust, a weight. A man's system is thought of as a kind of space into which he puts or arranges his experience. This is the old, visual pattern. Critics are looking for the space into which I fit my experiences. There is no such space.

There is no continuum except that which we impose on things. The only sense which has the effect of continuum is the visual sense. The world of the nineteenth-century dance floor—the ballroom—was a continuum. The world of the twentieth-century dance floor is a discontinuum—a Discothèque à Go-Go, in which a dancer makes his or her own space which does not fit into anybody else's space. It's like a physicist trying to encounter electronic particles with Newtonian concepts.

STEARN: You have been accused of having a philistine enthusiasm for devices, the machines of civilization. The corollary of this charge, of course, being that you are indifferent to man. Christopher Ricks, among others, questions your definition of work. In *Understanding Media* you said: "What the nineteenth century had delegated to servants and housemaids, we now do for ourselves." Switching on a washing machine and actually scrubbing are not considered similar in terms of "work."

McLUHAN: Ricks doesn't consider that his wife's devotion to that electric washing machine is a meaningful substitution for the "navvy" or washerwoman of the nineteenth century. He assigns his wife cheerfully to the role of charwoman and feels himself quite superior to the whole operation. Electric media, for example, create learning for everybody instead of assigning it to specialists. They create an environment of knowledge. Just as work becomes diffused through the total population with electric devices, so does learning. Where learning before had been locked up in little, citational cells and classified slots, under electric conditions all that had been previously cherished, precious, erudite now become general, mass-oriented, diffuse—environments. What had previously been the content of a select environment becomes an environment itself. Work becomes an environment. Knowledge, learning become an environment of toil. That is the future work of mankind—just processing the data of the electronic environment. "Labor-saving" is a nineteenth-century concept of work. Jacques Ellul says that the twentieth-century child works harder than any child in human history. What is he working at? Just data processing.

Elizabeth Hardwick told me that in New England toilet-training was abandoned upon the discovery of the electric washing machine. Moral responsibility was shifted to the washing machine.

STEARN: When you speak about environment aren't you actually making value judgments or, at least, content analysis? For example, your much-quoted statement that the space program makes the earth seem like a used nose-cone.

McLUHAN: The safety car—I always like to talk about things which are to me puzzles—is in a certain degree, the death sentence of the existing motorcar. Just as much as the motorcar was the death sentence of the horse and buggy. The motorcar's environment creates roads and surfaces. It doesn't simply occupy a space. It creates its own space. The safety car is a bump car. It will create a totally different environment. When things began to happen all at once, people began to notice the effects of cars. They began to notice what cars do to people. All our technologies in the Western world are built on the assumption that they have complete immunity from inspection. You inspect their content—the old one, not the new one. When you look at the car in terms of what it does to people, it becomes a horrifying story—as bad as the death camps. People were unable to see the road system that came with the car. It was one thing to put the car in the old environment— horse and buggy, old mud roads.

People are now aware of consequences because of electronic information. Why are people suddenly unhappy with capital punishment? Why are they suddenly aware that crime is not committed by private individuals but by the whole society? Now the satellite or space capsule world is only possible as a result of intense study of consequences. This is a new stress in our time. To build a capsule you must foresee all the possible effects on the human form. Buckminster Fuller has remarked that the space capsule is the first completely designed human environment. Up to the present, we have not been designing environments. We have been designing things to put into the environment. It's like finding the right picture for the right room. Now one says, "What kind of a room will grow out of this picture?" The space capsule is an extension of the planet. The safety car is not an event; it's a Happening.

STEARN: Is it possible that self-appointed disciples will somehow distort your work? Are you a McLuhanite?

McLUHAN: You can be quite sure that if there are going to be McLuhanites, I am not going to be one of them. I know that anyone who learns anything will learn it slightly askew. I can imagine that having disciples would become a very great bother. It would disturb one's freedom, privacy, work. If I just keep writing with great energy, no McLuhanite will ever be able to digest it all. My areas of probing, of exploring are very personal. But of course my work might produce considerable consequences for other people. Most of what I have to say is secondhand, gathered however from esoteric sources. My favorite stomping grounds are areas that very few people have ever stomped.

STEARN: Is there a real danger in the new media?

McLuhan: It seems to me that the great advantage in understanding the operational dynamics of various media is to quiet them down, not exploit them. If you understand these dynamics, you can control media, eliminate their effects from the environment. And this is most desirable. I think we would do ourselves a considerable kindness if we closed down TV operations for a few years. If TV was simply eliminated from the United States scene, it would be a very good thing. Just as radio has a most malignant effect in Africa or Algeria, or China—in highly auditory cultures, radio drives these people nearly mad with paranoia and tribal intensity—TV, in a highly visual culture, drives us inward in depth into a totally nonvisual universe of involvement. It is destroying our entire political, educational, social, institutional life. TV will dissolve the entire fabric of society in a short time. If you understood its dynamics, you would choose to eliminate it as soon as possible. TV changes the sensory and psychic life. It is an oriental form of experience, giving people a somber, profound sense of involvement.

Stearn: When an admirer called him a poet, Freud considered the judgment harmful in that it took away from his scientific intent. A Canadian writer suggests that you are not literary critic, sociologist, historian, or whatever, but, simply, a poet.

McLuhan: All poets have to probe to discover anything. In our world, there is so much to discover.

Stearn: Can we excuse methodological lapses in the name of poetic and/or artistic license?

McLuhan: Our sensory modes are constituents, not classifications. I am simply identifying modes of experience. We need new perceptions to cope. Our technologies are generations ahead of our thinking. If you even begin to think about these new technologies you appear as a poet because you are dealing with the present as the future. That is my technique. Most people look back for security. Much greater perceptions and energies are needed than simply mine in the world in which we exist. Better developed talents are needed. James Joyce had these talents in a much more refined state. Joyce had a complete ecology of manmade environments which these critics should have read and studied long ago.

STEARN: Will there ever be silence?

McLUHAN: Objects are unobservable. Only relationships among objects are observable.

STEARN: Are you disturbed by the sometimes harsh critical responses your work excites?

McLUHAN: Even Hercules had to clean the Augean stables but once!

SOURCES

Part One: The New World of Marshall McLuhan

1. Howard Luck Gossage, "Understanding Marshall McLuhan," *Ramparts,* April, 1966.
2. Tom Wolfe, "The New Life Out There," New York *Herald Tribune,* November 21, 1965.
3. John Culkin, S.J., "A Handful of Postulates," unpublished manuscript, Copyright, 1966.
4. Dean Walker, "McLuhan Explains the Media," *Executive* (Toronto), August, 1964.
5. Kenneth E. Boulding, "The Medium and the Message," *Canadian Journal of Economics and Political Science,* May, 1965.
6. George P. Elliott, "Marshall McLuhan: Double Agent," *The Public Interest,* Summer, 1966.

Part Two: The Honeymoon of the Mechanical Bride

7. Rudolph E. Morris, untitled review, *Renascence,* Spring, 1952.
8. Walter Ong, S.J., "A Modern Sensibility," *Social Order,* February, 1952.
9. "The Picture on Your Mind," *Ammunition,* December, 1951.

Part Three: Explorations In The New World

10. "Marshall McLuhan," Verbi-Voco-Visual," *Explorations* No. 8, December, 1957.
11. Marshall McLuhan, "Classroom Without Walls," *Explorations* No. 7, May, 1957.
12. William Blissett, "Explorations," *Canadian Forum,* August, 1958.
13. Marshall McLuhan, "Joyce, Mallarmé and the Press," *The Sewanee Review,* Winter, 1954.
14. Marshall McLuhan, Harley Parker, and Robert Shafer, "The Gutenberg Galaxy: A Voyage Between Two Worlds," reprinted as Appendix in *Report on Project on Understanding New Media,* Office of Education, United States Department of Health, Education and Welfare, (n.p.), 1960.
15. H. Marshall McLuhan, *Report on Project on Understanding New Media, op. cit.,* 1960.

Part Four: The Galaxy Reconsidered

16. John Freund, "McLuhan's Galaxy," *Journal of Conference on College Composition and Communication*, May, 1963.
17. Patrick D. Hazard, untitled review, *The Annals*, November, 1964.
18. Dell Hymes, untitled review, *American Anthropologist*, April, 1963.
19. Frank Kermode, "Between Two Galaxies," *Encounter*, February, 1963.
20. A. Alvarez, "Evils of Literacy," *New Statesman*, December 21, 1962.
21. Dan M. Davin, a review of *The Gutenberg Galaxy*, *Toronto Globe and Mail*, July 14, 1962.
22. Raymond Williams, "A Structure of Insights," *University of Toronto Quarterly*, April, 1964.

Part Five: Understanding M.

23. Harold Rosenberg, "Philosophy in a Pop Key," *The New Yorker*, February 27, 1965.
24. Dwight Macdonald, "Running It Up the Totem Pole," Book Week, New York *Herald-Tribune*, July 7, 1964.
25. Christopher Ricks, "Electronic Man," *New Statesman*, December 11, 1964.
26. Jack Behar and Ben Lieberman, "Paradise Regained or McLuhanacy?" Teacher's College *Record*, April, 1966.
27. John M. Johansen, "An Architecture for the Electronic Age," *The American Scholar*, Spring, 1966.
28. George Steiner, Jonathan Miller, and Andrew Forge," The World and Marshall McLuhan," British Broadcasting Corporation, transcript of program of May 24, 1966.
29. Benjamin DeMott, "King of Popthink," *Esquire*, August, 1966. The author's original title was "Against McLuhan."
30. Susan Sontag, "One Culture and the New Sensibility," *Against Interpretation*, Chapter X (New York: Farrar, Straus and Giroux, 1965).

A SELECTED BIBLIOGRAPHY

The Writings of (Herbert) MARSHALL MC LUHAN

BOOKS:

The Mechanical Bride: Folklore of Industrial Man (New York: The Vanguard Press, Inc., 1951).

(As editor) *Selected Poetry of Tennyson* (New York: Rinehart & Co., Inc., 1954).

Report: Project On Understanding New Media, National Association of Educational Broadcasters, 1960. N.D., N.P.

Explorations in Communication (with E. S. Carpenter) (Boston: The Beacon Press, 1960).

The Gutenberg Galaxy: The Making of Typographic Man (Toronto: The University of Toronto Press, 1962).

Understanding Media: The Extensions of Man (New York: McGraw-Hill, Inc., 1964).

Voices of Literature, Vol. 1, an anthology of verse in 2 volumes, Marshall McLuhan and Richard J. Schoeck, eds. (New York: Holt, Rinehart & Winston, 1964).

Ibid., Vol. 2, 1965.

The Medium Is the Massage (with Quentin Fiore) (New York: Random House, Inc., 1967).

ARTICLES:

1934 "George Meredith as a Poet and Dramatic Parodist," M.A. thesis.

1936 "G. K. Chesterton: A Practical Mystic," *Dalhousie Review,* Vol. 15 (1936).

1937 "The Cambridge English School," *Fleur de Lis* (student magazine), St. Louis University (1937).

"Creative Thought vs. Pragmatism," *ibid.*

"The Non-Being of Non-Being," *ibid.*

1943 "Aesthetic Patterns in Keats' Odes," *University of Toronto Quarterly,* Vol. 12 (Jan. 1943).

"Education of Free Man," *Studies in Honour of St. Thomas Aquinas* (St. Louis University), Vol. 1 (1943).

"Herbert's Virtue," *The Explicator,* Vol. 1, No. 2 (Oct. 1943).

1944 "Dagwood's America," *Columbia,* Vol. 23 (Jan. 1944).

"Edgar Poe's Tradition," *Sewanee Review,* Vol. 52, No. 1 (Jan. 1944).

"Eliot's Hippopotamus," *The Explicator*, Vol. 2, No. 7 (May 1944).

"Kipling and Forster," *Sewanee Review*, Vol. 52, No. 3 (July 1944).

"Lewis," *Studies in Honour of St. Thomas Aquinas, op. cit.*, Vol. 2 (1944).

"Poetic vs. Rhetorical Exegesis," *Sewanee Review*, Vol. 52, No. 2 (April 1944).

1945   "The New York Wits," *Kenyon Review*, Vol. 7, No. 1 (1945).

1946   "The Analogical Mirrors," in *Gerard Manley Hopkins, Kenyon Review*, eds. (New York: New Directions, 1946).

"An Ancient Quarrel in Modern America," *The Classical Journal*, Vol. 41, No. 4 (Jan. 1946).

"Footprints in the Sands of Time," *Sewanee Review*, Vol. 54, No. 4 (Oct. 1946).

"Out of the Castle Into the Counting-House," *Politics* (1946).

1947   "American Advertising," *Horizon*, Nos. 93–94 (1947).

"Inside Blake and Hollywood," *Sewanee Review*, Vol. 55, No. 4 (Oct. 1947).

"Mr. Connolly and Mr. Hook," *ibid.*, No. 1 (July 1947).

Introduction to *Paradox of Chesterton* by Hugh Kenner (New York: Sheed and Ward, 1947).

"The Southern Quality," *Sewanee Review*, Vol. 55, No. 1 (July 1947).

"Time, Life and Fortune," *View* Magazine (Spring 1947).

1948   "Henry IV, a Mirror for Magistrates," *University of Toronto Quarterly*, Vol. 17 (Jan. 1948).

"On Herbert's Virtue," in *Readings for Liberal Education*, L. G. Locke, W. M. Gibson, and G. Arms, eds. (New York: Rinehart, 1948). *Op. cit.*, 1943

1949   "Color-bar of BBC English," *Canadian Forum*, Vol. 29 (April 1949).

"Mr. Eliot's Historical Decorum," *Renascence*, Vol. 2, No. 1 (Autumn 1949).

1950   "Pound's Critical Prose," in *Examination of Ezra Pound: A Collection of Essays*, Peter Russell, ed. (New York: New Directions, 1950).

"T. S. Eliot," *Renascence*, Vol. 3, No. 1 (Autumn 1950).

1951   "American Novel Through 50 Years: John Dos Passos," *America*, Vol. 85, No. 3 (June 1951).

"The Folklore of Industrial Man," *Neurotica*, Vol. 8, No. 3 (Spring 1951). (Abstracted from *The Mechanical Bride*.)

"John Dos Passos: Technique vs. Sensibility," in *Fifty Years of the*

American Novel: A Christian Appraisal, Charles Gardiner, ed. (New York: Charles Scribner's Sons, 1951).

"Joyce, Aquinas, and the Poetical Process," *Renascence,* Vol. 4, No. 1 (Winter 1951).

"Poetry and Opinion: Examination of Ezra Pound and Letters of Pound," *ibid.,* Vol. 3, No. 2 (Spring 1951).

"Tennyson and Picturesque Poetry," *Essays in Criticism,* Vol. 1, No. 3 (July 1951).

1952   "Advertising as a Magical Institution," *Commerce Journal* (Univ. of Toronto), (Jan. 1952).

"The Aesthetic Moment in Landscape Poetry," in *English Institute Essays 1951,* Alan Downe, ed. (New York: Columbia University Press, 1952).

"Baseball Is Culture," *CBC Times,* Oct. 25,Nov.1, and Nov. 8, 1952.

"Defrosting Canadian Culture," *American Mercury,* Vol. 74, No. 339 (March 1952).

"Technology and Political Change," *International Journal,* Vol. 7 (Summer 1952).

1953   "The Age of Advertising," *Commonweal,* Vol. 58, No. 23 (Sept. 11, 1953).

"Comics and Culture," *Saturday Night,* Vol. 68, No. 1 (Feb. 28, 1953).

"Culture Without Literacy," *Explorations,* Vol. 1 (Dec. 1953).

"James Joyce: Trivial and Quadrivial," *Thought,* Vol. 28, No. 108 (Spring 1953).

"The Later Innis," *Queen's Quarterly,* Vol. 60, No. 3 (Autumn 1953).

"Maritain on Art," *Renascence,* Vol. 6 (Autumn 1953).

"The Poetry of George Herbert and Symbolist Communication," *Thought* (Autumn 1953).

"Wyndham Lewis: His Theory of Art and Communication," *Shenandoah,* Vol. 4, Nos. 2–3 (Autumn 1953).

1954   "Catholic Humanism and Modern Letters," in *Christian Humanism in Letters: The McAuley Lectures, Series 2, 1954* (West Hartford, Conn.: St. Joseph College, 1954).

"Comics and Culture," in *Our Sense of Identity: A Book of Canadian Essays,* Malcolm Ross, ed. (Toronto: Ryerson Press, 1954). *Op. cit.,* 1953.

"Joyce, Mallarmé and the Press," *Sewanee Review,* Vol. 62, No. 1 (Winter 1954).

"Media as Art Forms," *Explorations,* Vol. 3 (Aug. 1954).

"New Media as Political Forms," *ibid.* Also in *The Creative Reader:*

An Anthology of Fiction, Drama, and Poetry, R. W. Stallman, R. E. Waters, eds. (New York: Ronald Press, 1954).
"Poetry and Society," *Poetry*, Vol. 84, No. 2 (May 1954).
"Sight, Sound and the Fury," *Commonweal*, Vol. 60 (April 9, 1954).

1955 "Five Sovereign Fingers Taxed the Breath," *Shenandoah*, Vol. 7, No. 1 (Autumn 1955).
"An Historical Approach to Media," *Teacher's College Record*, Vol. 57, No. 2 (Nov. 1955).
"The Poetry of T. S. Eliot," *Renascence*, Vol. 3, No. 3 (Spring 1955).
"Psychopathology of *Time* and *Life*," in *The Scene Before You: A New Approach to American Culture*, Chandler Brossard, ed. (New York: Rinehart, 1955).
"Radio and Television vs. the ABCED-Minded," *Explorations*, Vol. 5 (June 1955).
"Space, Time and Poetry," *ibid.*, Vol. 4 (Feb. 1955).

1956 "Educational Effects of Mass Media of Communications," *Teacher's College Record*, Vol. 57, No. 6 (March 1956).
"The Media Fit the Battle of Jericho," *Explorations*, Vol. 6 (July 1956).
"Mimesis," *Renascence*, Vol. 9, No. 2 (Winter 1956).
"The New Languages," *The Changing Review*, Vol. 10, No. 1 (Spring 1956).

1957 "American Advertising," in *Mass Culture: The Popular Arts in America*, Bernard Rosenberg and David Manning White, eds. (Glencoe, Ill.: Free Press, 1957). *Op. cit.* 1947.
"Classrooms Without Walls," *Explorations*, Vol. 7 (March 1957).
"Coleridge as Artist," in *The Major English Romantic Poets: A Symposium in Reappraisal*, Clarence D. Thorpe, Carlos Baker, and Bennet Weaver, eds. (Carbondale, Ill.: Southern Illinois University Press, 1957).
"David Riesman and the Avant-Garde," *Explorations, op. cit.*
"The Effect of the Printed Book on Language in the Sixteenth Century," *ibid.*
"Jazz and Modern Letters," *ibid.*
"Sight, Sound and the Fury," in *Mass Culture, op. cit.* Also see 1954.
"Subliminal Projection on Project," *Canadian Forum*, Vol. 37 (Dec. 1957).
The following articles appeared in *Explorations*, Vol. 8 (Oct. 1957):
"The Alchemy of Social Change"
"American Model, 1795"

"The Bathroom Baritone and the Wide-Open Spaces"
"The Be-Spoke Tailor"
"Brain Storming"
"Characterization in Western Art, 1600–1900"
"Churchill Mobilizes the English Language"
"Electronics as ESP"
"Eminent Extrapolators"
"The Journalist's Dilemma"
"The Liturgical Review"
"Milton Had His Daughters, I Have My Dictaphone"
"No Upside Down in Eskimo"
"The Old New Rich and the New New Rich"
"Oral-Anal"
"The Organization Man"
"The Pattern of Oral Strategy in the USSR"
"Picture of the World"
"Print as Patterkiller"
"Sherlock Holmes vs. the Bureaucrats"
"Stress"
"Television Murders Telephony"
"The Third Program in the Human Age"
"Verbi-Voco-Visual"

1958 "Eliot's Poetry and Plays," *Renascence*, Vol. 10, No. 2 (Winter 1958).
"The Electronic Revolution in North America," *International Literary Annual No. 1*, John Wain, ed. (London: John Calder, 1958).
"Knowledge, Ideas, Information, and Communication," *Yearbook of Education*, 1958.
"Media Alchemy in Art and Society," *The Journal of Communication*, Vol. 8, No. 2 (Summer 1958).
"One Wheel, All Square," *Renascence*, Vol. 10, No. 4 (Summer 1958).

1959 "Joyce or No Joyce," review of *Joyce Among the Jesuits*, in *Renascence*, Vol. 12, No. 1 (Autumn 1959).
"The Letters of William Butler Yeats," *Renascence*, Vol. 11, No. 3 (Spring 1959).
"Myth and Mass Media," *Daedalus*, Vol. 88 No. 2 (Spring 1959).
"Printing and Social Change," in *Printing Progress: A Mid-Century Report*, by The International Association of Printing House Craftsmen, Inc. (Cincinnati, 1959).
"On Poetry and Poets," *Renascence*, Vol. 11, No. 2 (Winter 1959).

1960 The following articles appeared in *Explorations in Communication*, see "Books":

"Acoustic Space."

"Classrooms Without Walls," *op. cit.* 1957.

"The Effect of the Printed Book on Language in the 16th Century."

"Five Sovereign Fingers Taxed the Breath," *op. cit.*, 1955.

"Media Log."

"Another Eliot Party," review of *T. S. Eliot: A Symposium for His 70th Birthday*, by N. Braybrooke, in *Renascence*, Vol. 12, No. 3 (Spring 1960).

"Around the World, Around the Clock," review of *The Image Industries*, by William Lynch, *ibid.*, No. 4 (Summer 1960).

"A Critical Discipline," review of *A Portrait of the Artist as the Enemy*, by Wyndham Lewis, *ibid.*, No. 2 (Winter 1960).

"The Effects of the Improvement of Communication Media," *Journal of Economic History*, Vol. 20 (Dec. 1960).

"Electronics and the Changing Role of Print," *Audio-Visual Communication Review*, Vol. 8 No. 5 (Sept.-Oct. 1960).

"Flirting with Shadows," review of *The Invisible Poet: T. S. Eliot*, by Hugh Kenner, *Renascence*, Vol. 12, No. 4 (Summer 1960).

"The Medium Is the Message," *Forum* (Spring 1960).

"Melodic and Scribal," review of *Song in the Works of J. Joyce*, by M. J. C. Hodgart and M. P. Worthington, *Renascence*, Vol. 13, No. 1 (Autumn 1960).

"Myth and Mass Media," in *Myth and Mythmaking*, Henry A. Murray, ed. (New York: George Braziller, 1960).

"New Media and the New Education," in *Christianity and Culture*, J. S. Murphy, ed. (Baltimore: Helicon Press, 1960). Also appeared under the title "Electronics and the Changing Role of Print," *op. cit.*, 1960, and in *The Basilian Teacher*, Vol. 6, No. 3 (Dec. 1961).

"The Personal Approach," review of *Shakespeare and Company*, by Sylvia Beach, *Renascence*, Vol. 13, No. 1 (Autumn 1960).

"Romanticism Reviewed," review of *Romantic Image*, by Frank Kermode, *ibid.*, Vol. 12, No. 4 (Summer 1960).

"Tennyson and Picturesque Poetry," in *Critical Essays on the Poetry of Tennyson*, John Kilham, ed. (London: Routledge and Kegan Paul, 1960). *Op. cit.*, 1951.

"Tennyson and the Romantic Epic," *ibid.*

1961   "The Books at the Wake," *Renascence*, Vol. 13, No. 4 (Summer 1961).

"The Humanities in the Electronic Age," *Humanities Association Bulletin* (Canada), Vol. 34, No. 1 (Fall 1961). Also in *Thought from the Learned Societies of Canada* (Toronto: W. J. Gage, 1961).

"Inside the Five Sense Sensorium," *Canadian Architect*, Vol. 6, No. 6 (June 1961).

"James Joyce," *Renascence*, Vol. 13, No. 4 (Summer 1961).

1962 "The Electronic Age—The Age of Implosion," in *Mass Media in Canada*, John A. Irving, ed. (Toronto: Ryerson Press, 1962).

"A Fresh Perspective on Dialogue," *The Superior Student*, Vol. 4 (Jan.-Feb. 1962).

"Joyce, Aquinas and the Poetic Process," in *Joyce's Portrait: Criticisms and Techniques*, Thomas E. Connolly, ed. (New York: Appleton-Century-Crofts, 1962).

"Prospect," *Canadian Art*, Vol. 19 (Sept.-Oct. 1962).

"Prospect of America," *University of Toronto Quarterly*, Vol. 32, No. 1 (Oct. 1962).

"Two Aspects of the Communications Revaluation," *Canadian Communications*, Vol. 2, No. 2 (1962).

1963 "The Agenbite of Outwit," *Location* Magazine, Vol. 1, No. 1 (Spring 1963).

"We Need a New Picture of Knowledge," in *New Insights and the Curriculum Development* (Washington: National Education Association, 1963).

1964 "Decline of the Visual," *Dot Zero* Magazine (New York: National Society of Art Directors) (May 1964).

"John Dos Passos: Technique vs. Sensibility," in *Modern American Fiction: Essays in Criticism*, A. Walton Litz, ed. (New York: Oxford University Press, 1964). *Op. cit.*, 1951.

"Masks and Roles and the Corporate Society," *Varsity Graduate*, Vol. 11, No. 2 (Summer 1964).

"Murder by Television," *The Canadian Forum*, Vol. 43, No. 516 (Jan. 1964).

"New Media and the Arts," *Arts in Society* Magazine (University of Wisconsin Press) Vol. 3, No. 2 (Sept. 1964).

"Notes on Burroughs," a review of *The Naked Lunch* and *Nova Express*, by William Burroughs, in *Nation*, Vol. 199 (Dec. 28, 1964).

"Printing and the Mind," *Times Literary Supplement* (London), June 19, 1964.

"Radio: The Tribal Drum," *AV Communication Review*, Vol. 12, No. 2 (1964).

"The University in the Electric Age: The End of the Gap Between Theory and Practice," *Varsity Graduate*, Vol. 11, No. 3 (Dec. 1964).

Foreword to "Vision and Reading Achievement," by W. A. Hurst,

in *Canadian Journal of Optometry*, Vol. 25, No. 4 (April 1964).
Preface for the reprinting of *The Bias of Communication*, by H. A.
Innis (Toronto: University of Toronto Press, 1964).

1965   "Art as Anti-Environment," *Art News Annual*, Vol. 31 (Feb. 1965).
Preface to paperback edition of *Understanding Media* (New York:
McGraw-Hill, 1965).

1966   "Address at Vision '65," *The American Scholar* (Spring 1966).
"The Crack in the Rear-View Mirror," *McGill Journal of Education*
(Spring 1966).
"Electronics and the Psychic Drop-Out," *This Magazine Is About
Schools*, Vol. 1, No. 1 (April 1966).
"The Emperor's Old Clothes," in *The Man-Made Object*, Gyorgy
Kepes, ed. (New York: George Braziller, 1966).
"Environmental Change and the New Technology," *Dicta* Magazine,
No. 8, (Oct. 1966).
"From Instruction to Discovery," *Media and Methods*, Vol. 3, No.
2 (Oct. 1966).
"Great Change-overs for You," *Vogue*, Vol. 148 (July 1966).
"Guaranteed Income in the Electric Age," *The Guaranteed Income:
A Symposium in Income Distribution in a Cybernated Era*, by
Robert Theobald (New York: Doubleday, 1966).
"The Invisible Environment: The Future of Consciousness," *Per-
specta* (Yale Architectural Journal), No. 11 (Fall 1966).
"Questions and Answers with Marshall McLuhan," *Take One*
Magazine, Vol. 1, No. 2 (Nov.-Dec. 1966).
"The Relation of Environment to Anti-Environment," University of
Windsor *Review*, Vol. 11, No. 1 (Autumn 1966).
Review of *Cybernetic Principles of Learning and Educational De-
sign*, by Karl U. Smith and M. F. Smith, New Society (London),
(Sept. 1966).

1967   "The Humanities in the Electronic Age," *The Book of Canadian
Prose*, Vol. 11 (Toronto: W. G. Gage, Ltd., 1967). *Op. cit.*, 1961.
"Love," *Saturday Night*, Vol. 82, No. 2 (Feb. 1967).
"The New Education," *The Basilian Teacher*, Vol. 2, No. 2 (1967).
"The Relation of Environment to Anti-Environment," in *The Human
Dialogue*, Floyd Matson and Ashley Montagu, eds. (New York: The
Macmillan Company, 1967).
Review of *The Art of Memory*, by Frances A. Yates, *Encounter*
(Feb. 1967).
"Technology and Environment," *Artscanada* Magazine, No. 105
(Feb. 1967).
"What TV Is Really Doing to Your Child," *Family Circle* (March
1967).